Forgiveness

Vladimir Jankélévitch

Forgiveness

Translated by Andrew Kelley

The University of Chicago Press / Chicago and London

Vladimir Jankélévitch (1903–1985) held the Chair in Moral Philosophy at the Sorbonne from 1951 to 1978. He was the author of more than twenty books on philosophy and music, including the recently translated *Music and the Ineffable.*

Andrew Kelley is assistant professor in the Department of Philosophy and Religious Studies at Bradley University. He is also the translator of Josef Popper-Lynkeus's *The Individual and the Value of Human Life.*

The University of Chicago Press, Chicago 60637
The University of Chicago Press, Ltd., London
© 2005 by The University of Chicago
All rights reserved. Published 2005
Printed in the United States of America

14 13 12 11 10 09 08 07 06 05   1 2 3 4 5

ISBN: 0-226-39213-9 (cloth)

First published as *Le Pardon* by Aubier-Montaigne in 1967.

Library of Congress Cataloging-in-Publication Data

Jankélévitch, Vladimir.
  [Pardon. English]
  Forgiveness / Vladimir Jankélévitch ; translated by Andrew Kelley.
    p. cm.
  Includes bibliographical references and index.
  ISBN: 0-226-39213-9 (hardcover : alk. paper)
  1. Forgiveness of sin. I. Title.
  BT795.J313 2005
  179'.9—dc22

                                                2004057961

Contents

Translator's Introduction

> What is hard to comprehend is that Jankélévitch was and still
> is so little appreciated, even ignored, in [France] . . . We know,
> however, and we are tempted to say, that under different
> circumstances the teaching of Jankélévitch could have had
> the resonance of a Bergson, a Bachelard, or, even closer to us,
> of a Lacan. —*Josef Sivak*[1]

The originality, profundity, breadth, and beauty of the
writings of Vladimir Jankélévitch (1903–1985) merit that he be mentioned
in the same breath as such renowned figures as Lacan, Merleau-Ponty,
Foucault, Lévinas, and Derrida. Because his thought in large part cannot
be pigeonholed and because he never belonged to any particular school of
thought, Jankélévitch never achieved wide recognition. After World War II,
his writings were for the most part neglected by professional philosophers
in France. Although his work was not completely overlooked during his lifetime, it is now experiencing a posthumous "rebirth." Although it is unfair to
the very spirit of his thinking and writings, the following attempt to summarize Jankélévitch's life and work serves the purpose of introducing the
man and the general themes and problematics of his writings to an English-
speaking world in which he is an even more obscure figure than he was in
France during his lifetime.

---

1. Josef Sivak, "Nécrologie," *Revue Philosophique* 4 (1985): 580.

An Overview of Jankélévitch's Life

Given his background, it is not surprising that Vladimir Jankélévitch followed a life of intellectual pursuits. He was born to Russian parents in Bourges, France, on August 31, 1903. His father, Samuel Jankélévitch, a physician by vocation and a person of letters by avocation, translated works by Freud, Schelling, Simmel, Croce, and Hegel into French. The elder Jankélévitch was to have a significant influence on the development of his son's intellectual interests.

The Jankélévitch family relocated to Paris after Vladimir was born. He attended the prestigious Lycée Louis le Grand, followed in 1922 by the even more prestigious École Normale Supérieure. After two years there, he defended the equivalent of a master's thesis on Plotinus's *Enneads,* under the direction of the noted historian of philosophy Émile Bréhier. Four years after beginning at the École Normale Supérieure, Jankélévitch took first place in the *aggrégation,* a nationwide examination required in order to teach philosophy at any level. After fulfilling his military service in 1927, he was given a teaching position at the French Institute of Prague. This appointment allowed him to finish a noteworthy book on Henri Bergson, which, when published in 1931, had the distinction of including a foreword by Bergson himself. During Jankélévitch's time in Prague, he was also able to complete most of his doctoral thesis on Schelling and a supplemental thesis on the bad conscience; both of these works were defended and then published in 1933. In this period prior to his doctoral defense, Jankélévitch wrote many shorter articles on Bergson, Simmel, and Russian mysticism. It was during this period in Prague that he began to feel a distance opening up between himself and the French philosophical mainstream.[2]

In 1932, Jankélévitch returned to France. He wedded a young Czech woman, but the marriage fell apart after only a few months. In 1936, he began to lecture at the University of Toulouse, after having taught in lycées in Caen and Lyon for four years. This era of his life saw the publication of two books of philosophy and two on music, and he was beginning work on his monumental *Traité des vertus* (Treatise on the Virtues). When he obtained a post at the University of Lille in 1938, the young academic had achieved

2. Vladimir Jankélévitch to Louis Beauduc, September 15, 1931, in Vladimir Jankélévitch, *Une Vie en toutes lettres* [letters to Louis Beauduc], ed. Françoise Schwab (Paris: Liana Levi, 1995), 197.

some notoriety. Although his teaching position was two hours away by train, he still made his home in Paris in an apartment on the Quai aux Fleurs in the shadow of Notre Dame Cathedral. With the exception of the war years, this was to be his address until his death.

The events surrounding World War II had a profound effect on Jankélévitch. When Germany attacked France in 1940, he took part in the French effort to repel the advance and was wounded. Jankélévitch took advantage of his hospital stay to draft a manuscript of *Le Mensonge* (The Lie), which was published two years later. However, his Jewish background hindered his ability to be appointed to an academic position in the French universities. Fortunately, at that time there was a provision in French law that extended the benefits of French citizenship to former soldiers. Unfortunately, this provision was abolished in late 1940, and he was subsequently stripped of his permission to teach on account of his Jewish background.

Prior to the revocation of this exemption for former soldiers, Jankélévitch had relocated to Toulouse with the hope of being named, if only temporarily, to a position there. When he lost the right to teach in public institutions, he began to work as a tutor for hire as well as holding philosophy lectures secretly at various cafés in Toulouse. For the duration of the war, Jankélévitch remained in Toulouse, secretly giving lectures, helping the efforts of the Resistance, and trying to elude deportation. Despite the precarious nature of his existence during these years, Jankélévitch still managed to write, with a treatise on music, *Le Nocturne,* and a philosophical work, *Le Mensonge,* both appearing in 1942. (Perhaps foreshadowing future events, it is important to note that it was Jankélévitch's former students and not colleagues from the university who were responsible for securing the publication of these books.) In several letters from 1942, he alludes to the possibility of a teaching position in New York.[3] Nothing ever came of this.

After the war, Jankélévitch anxiously waited to be reinstated as a professor. In the meantime, he accepted a post as director of music programs at Radio Toulouse, a job that was not repugnant to Jankélévitch given his love of music. He was reappointed to the University of Lille in October 1947. The long delay served only to deepen the wound that he suffered by being barred from teaching during the war. To make matters worse, the publisher Aubier withdrew its agreement to publish the *Traité des vertus,* which Jankélévitch had completed in 1946; the reasons remain unclear. In a letter to his friend

3. Ibid., 280, 286. The letters are dated June 29, 1942, and November 27, 1942, respectively.

Louis Beauduc, Jankélévitch cynically claims that he should just mimeo-
graph the manuscript, with his own money, in the hope that later generations would publish it.[4] Eventually, the work was published. It would
become Jankélévitch's most famous book.

The decade after World War II saw several major changes in Jankélévitch's personal life. At the age of forty-four, in April 1947, Jankélévitch
married again. This time the relationship succeeded. In 1953, Lucienne and
Vladimir Jankélévitch would have their only child, Sophie, who followed in
her father's footsteps as a philosopher.

Unfortunately, the notoriety and status for which Jankélévitch had
seemed destined before the war never arrived. From this point on, Jankélévitch would be an outsider in the world of French academic philosophy. Op-
portunities for him to contribute to conferences and colloquia in France became scarce, although he was regularly asked to lecture abroad. In 1947, Jean
Wahl invited Jankélévitch to give a series of lectures at his famed "College
Philosophique." Jankélévitch was grateful to Wahl for this opportunity because, as Jankélévitch wrote, "such occasions in Paris are rare for those who
are not part of anything."[5] Not only was the style in which Jankélévitch wrote
unique—even for a nation that so values its literature—but the thinkers to
whom he often referred were well out of the philosophical mainstream.
What was worse, a main emphasis of his writings (ethics) and a main feature of this emphasis (the virtues) were literally dead topics in the climate
of phenomenology and existentialism that dominated postwar French
thought.

Jankélévitch was profoundly affected by the Holocaust and by his wartime experiences.[6] As a result, he made a conscious effort to purge his life of
all things German. In an interview with Robert Hébrard, Jankélévitch acknowledged that after the war he "forgot the German language, and repudi-
ated nearly all of German culture."[7] He would not perform or write about
German music, and when he published reeditions of his earlier writings, he
often deleted references to German thinkers. What he called the "great sep-
aration [*coupure*] of his life" is even more significant because his refusal to

4. Ibid., 313. The letter is dated January 3, 1947.

5. Ibid., 315. The letter is dated March 6, 1947.

6. Jacques Madaule, "Vladimir Jankélévitch," in *Écrit pour Vladimir Jankélévitch*, ed.
Monique Basset (Paris: Flammarion, 1978), 9.

7. "Entretien," *Arc* 75 (1979): 9.

engage with recent German philosophy would alienate him from postwar French thought, which drew heavily from Nietzsche, Husserl, and Heidegger. At the end of his life there was the beginning of a reconciliation or thaw in Jankélévitch's attitude toward Germany. A young German schoolteacher, Wiard Raveling, heard Jankélévitch speak and wrote to him in order to apologize for Germans and Germany. Jankélévitch was deeply touched by Raveling's gesture. The two met at Jankélévitch's apartment in Paris and began a correspondence.

Perhaps one positive effect of his wartime experiences was that it forced Jankélévitch to take stock of his own relationship with Judaism. It was only at this point that he began to write essays on Israel and what it means to be Jewish. However, although he acknowledged his own Jewish ancestry and wrote on the subject, he did not look to the Torah or the Talmud for philosophical insight as did thinkers such as Rosenzweig, Buber, or Lévinas.

After being passed over three years earlier, Jankélévitch was given a position at the Sorbonne in 1951. He would maintain a chair in moral philosophy there until his partial retirement in 1975; he fully retired from all teaching duties in 1979. Almost every year during this period saw the publication of a book on philosophy or music or a revised edition of an earlier book on philosophy or music. He regularly lectured outside France and was awarded a doctorate *honoris causa* by the Free University of Brussels in 1965.

Despite these successes, Jankélévitch felt increasingly isolated from the world of academic philosophy in France. He commented to Louis Beauduc that "[m]ore and more I flee from my colleagues, who don't interest me any more than I interest them. The epoch and I are not interested in one another."[8] He struggled to find publishers for his philosophical texts. Influential French journals, such as *Esprit* or *Les Temps Modernes,* which was linked to Sartre, would not review his works.[9] At the end of his life, Jankélévitch noted that his books were not given even a simple mention in *Le Monde*'s list of recent publications.[10] He rarely lectured or presented papers in France. In fact, in August 1954 he wrote to Beauduc about lecturing in Italy, where, he said, he had a few readers and felt at home.[11] An important

8. Jankélévitch, *Une Vie en toutes lettres,* 331.
9. Ibid., 357.
10. Ibid., 374. The letter is from January 2, 1975.
11. Ibid., 331.

reason for this distance between Jankélévitch and his contemporaries grew out of Jankélévitch's suspicion of groups and rigidly defined schools of thought, which is reflected in his claim that "now there is room in France only for herds: Marxists, Catholics, existentialists. And I am not from any parish."[12]

Despite these obstacles Jankélévitch was able to secure publishers, and his writing was nothing short of prolific. His books are difficult to categorize because he often interwove moral, metaphysical, spiritual, and psychological analyses within the same work; in fact, for him these issues are inseparable. Nevertheless, one of the books for which he is most well known, *Philosophie première,* which appeared in 1953, deals primarily with metaphysics. His monumental *Traité des vertus*—which was revised and expanded to 1,500 pages between 1968 and 1972—remains his signature piece. At the end of his career, much of his effort was devoted to reworking previous texts that he had written.

Although Jankélévitch shied away from many of the bureaucratic duties and petty power politics that took him away from teaching and writing, he gave significant amounts of his time to causes that he viewed as important. In May 1968, Jankélévitch protested for reforms in higher education alongside his students, and this elicited charges of demagoguery from many of his colleagues.[13] He also took a passionate stand against euthanasia and was important in the fight against the initiative to discontinue the instruction of philosophy in French high schools.

In spite of the cold shoulder that Jankélévitch seemed to receive from his colleagues, his students continued to revere him. Former students often describe his lectures as one-time "events" (instead of simply as sessions in which information is passed on to others). Likewise, Jankélévitch unlike many professors seemed to view students as compatriots instead of rabble. By the end of his career, his status with students was such that he often had more than one hundred masters theses to direct during a year.

By no means did Jankélévitch live in an ivory tower. His gift for philosophy was matched by his passion for music. In addition to being a talented pianist, he wrote extensively about music. According to Xavier Tilliette, Jankélévitch played no small role in bringing figures such as Satie, Albeniz, and

12. Ibid., 339. The letter is dated January 2, 1958.
13. Ibid., 361. The letter is from January 2, 1969.

Mompou to a wider French audience.[14] His love of music and dancing and his commitment to moral and political issues show that he very much lived and loved life outside of the academy. By all accounts, he was a kind, caring person. His demeanor is often described as humble, yet exuding an obvious passion for those things in which he was interested. One former student, Catherine Clément, writes that friendship was his most striking quality, that he was the incarnation of *philia,* and that he resembled a Saint Francis of philosophy.[15]

Jankélévitch died on June 6, 1985, and was laid to rest outside of Paris at Châtenay-Malabry cemetery, where his parents are buried. He once commented to Louis Beauduc, "I am writing for the twenty-first century, which will discuss my ideas with passion, as opposed to the twentieth century."[16] This prophecy is perhaps now coming true.

General Themes in Jankélévitch's Philosophy

Any attempt to summarize Jankélévitch's philosophy, including this one, is potentially misleading. Jankélévitch does not have a strict system of thought in which there is some ultimate beginning point from which all of the other aspects or tenets of his system can be deduced. In fact, Jankélévitch explicitly denies that he even has "a philosophy": "You know, I do not have a philosophy, a system of which I am the proprietor as one holds a chair that was given to one by the state. And I cannot make myself the spectator of my own doctrine since I don't have one."[17] His writings, therefore, have an affinity with those of Nietzsche or Kierkegaard, whose works explore various themes and horizons without forming a closed system. One commentator even refers to Jankélévitch's writings in terms of an "asystematic systematicity, in which the accent falls not so much on the systematicity as on the asystematicity."[18] However, even given Jankélévitch's caveats, it is still possible to discern some main themes and strategies in his writings.

14. Xavier Tilliette, "Une Kitiège de l'âme: L'éthique de Vladimir Jankélévitch," *Arc* (75): 66.
15. Catherine Clément, "L'Amour de la vie," *Arc* 75 (1979): 1.
16. Vladimir Jankélévitch, *Une Vie en toutes letters,* 332. The letter is dated January 1, 1955.
17. Vladimir Jankélévitch, "Entretien avec Robert Hébrard," *Arc* 75 (1979): 9.
18. Marie Louise Facco, "Il 'Traité des vertus' di Vladimir Jankélévitch," *Giornale di metafisica* 30 (July–August 1975): 405.

Jankélévitch's inimitable writing style is one of the most striking features of his texts. His sentences are often extremely long by today's standards. Yet at the same time they are uncharacteristically clear and to the point. This is not an attempt on his part to be ostentatious or pedantic. Rather, his sentences follow along like musical lines, ending when the phrase is over or when a breath is needed. In the same manner, his paragraphs often go on for pages. They function and unfold in the same way a movement develops in a piece of music; there literally are crescendos, repetitions, and pianissimos.

Jankélévitch is also well known for his unique terminology, and for many readers this can be intimidating. His facility with foreign languages is evident by the way in which he cites texts in the original, especially Greek and Latin texts. He draws many of the terms that he uses—"hapax," "philauty," "quoddity," "quiddity," and so on—from classical philosophy. Again, this is not pedantry on his part. Unlike Kant or Hegel, whose neologisms form part of a technical vocabulary that is often as ambiguous as it is dry, Jankélévitch employs these terms because he sees them as being more concrete and pregnant with meaning than terms out of contemporary French philosophical language or contemporary French. Once one understands the origin of Jankélévitch's neologisms, one sees that they are very lucid and concrete.

Jankélévitch did not view his texts simply as a neutral medium through which to communicate his "position." His writings are just as much about challenging our notions concerning some theme or topic as about trying to provide any "definitive" answer to some given question. His method is more often than not negative—or "apophatic," as he describes it—in that he devotes a large portion of his text to leading his reader step by step to what the answer to the issue or topic cannot be. He will assume a position or view only to demonstrate why such a position or view is not cogent. By the end of the work, Jankélévitch will bring out positive conclusions, but often these conclusions are open-ended. When one begins to read a text by Jankélévitch, one is not sure how the text will end. In no way should this be taken to mean that Jankélévitch's texts lack philosophical depth or rigor. While his books are written in the traditional academic style, they reflect a tremendous amount of scholarship as well as Jankélévitch's mastery of the history of philosophy. One of the extraordinary aspects of Jankélévitch's writings is that they combine aesthetic beauty with logical rigor.[19]

19. Sivak, "Nécrologie," 577.

Not only does his style of writing and speaking break with the academic norm, but the authors whom Jankélévitch cites are not necessarily the major authors from the canon. To be sure, Jankélévitch refers to standard authors such as Aristotle, Plato, Spinoza, Kant, Kierkegaard, and Bergson. However, he routinely makes references to authors and works that are rarely cited in philosophical texts: Philo, Fénelon, Baltasar Gracián, the early Church Fathers, Saint Francis de Sales, mystics from both Eastern and Western Christian traditions, philosophers of Slavic origin such as Shestov and Berdiaev, and Russian writers such as Tolstoy and Dostoevsky. For him it was possible to find philosophically relevant material wisdom in a piece of music, a poem, a play, a story, or a religious work.

At the heart of Jankélévitch's philosophizing, from the beginning of his career to the end, is his conception of the nature of reality and hence of time. Beginning with his years at the École Normale Supérieure, Jankélévitch was drawn to vitalist thinkers such as Simmel, Guyau, and Bergson, writers who interpreted life in terms of temporality.[20] As a result, Jankélévitch saw the primary feature of life—and thus time—as irreversibility.[21] In those early days, Jankélévitch also absorbed another vitalist notion that was to become important in his work: life is a continual destruction of forms.[22] That is, he saw the essence of life as being a continual process of rupture and redefinition.[23]

In addition to so-called vitalist thinkers, in the early 1920s Jankélévitch was also reading and teaching idealism, mysticism, romanticism, Plotinus, Dostoevsky and Tolstoy, and Schelling. But it was Bergson's thought that laid the foundation for Jankélévitch's philosophizing. In Bergson's view, discursive thought—thought involving concepts—cannot grasp objects as wholes because it parcels them up; intuition, on the other hand, grasps realities as complete and whole. This suspicion about discursive thought would stay with Jankélévitch for the rest of his career. Jankélévitch also followed Bergson in the belief that time is not an object that discursive thought can understand in the way that it might understand a table, a chair, a watch, or a book. "Time is not an object, *res*, nor a 'given.' It is evasive. It flees,"

20. Carlo Migliaccio, "Bergson pour maître," *Magazine Littéraire* 333 (1995): 36.
21. Jankélévitch, *Une Vie en toutes lettres,* 172–73. The letter is dated October 8, 1929.
22. Ibid., 63. The letter is dated September 4, 1923.
23. Ibid.

Jankélévitch wrote.[24] Accordingly, time is something that we live; it can be experienced only intuitively.

Jankélévitch, however, broke from Bergson's view that time involves a continuous duration that evolves organically. Jankélévitch did not deny duration. However, he believed that this very duration was punctuated with and delineated by what he called "instants." This theme of the instant occupies a central role throughout Jankélévitch's works. As is the case with time, the instant also turns out to be an "almost nothing."[25] An "almost nothing" is not equivalent with nothingness, or the void, or complete negation because this would make the instant into an illusion or something unreal. Nor is the instant a very brief duration or the smallest possible interval of time because these, too, are still aspects of duration, that is, of the interval. Furthermore, the instant is not the negation of duration or the interval because the negation of duration is still measured by—and thus is of the order of—duration. According to Jankélévitch, the instant is of a "wholly different order"[26] than being, and being is the measure of duration.[27] According to Jankélévitch, the instant "designates the ungraspable threshold where being ceases to be something and where nothing ceases to be nothing, where each contradictory is at the point of and even in the middle of becoming its contradictory."[28] It is the very limit or border or threshold at which a change comes to pass. It is the border or change where a being goes out of existence and another being comes into existence. As one commentator describes it, the instant is a "rupture, fission, or discontinuity."[29] It neither exists nor does not exist (for not-being is the negation of being). It is both being and not-being and yet neither being nor not-being; it almost is. In order to allude to the instant, Jankélévitch employs terms such as "threshold" (*seuil*), "summit" (*sommet*), or "peak" (*cime*). What the instant is or presents is a qualitative

24. Vladimir Jankélévitch, *Le Je-ne-sais-quoi et le presque-rien*, vol. 2: *Le Méconnaissance, le malentendu* (Paris: Éditions du Seuil, 1980), 92–93.

25. Vladimir Jankélévitch, *Philosophie première: Introduction à la philosophie du presque* (Paris: Presses Universitaires de France, 1953), 210.

26. Emmanuel Lévinas acknowledges that his notion of the "wholly other" or "absolutely other" comes from Jankélévitch. See Emmanuel Lévinas, "Phenomenon and Enigma," in *Collected Philosophical Papers*, trans. Alphonso Lingis (Pittsburgh: Duquesne University Press, 1998), 47.

27. Jankélévitch, *Philosophie première*, 210.

28. Ibid.

29. Migliaccio, "Bergson pour maître," 38.

difference, not a quantitative one, or an abrupt change from one quality to another.[30]

What is more important, however, is the connection that Jankélévitch establishes between the instant, the act of creating, and ethics. In the quote cited a few lines above, Jankélévitch talks about the instant in terms of one thing that is going out of existence just as something new is brought into existence. This is nothing other than creation plain and simple, and therefore he equates the instant with creation.[31] Thus, creation involves the positing of something's essence and existence, both of which were not there previously.[32] Creation—or, the instant—stands outside of categories and discursive thought.[33] It is metalogical, meta-empirical, and even prior to metaphysics.[34]

For Jankélévitch, life—and, thus, time—appears as a succession of choices that we make.[35] Life, then, is the interplay between the instant where we create and the intervals in which what was created is maintained. The instant—creation—is the demarcation between intervals. It sets the stage for the interval that follows upon it, so to speak. This is why Jankélévitch refers to the instant as "an explosive atom."[36] It is miraculous because it brings into existence something that was not there before; it breaks with what was there and institutes something new.[37] Jankélévitch sees generosity as "giving that which one is not," and because creation is nothing more than making something that was not there come into existence, he understands the instant of creation as that which is "most sovereignly generous."[38] Hence, he relates the instant of creation to grace, to a gift and a giving. In short, there is an ethical aspect to creation, and thus first philosophy necessarily concerns the ethical.

30. See ibid.; and Jankélévitch, *Le Je-ne-sais-quoi,* 94.

31. Jankélévitch, *Philosophie première,* 209.

32. Ibid., 218–19.

33. Ibid., 202, 208, 218.

34. Ibid., 205. See also Colin Smith, "The Philosophy of Vladimir Jankélévitch," *Philosophy* 32, no. 123 (October 1957): 321; and John Llewelyn, "In the Name of Philosophy," *Research in Phenomenology* 28 (1998): 41, 48.

35. Anne-Elizabeth Fernandez, "Vladimir Jankélévitch," *Dictionnaire des philosophes* (Paris: Presses Universitaires de France, 1984), 1336.

36. Jankélévitch, *Philosophie première,* 211.

37. Ibid., 213.

38. Ibid., 212.

Yet Jankélévitch's views about the ethical differ somewhat from our post-Enlightenment conception of the field. He worries that modern systems of ethics conceptualize moral behavior only in terms of some type of economic transaction in which someone receives what he or she is owed. In reaction to this, Jankélévitch looks back to classical philosophy, whose notion of morality centered on character and virtues, which he understands in terms of dispositions.[39] For Jankélévitch, there are two kinds of virtue: virtues of initiation and virtues of continuation.[40] Because life is a dialectic between the instant and the interval, some virtues such as fidelity, friendship, justice, and modesty pertain to the interval, whereas some virtues—courage, love, charity, and humility—relate to initiation, creation, and the instant.[41] Because of the importance of the notion of the instant across Jankélévitch's writings, it comes as no surprise that he favors virtues of initiation.

One never finds a set of rules or principles in his writings, because, as he says, "morality is neither inscribed in tables nor prescribed in commandments."[42] For Jankélévitch, one does not first grasp the moral law (as one would in Kant's view), or first contemplate the form of the Good (as one would with Plato), and then subsequently act. For him, through acting or willing we create virtues, we create the moral law, we create the Good. However, for Jankélévitch, moral work and moral action must be endlessly begun again. As soon as one acts—whether morally or not—the slate is wiped clean, so to speak, and one must now create something in this new moment. But it is not just the action itself that must be created or re-created in the new moment; the value or virtue itself must be chosen, that is re-created, too. Jankélévitch commented to Beauduc, "As soon as one wants to seize virtue, it becomes a caricature . . . as a result of its musical nature, virtue exists only in escaping us."[43]

In Jankélévitch's philosophy, one notices a recurring theme of love and the good will and their constant battle with evil. But these are not first principles. For Jankélévitch, there is no system or recipe for loving or willing

39. Jankélévitch, *Une Vie en toutes lettres,* 208. The letter is dated March 18, 1932.

40. See Smith, "Philosophy of Vladimir Jankélévitch," 321; and Monique Perigord, "Vladimir Jankélévitch ou improvisation et 'Kaïros,'" *Revue de Métaphysique et de Morale* 79 (April–June 1974): 245.

41. Smith, "Philosophy of Vladimir Jankélévitch," 321.

42. Vladimir Jankélévitch, *Quelque Part dans l'Inachevé* (with Béatrice Berlowitz) (Paris: Gallimard, 1978), 68.

43. Ibid., 68.

well.[44] With each instant, one must begin again not only at loving and willing well, but also at coming up with what these things are. Thus, Jankélévitch did not have a strict definition of love, with perhaps the one condition that love makes a person look beyond himself or herself. In *L'Austérité et la vie moral,* from 1956, Jankélévitch wrote: "only love finds sur-nature, which decidedly and in one fell swoop with the sovereign simplicity and the suddenness of genius places the man in the wholly other order of the forgetting of the self and the absolute by grace as it excludes it from the law."[45] Love, for Jankélévitch, is the beginning of the moral, but it is only the beginning. Given our freedom, we can just as easily will evil as we can will good, so his philosophy calls for us continually to create, define, and redefine love in the face of what we confront with each minute.

Jankélévitch on Forgiveness

The subject of forgiveness begins to appear in Jankélévitch's works after World War II. In the last chapter of a book-length discussion of evil from 1947—entitled *Le Mal* (Evil)—Jankélévitch began to formulate many of the ideas that would appear in the book that is translated here. He also discusses forgiveness in his monumental tome on ethics the *Traité des vertus* from 1949 and in a paper presented at the 1963 colloquium for Jewish intellectuals entitled "Introduction au thème du pardon" (Introduction to the Theme of Forgiveness). The French publisher Aubier wanted Jankélévitch to rework his public lecture courses on moral issues into a series of books. *Forgiveness,* which appeared in 1967, was the only title ever to appear. Unfortunately, this philosophical text has not received the same level of attention as has his polemical essay "Should We Pardon Them?" which was originally based on a letter to the newspaper *Le Monde,* and which later reappeared in book-length form in an edition entitled *L'Imprescriptible.* During the 1970s, Jankélévitch also authored other articles and gave interviews pertaining to forgiveness.

Traditionally, philosophers have not given much attention to the topic of forgiveness because it was taken to be first and foremost a religious or

44. Perigord, "Vladimir Jankélévitch ou improvisation et 'Kaïros,'" 243.

45. Vladimir Jankélévitch, *L'Austérité et la vie moral,* in *Philosophie morale,* ed. Françoise Schwab (Paris: Flammarion, 1998), 581.

theological issue. The topic of forgiveness is important because it concerns the broader problem of how to respond to injustice and evil. In this regard, it must be remembered that for Jankélévitch life, time, and the universe move in one irreversible direction. In a letter to Louis Beauduc, Jankélévitch both sets up the problem and provides a possible resolution. He writes: "The will can do all—except one thing: undo that which it has done. The power of undoing is of another order: of the order of grace, if you will. It is a miracle."[46] Forgiveness becomes an issue precisely because we cannot go back and undo what has been done. Furthermore, Jankélévitch foreshadows what seems to be his own view of forgiveness when he writes that this power of undoing is miraculous and of the order of grace. Forgiveness, as will be seen, cannot literally undo the past misdeed, but it can make it *as if* the misdeed never had occurred.

Forgiveness, like most of Jankélévitch's texts, is not merely a treatise on one topic. Herein lie both the importance and the beauty of the work. Not only does Jankélévitch provide a seminal "analysis" of forgiveness in this book, but he also provides a lucid assessment of the relationship between time and ethics (chapter 1), an important study of love (chapter 3), and a brilliant treatment of the contradictory poles of love and justice between which the moral agent finds himself or herself (conclusion). Jankélévitch effortlessly interweaves metaphysical, moral, psychological, legal, and theological discussions into a piece that transcends standard treatments of moral problems.

At first, the reader may be somewhat befuddled by Jankélévitch's manner of treating forgiveness; he literally devotes most of the book to a discussion of what forgiveness is not. Because true forgiveness resists standard attempts at analysis and elucidation, Jankélévitch claims that only a negative analysis of forgiveness is possible. So he proceeds by first considering acts that we often deem equivalent to forgiveness. Given his views about the nature of reality and the importance of the instant, it should come as no surprise that Jankélévitch is wary of attempts to pin down forgiveness to some specific concept or to a set of necessary and sufficient conditions. In several places throughout the book, Jankélévitch reiterates his idea that forgiveness is not one "thing" or "action" but rather a "horizon" or an "ideal limit" that we can only approach. In short, there is no criterion for forgiveness

---

46. Jankélévitch, *Une vie en toutes lettres,* 195. The letter is from 1931.

and—luckily—nothing like one. Every time one attempts to forgive, one creates forgiveness anew.

This is not to say that Jankélévitch cannot mention anything positive or definitive about forgiveness qua ideal-limit or qua horizon. In his discussions of why the actions that we often confuse with forgiveness are not really forgiveness, Jankélévitch actually articulates important—if not ground-breaking—considerations pertaining to forgiveness. In fact, it is precisely in these positive aspects that the importance and originality of Jankélévitch's treatment of forgiveness come to light. In the last paragraph of chapter 3, Jankélévitch writes: "Forgiveness itself forgives in one fell swoop and in a single, indivisible *élan,* and it pardons undividedly; in a single, radical, and incomprehensible movement, forgiveness effaces all, sweeps away all, and forgets all. In one blink of an eye, forgiveness makes a *tabula rasa* of the past, and this miracle is for forgiveness as simple as saying hello and good evening." In writing this, he relates forgiveness to his idea of the instant. From the very outset of the book, Jankélévitch maintains that forgiveness is not an attitude, mindset, ideology, and so on, but rather an event; it happens once and then it is gone.

Jankélévitch ultimately holds that true forgiveness must involve a real relation with another person. Forgiveness recognizes the person behind the bad action. If one merely forgets what the other person has done, or if one allows time to "heal" the wounds, or if someone simply says, "enough with this," then the effects of such actions may be similar to those of forgiveness. But unlike true forgiveness, these acts do not necessarily involve any type of connection with the wrongdoer. This is precisely why many contemporary accounts of forgiveness, whereby it is understood as the overcoming of hatred for another person, would not be true instances of forgiveness for Jankélévitch. For if a person forgives in order to overcome hatred, then the wrongdoer himself or herself is not the true concern for the victim, but rather the attempt to overcome hatred is the true concern.

Yet, these first two "conditions" or descriptions of forgiveness point toward what is the definitive aspect of forgiveness for Jankélévitch: the miraculous, ineffable, and extrajuridical nature of forgiveness. When an action is required or commanded, then one can give reasons as to why one should perform that action. Jankélévitch astutely points out that as soon as reasons are given as to why one should forgive, then forgiveness collapses back into something else such as excusing, clemency, or reconciliation. For example, if one is hardened by anger or stuck in one's anger, then forgiveness—qua forgetting—is to be recommended. In this case, forgiveness would amount to a type of mental hygiene. Or if there are mitigating circumstances, then the supposed wrongdoer should be excused. That is, if the circumstances made it such that the person accused of doing the wrong could not have done otherwise, then the person did not intend to perform the wrong act; he or she should be excused. Similarly, if one "forgives" the wrongdoer in order to rehabilitate him or her—because one thinks that wrongdoer will profit from this chance—then forgiveness merely becomes the means for reconciliation or rehabilitation. Rehabilitation is then at issue and is that which is valued. This is not to indicate in any way that there is something wrong with excusing, clemency, or reconciliation. But if there is something to be gained by reconciling with a wrongdoer, by forgetting about the past, by kissing and making up, or by realizing that there were mitigating circumstances surrounding the misdeed, then we do not need forgiveness because we already have ways of dealing with these situations: forgetting, reconciling, excusing, and so on.

Hence, Jankélévitch claims that the only way in which forgiveness can have meaning or play a role that is exclusive to it is precisely in those situations in which there is nothing to excuse or when forgetting is not possible. He writes: "Forgiveness absurdly, supernaturally, and unjustly forgives the inexcusable and the unforgivable which is the limit of the inexcusable. Such is the miracle. If evil were excusable, if there were attenuating circumstances, thus if evil were not evil, forgiveness would be superfluous; the indulgence founded on reason would suffice."[47] In a word, forgiveness by its very nature is reserved for those situations in which a person has no valid excuses as to why he or she committed a misdeed. If there are reasons or excuses and if something good is to come from forgiveness, then forgiveness automatically collapses back into one of the aforementioned actions that Jankélévitch claims are often confused with forgiveness.

Because forgiveness forgives that which cannot be excused or forgotten, it stands outside of what any system of ethics could prescribe, and as such it is necessarily amoral or immoral. A system of normative ethics may require that someone who has committed a terrible act be punished and be made to make amends for his or her action. Justice would require that the person be held accountable and make restitution for his or her actions. Insofar as forgiveness abolishes the fact that one holds the crime against the person and

47. Jankélévitch, *Quelque Part dans l'Inachevé*, 125.

abolishes one's demands for reparation or restitution, it goes against justice or a system of legalistic ethics. Hence, in this respect forgiveness is amoral; it returns kindness, love, or good for evil. It is guilty of being kind to a person who by his or her actions merits being dealt with severely.

It is in its spontaneity and freedom, which are literally ineffable, that forgiveness finds what truly separates it from other actions that emulate its effects. Because it is a truly free act, there can be nothing like Mill's Principle of Utility or Kant's Categorical Imperative to which we can have recourse in order to instruct us when or when not to forgive. One cannot deliberate or weigh out alternatives and then forgive. There are no reasons to forgive, per se; we cannot command or even recommend forgiveness because this turns forgiveness into something else. Forgiveness just happens, spontaneously. In this respect, it truly is of the order of grace and the miraculous.

Given Jankélévitch's views about becoming and temporality, he cannot claim that forgiveness makes the misdeed go away or that the crime is forgotten. Strictly speaking, the evil act can never go away, and the person who committed the act at that specific point in time will still always be the one who committed the act. Jankélévitch clarifies his position when in chapter 3 he writes:

To forgive is neither to change one's mind on the score of the guilty person, nor to rally around the thesis of innocence . . . Quite the contrary! The supernaturality of forgiveness consists in this, that my opinion on the subject of the guilty person precisely has not changed; but . . . it is . . . my relations with the guilty person that [are] modified, it is the whole orientation of our relations that finds itself inverted, overturned, and overwhelmed! The judgment of condemnation has stayed the same, but an arbitrary and gratuitous change has intervened, a diametrical and radical inversion, *peristophē,* which transfigures hatred into love.

In this passage, Jankélévitch emphasizes that the one forgiving does not now proclaim that the criminal is innocent or that he or she in fact never committed the crime or the evil act. Instead, Jankélévitch claims that true forgiveness alters the relationship between the victim and the wrongdoer. The victim no longer holds the misdeed against the wrongdoer, no longer demands any form of restitution from the wrongdoer, and renounces any claims to a moral advantage or high ground.

The fact that forgiveness stands outside of any moral system—and, hence, any system of justice—on Jankélévitch's account does not mean that it should never be granted. Instead, the nature of forgiveness leads to a tension—or perhaps, better stated, a contradiction—between the order of justice and the order of love or grace. In fact, such a tension exists between Jankélévitch's philosophical text *Forgiveness* and his essay "Should We Pardon Them?" In the latter, Jankélévitch argues vehemently against a pardon by France—for which there was a formal vote in 1965—of Germany and the Germans in regard to Nazi war crimes. His claim is that "crimes against humanity are imprescriptible, that is, the penalties against them cannot lapse; time has no hold on them."[48] He makes the case that the Holocaust is unlike any other crime that has been committed. So to pardon the country that perpetrated the Holocaust—that is, to restore full relations with Germany and to move on after twenty years—"would be a new crime against the human species."[49] In *Forgiveness,* on the other hand, Jankélévitch explicitly writes that there is no such thing as that which is unforgivable. It is this apparent contradiction between these two specific texts that became the subject for several essays by Jacques Derrida.[50] However, Derrida's essays are not strict line-by-line analyses of these texts. Instead, he uses Jankélévitch's writings on forgiveness as places from which to begin his own reflections on this subject. Whether or not Derrida's arguments in these essays are cogent is an issue that is beyond the scope of this introduction; other scholars have done this work. What is important about Derrida's use of these texts is that it brings much-needed new exposure and credibility to Jankélévitch's work.

In the end, the "contradiction" that exists between Jankélévitch's position in "Should We Pardon Them?" and the one he takes in *Forgiveness* is not really one at all. In "Should We Pardon Them?" Jankélévitch looks at the issue of forgiving from within a system of ethics and laws. Given this fact, it should come as no surprise that Jankélévitch argues against any type of forgiveness or even reconciliation with Germans and Germany. The reason for this is simple: the German crimes during World War II were so horrible and so far-reaching that there is nothing that anyone could do even to begin to

48. Vladimir Jankélévitch, "Should We Pardon Them?" trans. Ann Hobart, *Critical Inquiry* 22 (Spring 1996): 556–57.

49. Ibid., 556.

50. See Jacques Derrida, "On Forgiveness," in *On Forgiveness and Cosmopolitanism,* trans. Marc Dooley and Michael Hughes (London: Routledge, 2001), 27–60. Jacques Derrida, "To Forgive: The Unforgivable and the Imprescriptible," in *Questioning God,* ed. John Caputo, Mark Dooley, and Michael Scanlon, trans. Elizabeth Rottenberg (Bloomington: Indiana University Press, 2001), 21–51.

make up for, to "pay back," or to make good the evil actions done. On the other hand, in *Forgiveness,* Jankélévitch continually makes the claim that there is no such thing as an unforgivable. It must be remembered, however, that forgiveness is a spontaneous, supernatural, and gracious act. Because of its nature, no one can deliberate about whether or not to do it, let alone require or even recommend it. It stands outside of systems of justice and normative ethics. When it comes to pass, it comes to pass spontaneously.

But simply the fact that forgiveness stands outside of systems of normative ethics and justice does not necessarily mean that it is immoral in the grand scheme of things. In this regard, for Jankélévitch, forgiveness is in the same situation as other actions such as love, courage, and charity. None of these, in their true form, fits into a systematic ethics because they are all spontaneous acts for Jankélévitch. As such, they can never be recommended. However, it may occur that in hindsight, when one looks back on any of these acts, one may see that they in fact did great good and perhaps more good than anything that a system of normative ethics could have recommended. Unfortunately, when one forgives, one also could be letting the wrongdoer off much too easily; naïve reconciliation or excusing could also be a slap in the face to the victims. This is Jankélévitch's worry in "Should We Pardon Them?" But it must be stressed that this worry pertains to issues of justice and arises from within a system of justice.

In the last passage from Jankélévitch cited above, Jankélévitch writes that forgiveness "transfigures hatred into love." This thought gives rise to an eternal problem that Jankélévitch discusses in the conclusion to *Forgiveness,* where he addresses the continual struggle between love and evil. Here Jankélévitch provides a compelling description of the human "moral" condition. At each moment when we have to make a moral decision, we are free to choose. The previous moment is gone and we must choose again in this moment. The problem that exists—and this shows the acuity and radicality of Jankélévitch's philosophizing—is that we can choose to act in any manner; we can love, we can forgive, we can follow some system of ethics, be it Kant's or Mill's or Aristotle's. However, we cannot forgive and be just or love and be just. The two are at odds with each other. Each can be moral in its own way and each can be immoral in its own way. Or, to put it differently, there are two ways to respond to evil and injustice: the path of loving and forgiveness or the path of moral systems and justice, which is sometimes severe. Unfortunately, there is no criterion or test that we can use to tell us when to be severe as opposed to when to love or forgive. Moral life or the moral human condition, for Jankélévitch, is the constant struggle between spontaneity—love, forgiveness, grace—and reason in the guise of following moral and legal systems. Not surprisingly, this very struggle is one of the main themes in his last book, *Le Paradoxe de la morale* (1981).

Notes on the Translation

In preparing this translation, I have used the original 1967 edition of *Le Pardon*, published in Paris by Aubier-Montaigne. *Le Pardon* also exists in a collection of six of Jankélévitch's writings on ethics, entitled *Philosophie morale*, edited by Françoise Schwab, which appeared in 1998 from the publisher Flammarion in Paris. Except for pagination and miscellaneous typographical errors, the versions are the same.

Because Jankélévitch's writing is unique, I have attempted to stay as close to the French version as possible insofar as clarity would allow. I did not break up Jankélévitch's often exceedingly long paragraphs into shorter paragraphs. However, on some occasions, when clarity was at issue, I chose to divide some of his long sentences into shorter ones. I have not altered Jankélévitch's use of ellipsis points; they appear as they do in the original French. Likewise, a dash in this translation reflects a dash in the original French version. I have provided a glossary in order to show how I have translated certain key terms or expressions. It should be noted that I have translated the French *pardon* as "forgiveness." While I could have rendered the French term with the English "pardon," I chose to use "forgiveness" because in contemporary parlance, "pardon" has the connotation of "clemency." Likewise, literature on the subject, both contemporary and going as far back as the Christian Scriptures, speaks of the issue at hand in terms of "forgiveness" or "forgiving" instead of "pardoning." In the few instances in which Jankélévitch uses the word *gracier,* I use "pardon" as the English term, but the reader should be aware of the obvious connection that this term has with "grace."

Jankélévitch makes frequent use of Greek and Latin words and phrases. In this translation, Greek terms and phrases have been transliterated. These words and phrases appear in italics. However, Jankélévitch sometimes transliterates the terms in the text; whenever this is the case, the words are not italicized. If Jankélévitch cites a text and an English translation of the text exists, then I make reference to the English version. Translations of citations from other texts are my own unless otherwise noted. Likewise, bracketed material in the footnotes represents my additions to Jankélévitch's own footnotes. Finally, I do not alter Jankélévitch's use of what is now considered to be gendered language. I do not pretend to know Jankélévitch's position on gender issues and gendered language. My goal in translating his book was to stay as close to the text as possible. Thus, I have followed Jankélévitch's use of "he" and "him" in rendering their corresponding French terms into English. No one should draw any conclusions about my own views on this subject—which in the case at hand are irrelevant—from the fact that I have followed the original text.

I need to thank several people without whose assistance this project never would have come to fruition. Alan Udoff, who has written on forgiveness, took an interest in this project from the beginning and put me in contact with the University of Chicago Press. John Tryneski and the staff at the University of Chicago Press have been extremely helpful and supportive. Arnold Davidson, who has taught a graduate seminar on Jankélévitch's *Le Pardon,* offered many useful suggestions for the improvement of the translation. Ryan Coyne arduously looked over an entire draft of the translation, found mistakes and omissions, and suggested alternative ways of rendering words and phrases. Michael Greene meticulously went through several versions of my translator's introduction and offered many thoughtful suggestions on how to improve it. Susan Tarcov provided helpful comments for improving the translation in the course of copyediting. Finally, I would like to thank my wife, Jennifer Brady, and our children, Eamon and Neve, for their patience with me.

Introduction

It is not difficult to understand why the duty to forgive has become our problem today. The forgiveness that one should grant to the offender and to the persecutor is, indeed, exceptionally difficult for a certain category of humiliated and offended people: to forgive is an effort to begin again continually, and no one will be astonished if we say that in certain cases the ordeal is at the limits of our strength. But this is because forgiveness in the strict sense is effectively a limit case, just as remorse, sacrifice, and the gesture of charity can be. It is very possible that a forgiveness free from any ulterior motive has never been granted here below, that in fact an infinitesimal amount of rancor subsists in the remission of every offense, such as the calculating self-interest that cannot be weighed, or that a microscopic motive of concern for the self subsists hidden in the underground of unselfishness, such as the imperceptible and small speculation that makes despair into a theatrical *disperato*[1] and that is the impure consciousness[2] of a guilty conscience. From this point of view, forgiveness is an event that has never come to pass in history, an act for which there is no place in space, a gesture of the soul that does not exist in our contemporary psychology ... However, and even if it is not a datum within psychological experience, the gesture of forgiving would still be a duty. What's more, it is only in the imperative because rightly it is not in the indicative! But the imperative itself is imperious only because the obligation prescribes something that is in theory capable of being performed. Here are two Kantian paradoxes that seem

1. [*Disperato de théâtre:* Jankélévitch often uses the Italian word *disperato* (desperate) untranslated.]

2. [*Conscience:* the French word *conscience* can mean either "consciousness" or "conscience."]

to contradict each other but that are both true at the same time. First, it is true, paradoxically true, that to will is to be able, and that if our will is infinite, then our ability in this sense is no less. The man of desire cannot magically and literally do all that he wishes, but the good will of the agent can do all that it wills. In this respect, the "omnivolent" being is omnipotent. If, then, the good will wills what is good, it can do it; and, consequently, the good is something that everyone can do on the condition of willing it. For the good is precisely something that it is necessary to do! From this we conclude that one can always do that which one should do if one sincerely wills it. And not only can one do it, a fortiori one can will to do it, the capacity to will being the only capacity that is absolutely discretionary, autocratic, and ecumenical that all men possess in virtue of their humanness. For in order to will, it suffices to will. And the will to will,[3] infinitely, depends only on our liberty, and it rests on an instant. What each person is capable of doing in principle is all the more reason that each person will have the strength to will to do it and will find the resources necessary to will this will. What good is it to *require* what no one can do? Even the apostle writes in Corinthians:[4] God will not permit that you are tempted beyond your strength, *ouk easei humas peirasthēnai huēer ho dunasthe,* but along with the temptation he gave us the capacity to endure it, *to dunasthai hupenegkein.* This capacity (*dunasthai*), which is the strength to resist, is the role of what is psychological. A fortunate possibility, *ekbasis,* is thus in store for us in all cases; thanks to it, the ordeal will always be humane (*anthrōpinos*) and the sinner always inexcusable. A commandment that commands the impossible is not a serious commandment but rather a Platonic recommendation without consequence, a simple folktale; worse yet: to require that which cannot be required, thus furnishing all sorts of pretexts and excuses for inaction, is a false intransigence, a Machiavellian sophism of ill will, or, who knows? a cunning act of sabotage. A purism that unconditionally requires purity without concessions of any kind, or an extremism that wills the end without the means, or a verism that preaches truth at all costs and in all cases, or a moral radicalism that wants an inaccessible perfection to the point of contradicting itself, these are the true clandestine enterprises of demoralization. The forgiving of offenses, then, would not be a serious task if the injured person lacked the strength necessary to forgive the one who in-

---

3. [*Le vouloir vouloir.*]
4. 1 Corinthians 10:13.

jured him. Forgiveness is certainly not a decision of the will, as is the victory over temptation, but like a decision it is an event that is initial, sudden, and spontaneous.—And here now is the opposite paradoxology: Kant questions if in the history of humankind there has ever been a single act of virtue that was purely selfless.[5] Similarly, La Rochefoucauld denounced altruism as a paraphrase of egoism, the virtues as variations on the theme of pride, self-lessness as a specious alibi for selfishness, and philanthropy as a clandestine philauty. Does not the "natural dialectic" threaten to discourage our confidence in a good will that can do all? The thing that is easiest in the world is thus the most difficult. In this impossible possibility lies all the ambiguity of "rigorism" . . . In fact, our abilities are effectively limited, but we have to ignore this and act as if we were capable of doing all that we will: for in this respect a good will that is innocent, sincere, and impassioned guards against usurping the perspective of the witness. Actually, the hero who not only attains but goes beyond the limits of his abilities, this hero, being annihilated by death, ceases to exist; such is the case of the hyperbolic sacrifice, which is *usque ad mortem.* But here *until (usque)* means both "to the death, excluding death" and "to the death, death included." At this highest point where existence touches nonexistence, where man, reaching the summit of his volition, is in the same instant stronger and weaker than death, the limit of human possibilities coincides with the superhuman, with inhumane impossibility. Pure love without a change of one's mind and a pure forgiveness without *ressentiment*[6] are, thus, not perfections that one might obtain in an inalienable fashion and the possession of which would be the source of a good conscience and contented complaisance for their possessor. The satisfaction of having done one's duty that is supposedly "accomplished," in the passive past tense, is a testament for which dogmatism actively claims responsibility. Indeed, many moral automata and virtuous parrots believe, that they possess a heart that is habitually pure, boast of their purity in the manner of a chronic habit, profess purism, and claim to enjoy the fruits of their merit. But a forgiving machine or something that automatically doles out graces and indulgences has undoubtedly only a distant relation to true forgiveness! In complete contrast, the grace of absolute selflessness, similar

---

5. [See Immanuel Kant, *Foundations of the Metaphysics of Morals,* trans. Lewis White Beck (Indianapolis: Bobbs-Merrill, 1981), 23.]

6. [*Ressentiment*—roughly translated as "resentment"—will be left in French throughout the text. It likely alludes to Nietzsche's use of *ressentiment.*]

in this regard to an impossible, Fénelonian pure love, is rather an ideal limit and an inaccessible horizon that one approaches asymptotically without ever attaining it in fact. This comes back to saying that the grace of forgiveness and of selfless love is granted to us in an instant and as a disappearing appearance—this is to say that at the same moment it is found and lost again. Is not a good impulse that is continued just as contradictory as a permanent spark? Does not an inspiration that claims to perpetuity as a manner of being degenerate into drivel? This flabbiness of forgiveness has now become a spectacle that is, so to speak, daily.

I. Temporality, Intellection, Liquidation

The *élan*[7] of forgiveness is so impalpable, so debatable, that it discourages all attempts at analysis. In this fleeting shock, in this imperceptible flickering of charity, where are the points of contact[8] that would make a philosophical discourse possible? In the limpid transparency of this innocent movement, what would we be able to find to describe? Incredible is the briefest instant, indescribable is the simplest mystery of the cordial conversion. But if it is a question of relative forgiveness and not of absolute forgiveness, then very well! About the empirical substitutes for meta-empirical forgiveness, and about the natural forms of supernatural forgiveness, we will have a vast amount to say . . . Whether forgiveness is reticent or selfish, that is to say whether forgiveness does not completely liquidate the past or squints toward the future, whether it conceals a secret rancor or consists of a shameful speculation, or whether it is mixed with *ressentiment* or "*pressentiment,*" in either case it offers abundant material for psychological dissection; in the one or the other case it becomes possible to parse the factors together and thwart ulterior motives. A few seeds of poorly digested rancor or a few calculations that are overly diplomatic suffice to complicate, to

---

7. [The French term *élan*—roughly translated as "spirit," "momentum," or "energy"—will be left in the original French throughout the text because of its connection to Bergson's "*élan vital.*"]

8. ["Points of contact" is a rendering of *les prises*. The idea is that there needs to be something that one can grasp or of which one can take hold. An alternative rendering of *les prises* would be "the solid ground."]

thicken, and to trouble the diaphanous sincerity of true forgiveness. Indeed, the more that forgiveness is impure and opaque, the more that it lends itself to description. As a matter of fact, only an apophatic or negative philosophy of forgiveness is truly possible. To begin with, we will have especially much to say about what true, disinterested forgiveness is not. Three replacement products offer themselves to us from the start: *decay through time, intellective excuse,* and *liquidation,* which is a "passage to the limit," can take the place of forgiveness, that is, can serve as forgiveness. If we do not take the intentional movement into account, then these three forms of simili-forgiveness have almost the same exterior effects as pure forgiveness, just as the appearance of conformity to duty has the same exterior effects as duty done for the sake of duty. Simili-forgiveness without the intention of forgiving is as indiscernible from true forgiveness as the imitation is from the model. For the copy sometimes mimics the model so well that it is difficult to tell which is which! Whether we forgive out of weariness or charity, it means the same for the one who insults: the differential element will stay invisible . . . But the heart of forgiveness, where is it? Apocryphal forgivings nevertheless have something in common with authentic forgiveness: they put an end to a situation that is critical, tense, or abnormal and that would unravel one day or another, for a chronic hostility that is passionately rooted in a rancorous memory demands to be resolved, as does any anomaly. Rancor arouses cold war, which is a state of exception, and forgiveness, be it true or false, does the opposite: it lifts the state of exception, liquidates what the rancor maintained, and resolves vindictive obsession. The knot of rancor unravels.

II. The Event, Grace, and the Relation to the Other. On Clemency.

Temporality, intellection, and liquidation, however, do not constitute in themselves all the distinctive marks by which true forgiveness is recognized. Here are three aspects that are among the most characteristic: True forgiveness is a significant *event* that happens at such and such an instant of historical becoming. True forgiveness, which is at the margins of all legality, is a *gracious gift* from the offended to the offender. True forgiveness is a *personal relation* with another person. To begin with, the event is certainly the decisive moment of forgiveness, just as it is the decisive moment of a conversion. Does it occur always and everywhere? On the contrary, it blurs into certain condescending forms of clemency: the sage is exempted from the meritorious effort and from the harrowing sacrifice that permit the offended to surmount the offense; for this invulnerable person almost nothing occurs or comes of it; the injuries of the offender do not affect him at all. No one expects to find true forgiveness in Epictetus's *Discourses*. For this haughty Stoic, hardened by ataraxia,[9] analgesia, and apathy,[10] the dramatic instant hardly plays any role at all. Injuries, for the sage, are more insignificant than scratches; he hardly perceives their existence. By disregarding evil and wickedness, clemency minimizes the injury at the same time; in minimizing the injury, it renders forgiveness useless. There is no forgiveness because, so to speak, there was no offense and absolutely no offended party, even though there was an offender. But was there even an offender?— Clemency, which does not imply any determinate event, is still less a true relation to the ipseity[11] of the other person. In sum: almost nothing to forgive and almost no one whom to forgive! From the height of his altitude the magnanimous person is much too big to see the gnats and lice who harass him; moreover, megalopsychia[12] easily turns into disdain. Not only is the offender neglected, but, to put it in a better way, he is quasi-nonexistent. In turn, clemency is not only condescending, but even more so, it is "intransitive"; it is literally solitary in its magnanimity. Clemency is forgiveness that has no interlocutor. Moreover, the person granting clemency does not utter the word of forgiveness to a true partner of flesh and bones. This tête-à-tête is a solitude, this dialogue is a soliloquy, this relation is a solipsism. It is an understatement to say that the person granting clemency has never suffered

9. [*Ataraxie:* the term was used by the Epicureans and Pyrrho to mean "tranquility," "freedom from disturbance," or "quietude." This refers to a mental state, as opposed to *aponia*, which refers to physical tranquility.]

10. [*Apathie:* the reference is to the Stoic doctrine of *apatheia*, meaning "indifference to pleasure and pain."]

11. [*Ipséité:* "selfhood," the opposite of alterity.]

12. [*Mégalopsychie:* Several lines later when Jankélévitch writes of "magnanimity or magnificence" and then follows this with their respective Greek terms, the first term, transliterated into French, is "mégalopsychie." In book 4, chapters 2–3 of the *Nicomachean Ethics*, Aristotle writes of magnificence and magnanimity, respectively. "Megalopsychia," meaning "greatness of soul," is translated as "magnanimity." See Aristotle's *Nicomachean Ethics*, trans. and notes by Terence Irwin, 2nd ed. (Indianapolis: Hackett, 1999), 1122a18–1125a36.]

from the act of the one who insults him, that he never had time to hold a grudge, that he neither reproaches the person who insults him for anything, nor even gives him the honor of feeling the least bit of rancor, be this even a nascent rancor that is just as quickly suppressed by forgiveness . . . Actually, he does not even care for the person whom he absolves! He does not even perceive the existence of the gnat! Be it magnanimity or magnificence, *megalopsychia* or *megaloprepeia,* clemency excludes every truly transitive or intentional relation with the next person. Clemency is not forgiveness any more than generosity is love. The generous person is simply too rich in resources, and the resources overflow themselves or the generous person blindly distributes them around himself just as a cornucopia gives of the earth and benedictions. In this respect, the generous person resembles nature: nature as well does not love anyone in particular. In its vital superabundance, it squanders its liberalities indistinctly, blindly, and without any selective predilection for anyone, for nature does not have preferences and it neither chooses nor hierarchizes values; moreover, nature gives flowers to everyone, to good people as well as evil. And it is likewise without gratitude just as much as it is without rancor; ungrateful and forgetful, nature shows itself to be perfectly indifferent to our sorrows. Anonymous nature does not have intentions, and insofar as it is unaware of the alterity of the other, a fortiori it is unaware of the relation to the other. Consider the slightly mad billionaire who throws her dollars out the window or distributes them to passersby, or invites all the passersby to her table, not because she particularly likes her guests but simply because the guests had the luck of passing beneath her windows at the right moment. Consider the man who, happy from love, smiles at all of the unknown people whom he encounters, who sings, and who kisses the subway ticket taker. But his kiss does not go out to the ticket taker and his smile is not in my honor; he smiles at no matter whom; he just smiles at the person who happens to be there at the moment when he passes. The world is not big enough for this person who is full of smiles. This is how clemency is lavish with graces, with full hands and without even paying attention to the person receiving the graces! Aristotle, as we know, gives more attention to liberality than to forgiveness, friendship than to charity. Stoicism preaches a general philanthropy and an abstract philadelphy that loves all of humankind; but tender agape, but the immediate movement of allocution and the predilection of the first person for its beloved second person by and large remains foreign to ancient wisdom.

Nevertheless, Hellenism appreciates the virtue of poverty insofar as poverty implies prideful independence and substantial autarchy;[13] but it ignores mendicity in as much as mendicity implies a moment of humiliation and suppliant demand. Indeed, forgiveness and mendicity go in opposite directions from one another; for the former magnanimously concedes grace, whereas the latter humbly implores alms. The former gives and forgives, whereas the latter receives and asks for forgiveness . . . But they have in common that they both come to pass and that they transitively put two people in relation to one another. Clemency itself is not the privileged moment of a relation with the Other; that is, it is both indifferent to the wrongs of the Other and insensitive to the presence of the other. What insults you, Epictetus's *Handbook* tells us, is not the person, *ouch ho loidorōn hē tuptōn hubrizei*,[14] but simply the opinion (*dogma*) that you form of the insult. For the sage who is overwhelmed with humiliations and snubs, for the one who, himself, would have had much to forgive of persecutors and violent people, and finally for the slave from Epaphrodite, it is a matter of being invincible (*anikētos*) in a battle,[15] yes, a battle (*agōn*), instead of a dialogue! It is a matter of being the strongest, while being the weakest. The sage, taking refuge in the citadel of self-will, in effect ignores the susceptibility of weak people and in the face of the insult makes himself more insensitive than a stone. Are stones in the street susceptible? It is beautiful to vanquish when one is defeated! Stoic clemency has never abandoned this armor of sublime indifference.

The effectivity of the event does not disappear any less in temporal decay or in intellection. Time drags out the event throughout the interval, as the days and years go by; and as for intellection, even if it implies the discovery of a rational truth, it completely annuls the instant of forgiveness and makes it disappear. What has come to pass ceases to be sudden if one waits for absolution from duration; but if we appeal to intellection, then what has come to pass in general ceases to come to pass! On the other hand, the deci-

---

13. [*Autarkie:* in reference to the Stoic virtue of *autarkeia,* meaning "emotional and physical self-sufficiency."]

14. *Handbook,* §20. [*Handbook of Epictetus,* trans. and ed. Nicholas P. White (Indianapolis: Hackett, 1983), 16: "Remember that what is insulting you is not the person who abuses you or hits you, but the judgment about them that they are insulting."]

15. *Handbook,* §21. [Ibid., 16. Actually, Jankélévitch seems to be citing §19: "You can be invincible if you do not enter any contest in which victory is not up to you."]

sion to go to the limit always comes to pass as an arbitrary and instantaneous occurrence.—As for the relation with the person, it is not a true personal relation either in chronological decay or in the passage to the limit:
neither in the one case nor in the other does the person who takes himself
to be forgiving have someone before him whom he would truly forgive. The
person forgiven by this forgiveness is rather an anonymous person, a being
without a face toward whom the insulted person behaves negligently.—Forgiveness is, thus, a free gift from the offended person to the offender. This
third characteristic, which is perhaps the most essential because it implies
an event and a relation to someone, we find in temporality and even in the
passage to the limit. Indeed, forgiveness surfaces in the extralegal, extrajuridical domain of our existence. Like equity, but still more, it is an opening
in a closed morality, a type of halo around a strict law; is equity not the
welcome infringement that we sometimes make on strict justice?[16] The rigorous contours of the law become hazy, diffuse, and atmospheric because
of the effect of forgiveness; justice with its sanctions becomes completely
blurred in the fog of evasive approximations. Without a doubt, in regulating
amnesty, prescription, and the very exercise of the "right of grace," the law
endeavors to impose its delays and limits on generous illegality. This is how
a "tip" seems to lose its optional, spontaneous character and becomes part of
the bill, how little by little gifts become taxes. But cordial gratification infinitely reconstitutes itself outside of the contract and beyond the service for
which one pays. Unceasingly, law codifies and encompasses the gracious
movement of forgiveness. And unceasingly forgiveness escapes beyond the
limits where a massive codex claims to contain it. By refusing to be a post-
script to literal law and a jurisprudence of justice, forgiveness is a principle
of mobility and fluidity for the law. By the grace of forgiveness, this law will
remain pneumatic,[17] evasive, and approximate. Thus, simply the idea of a

16. *Laws,* 6.757d–e: *to gar epieikes kai suggnōmon tou teleou kai akribous para dikēn tēn or-
thēn estin ēaratethraumenon.* ["this is the kind of 'equality' we should concentrate on as we
bring our state into the world … He must always make *justice* his aim. It consists of granting
the 'equality' that unequals deserve to get. Yet on occasion a state as a whole (unless it is prepared to put up with a degree of friction in one part or another) will be obliged to apply these
concepts in a rather rough and ready way, because complaisance and toleration are the enemies
of strict justice." Trans. Trevor J. Saunders, in *Plato: Complete Works,* ed. John M. Cooper (Indianapolis: Hackett, 1997), 1433.]

17. [*Pneumatique:* from the Stoic term for "spirit" or "soul."]

right of forgiveness destroys forgiveness. Forgiveness finds its use when the injury remains unexpiated, the mistake remains uncorrected, and as long as the victim is not paid damages for the damage. We do not say of the condemned person who has done his time in prison and completely served his penalty without remission or amnesty, we do not say of this condemned person on the day of his release that he leaves forgiven ... That would be a mockery that is only too bitter! We say only that he is cleared. That is all. His debt is paid and he no longer owes anything to anyone. In principle, society has given him in the form of a sentence the evil that it received from him. Tit for tat! The status quo ante (on the condition of knowing neither of the police record, nor of the lost years, which are irreversible) is arithmetically reestablished by penal compensation, that is to say, by leveling off the unjust protrusion. An impurity purified according to the rigors of justice no longer has need of gifts from anyone ... On the other hand, forgiveness finds a raison d'être when the moral debtor is still a debtor: hurry up and forgive before the debtor is cleared! Forgive in haste while there still is a punishment to shorten and more generally in order still to dispose of a penalty for which you can give grace to the guilty person. If you wait too long forgiveness will be nothing more than a bad joke. To forgive is to release the guilty one from his punishment or from a part of his punishment, or to liberate him before the completion of his punishment, and all this for nothing and in exchange for nothing, gratuitously, from beyond the marketplace! But for that, it is still necessary that there be a punishment or a bit of punishment to remit ... The material for forgiveness, then, is the unexpiated offense or the unexpiated portion of the offense; in other words, it is the offense that is unexpiated or partially unredeemed that is the object of gracious remission. Just as a bonus is a gift that one grants in addition to and from beyond the marketplace or from outside of the balance sheet, and that is, so to speak, a fringe benefit around a commutative payment, so forgiveness, a negative gift, is this addition that is a subtraction and that remains on the margins of the *antipeponthos,* that is, corrective justice. Without being obliged, the offended person renounces any claim to what is due to him and any exercise of his right; he freely interrupts his pursuits and decides not to take into account the wrong that he has suffered. Forgiveness is the concavity of which the gift is the convexity.[18]

18. [*Le pardon est en creux ce que le don est en relief.*]

III. The Offense and the Sin

A third distinction will here serve to support the first two. Successively playing the part of the event, of grace, and of the relation to the other in temporality, in intellection, and in liquidation, we will place ourselves each time in
two different points of view. The act to be forgiven, indeed, can be of two
sorts, to which correspond two forms of forgiveness; one is more psychological, the other is more purely moral. First, one can forgive the affronts
that one has oneself suffered; self-love and self-interest alone are at stake
here. As for values, they are wronged only in the measure in which an attack
against the I can be an attack against human dignity, for otherwise values
themselves are not "capable of being wronged"! This forgiveness by which
the offended party decides to abstract from his own ego in renouncing all
reparations is neither the least costly nor the least heartrending: for the only
meritorious "disinterestedness" is the one that has expressly made the cruel
sacrifice of self-interest. It is of little importance if the offense that one has
suffered does not create an ethical situation, or if the absolution of the offender does not give rise to a moral dilemma: forgiveness is itself the moral gesture, even though my own injured interest or my injured susceptibility does
not constitute moral problems. But one can also forgive outside of every
offense and all personal snubs. Forgiveness, which was the forgetting of injuries a little while ago, is now grace conceded to sin; in this case I do not
forgive the evil that one has done to me but evil as such, not the injury that
has hurt me but the injustice that the guilty person committed in general.
This forgiveness, giving back to the sinner all or part of the punishment that
he merited, gives rise to an ethical problem; from the moment that the
wrong remains unpunished, or that the sinner is considered to be cleared as
concerns the moral law, forgiveness gives rise to a conflict of duties and provokes scruples in us.—The distinction that we have just made concerns, in
particular, the relation with the Other, for forgiveness is obviously more personalized when the insult pertains to oneself alone and when the insulted
person should forgive the one who has insulted him. We must carefully distinguish this forgiveness from the impersonal forgiveness that comes after
an offense to values.

In temporal decay, whether it erases a sin or whether it attenuates an
offense, will we find the event, the gratuitousness, and the relation with
others?

1   Temporal Decay

If decay is a natural effect of duration, then it is necessary to admit that forgiveness truly confirms and even ratifies the very intention of nature. It is not that the decay of material things or minerals results from the temporality of time, strictly speaking. It is not time itself that transforms things, nor that gradually erodes them (because time is impalpable). It is the action of certain physical factors in time; it is the wind and the sea over the course of years but it is not the years themselves. It is not the minutes that muffle the sound waves of an echo or the vibrations of a diapason that fade, but it is the resistance of the air! On the other hand, the decay of living organisms, if it is accelerated by physical or chemical agents, results above all from a qualitative and irreversible entropy that is essential to a lived becoming. No, certainly, man never bathes twice in a row in the same river. Rather, it is necessary to say more: it is not the same man who bathes two times in a row . . . If we believe Heraclitus, at least the bather would stay the same over the course of his baths, for even in mobility there is an immobile system of reference. We know that Bergsonian superevolutionism renounces this last kernel of substantiality and immutable fixedness. All is change, including the subject that changes. Situations are modified along with the people who are in these situations. Other times, other problems! In this respect, forgiveness is very much headed in the direction of evolution, which always forges ahead. Forgiveness is opposed to rancor as that which makes itself is opposed to what is ready-made. Let us show in what manner forgiveness confirms the natural dimension of becoming and annuls the obstinate resistance of men to this becoming. For in all temporality there is a recto and a verso, a position and a negation . . .

I. To Come Back Is Still to Come to Pass. Becoming Is Always Right Side Out.[1]

Becoming, in the first place, is essentially futurition and, secondarily, preterition. That is, depending on whether one looks toward the future or toward the past, becoming ceaselessly posits a future, and with the same stroke and at the same time it deposits a past behind it. Successively, it makes the future present and makes the present past, and it does this in the same movement and with the same continual renewal. Indeed, to construct a becoming, a *recollection* and an *appearing*[2] are necessary at the same time. But here there are not two opposite movements made for thwarting each other, for if appearing and "settling up" pulled in diametrically opposed directions, they would neutralize each other reciprocally, and, when all is said and done, becoming would come to a halt at dead center. Indeed, becoming qua advent of the future[3] is secondarily a factory of memories. But these souvenirs, which are the natural deposit of position just as valleys are the reverse of mountains, fill the imagination and normally print an *élan* and an increased push on futurition, the role of memory being to enrich experience and not to retard the action; on the trampoline of memories, the action leaps higher and more energetically. Such is the effect of the alternative![4] Alteration makes what is other come to pass by driving back what is the same. Innovation actualizes novelty by draining the overabundance of memories, by favoring the deflation of the memory. And while the Not-yet becomes a Now, the Now, ipso facto, becomes an Already-more. Tomorrow will be Today, and Today will be Yesterday, and all of this in one single and same direction; such is the intention of becoming, for irreversible becoming has one *direction* and one vocation! All that goes in the direction of the current and of history is, therefore, right side out. Everything that goes in the opposite direction or swims in the countercurrent, meaning upstream, is headed in reverse. It is a matter of becoming in the direction of time and not of coming back to a countertime or against the grain of time . . . Even if the "recollection" is not an "appearing" in reverse, it is more the "coming to pass" that

1. [*Revenir, c'est encore advenir. Le devenir est toujours à l'endroit.*]
2. [*Pour fair un devenir, il faut à la fois, le souvenir et le survenir.*]
3. [*Devenir, en tant que avènement de l'avenir.*]
4. [Jankélévitch authored a work entitled *L'Alternative* (Paris: Alcan, 1938), and the notion of the alternative is an important theme in his works.]

is the true "coming" right side out.[5] Does not what has come to pass express the Elpidian[6] essence of coming, which is entirely hope, adventure, and advent? Coming back is not so much coming in reverse, it is rather in the manner of ghosts[7] to feign coming, for "coming back" is a simulacrum and a phantom of what has come. As an inverted progression, regression especially is a fundamental immobility under the appearance of movement: it stays stationary more than it goes backward. Recollection is this false coming. But in certain cases it can appear as a wave of return that tends to neutralize futurition. Among all the forms of false coming and of anachronism, rancorous retrogradation, even though it is not literally regressive, is without a doubt the most passionate, for rancor is not a recollection like others; rancor does not consent to evolve, as does recollection; nor does it allow itself to be colored by the chronological succession of events, as does recollection. Rather, the man of *ressentiment,* being similar to the remorseful man, clings and clutches to the preterit and stubbornly hardens against futurition. Aggressive rancor resists becoming; and forgiveness, on the contrary, favors becoming by ridding it of impediments that weigh upon it, it cures us of rancorous hypertrophy. The conscience having liquidated its old objects of rancor resembles a voyager without baggage; with a light step, it goes out to meet life. Or, if one prefers the vertical dimension, conscience, lightened of the weight of memories and *ressentiments,* surmounts the weight like an astronaut and raises itself toward a height in one leap, after having jettisoned the ballast. Make way for novelties! In this way, forgiveness undoes the last shackles that tie us down to the past, draw us backward, and hold us down. By allowing the coming times to come to pass, and, in doing so, accelerating this coming, forgiveness indeed confirms the general direction and the sense of a becoming that puts the tonic accent on the future. Forgiveness helps becoming to become, while becoming helps forgiveness to forgive. In general, rancorous anachronism does not resist the

5. [*Même si le "souvenir" n'est pas un "survenir" à l'envers, c'est bien l'"advenir" qui est le veritable "venir" à l'endroit.* The phrase "'venir' à l'endroit" can mean either "coming right side out" or "coming into place," both of which allude to "appearing" (*survenir*) and "coming to pass" (*advenir*).]

6. [Saint Elpidius (d. 422 CE) is mentioned in book 5, chapter 11 of Augustine's *Confessions.* There, Augustine mentions that he was impressed, already when he was in Carthage, with Elpidius's arguments against the Manicheans.]

7. [*Revenants:* Jankélévitch is playing on two senses of the word *revenant.* Taken as a noun, it means "ghost." However, understood as a gerund, it means "coming back."]

irresistible force of futurition for very long ... —In truth, becoming is always right side out, even when it seems to come back. Becoming always forges ahead even when it seems to retrace its steps: apparent steps backward follow in a chronological succession invariably directed toward the future, and that is that. In this way, everyone is in the direction of history, including those who seem to move against the current. The movement that posits in depositing and deposits in positing is position, in the end: this is its last word. Futurition-preterition is futurition in the end, and it is only this. Better yet, preterition itself is a moment of futurition, a futurition that is more rapid in growth, more laborious in aging, a futurition all the same and in every case! *Erchomenos ēxei, veniens veniet!*[8] *Idou erchetai, ecce venit.*[9] There is only one sole "coming," and this coming, positive or apparently negative, is becoming itself! For example, however much the events of which our memory holds a recollection have taken place in times past, nevertheless the act by which we remember them surely comes to pass now. The recollected event indeed carries its date in the past of chronicles, but recollection itself is each time a novelty in the present of the chronology. My present memories are an event of this very day. Saint Augustine said this using other terms. And thus, even anachronism too in its way, in its turn, and in its anachronistic manner is a piece of the chronology of which it is an anachronism: anachronism is an untimely episode of temporality. But if anachronism does not reverse the irreversible, then it slows down the tide. Reactionary forces hinder progress without, however, stopping it and a fortiori without inverting its course; on the whole, they do not change anything in the general tendency of evolution. Regression does not go in the opposite direction of progression, regression is simply a retarded progression. Retrogression that believes itself to be retrograde is simply a sluggish progress. Regressive progress, then, only differs from progressive progress in its qualitative tonality. The souvenir is this rallentando of becoming; it does not make becoming come back and it just barely slows it down. And as for rancor, it too acts only as an obstacle and as a retarding cause. Sooner or later, the rancorous person will give in to the omnipotence of time and to the weight of the accumulated years, for time is almost as omnipotent as death, and time is more tenacious than the most tenacious of wills, for it is irresistible! And the rancorous person will grow weary of holding a grudge

8. [See Habakuk 2:3: "It will surely come."]
9. [See Ezekiel 7:5–6: "Behold, it comes."]

against his offender before becoming grows weary of becoming . . . No, nothing resists this silent, continuous, and implacable force, this truly infinite pressure of progressive forgetting. No *ressentiment,* no matter how stubborn it is, can hold fast in the face of this mass of indifference and disaffection. Everything counsels forgetting! The memory, which is conquered in advance, can oppose futurition only by a defensive measure that is always provisional and generally hopeless . . . One day or another, in the long run, oceanic forgetting will submerge all rancor underneath its leveling grayness, just as the desert sands finish by burying dead cities and defunct civilizations, and just as the accumulation of centuries and millennia ultimately will envelop inexpiable crimes and undying glories in the immensity of nothingness. We know that Marcus Aurelius cast an eagle's eye view on this infinity of history that crushes even the most long-lasting renowned figures and on this infinity that annihilates the most memorable exploits: *mikron de hē mēkistē husterophēmia.*[10] Minimal is the longest posthumous glory. By comparison with infinite history, every memory goes toward zero, like a point in space. Centuries follow upon centuries; in the end, it is as if the exploit never took place, as if the hero never existed. And in the end we come to doubt whether the unforgivable crime was ever actually committed. The fact and the nonfact, *factum* and *infectum,* reabsorbed in the one same nonbeing, become indiscernible from each other. *Ducunt fata volentem, nolentum trahunt*[11] . . . This amounts to saying: *volens nolens,*[12] and whether you like it or not, the person has to march in the direction of futurition, to go where time leads him. Sooner or later, time will have the last word. *Volens nolens*? Then, rather *volens*! Since in the two cases the result will be the same, it is better to consent to time and be in full agreement with history. It is better spontaneously to assume one's destiny, in order not to have to suffer it. Sooner or later? Then, better sooner than later, right away is even better; and in any case as soon as possible! Yes, the sooner the better. Since it

10. Marcus Aurelius, *Meditations,* 3.10. ["Discard all else: cling to these few things only. Remember, moreover, that each man lives only this present moment; as for the rest, either it has been lived in the past or it is but an uncertain future. Small is the moment which each man lives, small too the corner of the earth which he inhabits; even the greatest posthumous fame is small, and it too depends upon a succession of short-lived men who will die very soon, who do not know even themselves, let alone one who died long ago." Marcus Aurelius, *Meditations,* trans. G. M. A. Grube (Indianapolis: Hackett, 1983), 22.]

11. ["The fates guide the willing and drag the unwilling."]

12. ["Whether willing or not."]

decidedly concerns a dilemma, since temporality in any case will be the strongest, since in any case forgetting will one day or another do its job, and since memory is a lost cause, one might as well forgive forthwith and finish once and for all with the lost cause and a condemned memory. Forgiveness, forestalling inevitable forgetting and inevitable obsolescence, recognizes in sum the invincibility of inexorable destiny, for we can apply what Aristotle and after him Leon Shestov said about the *ametapeistos anagkē*.[13] In order not to be crushed by the machine of the temporal process, the good memory anticipates its certain defeat, it takes the part of forgetting without getting to the point where becoming compels it, and as a consequence it hastens to forgive. It does not persist stubbornly in conserving outdated modes, in keeping in circulation decirculated currencies, in remaining stuck on outdated hatreds: it favors becoming by accelerating it.

II. Forgetting

And besides, even if the rancorous person does not forget the offense, those around him and new generations have already forgotten in his place. The latecomer, risking being swept up by his epoch, must thus compensate for the anachronism and salvage the general movement. He resembles an instrumentalist who is late and who runs and even leaps several measures ahead in order to get back in sync with the orchestra. In its own way, forgiveness erases a sort of dissonance. Before the discrepancy becomes irremediable, the rancorous person hurries to forgive . . . for history marches on more quickly than the healing of our wounds. The man who has been passed up will survive if he remains contemporary with his time or places himself in the same time as that of his contemporaries. We often say: the circumstances have changed, actuality and opportunity have been displaced, problems today arise in a completely different manner, and so on. Old feelings of

---

13. [*Ametapeistos anagkē:* the inexorable or that which cannot be persuaded. See Leon Shestov,] *Athens and Jerusalem,* [trans. Bernard Martin (Athens: Ohio University Press, 1966), Second Foreword and also book 4, §66. The reference is to a passage in Aristotle's *Metaphysics.* See *Metaphysics* in *Basic Works of Aristotle,* ed. and trans. Richard McKeon (New York: Random House, 1941), 5.5.1015a31–33: "And necessity is held to be something that cannot be persuaded—and rightly, for it is contrary to the movement which accords with the purpose and with reasoning."]

rancor, inhibited by the present and by the transformation of the historical context, become just as unreal as ghosts, as unreal as superstitious relics, as ridiculous as the outdated dresses of our grandmothers.—The evolution of each individual, including the offender himself, sums up, in its own way, that of successive generations. The person against whom I hold a grudge today is no longer the person who offended me earlier; in short, I continue to have rancor toward someone who no longer exists, toward the shadow of a guilty person, toward a phantom of the sinner. The refusal to forgive immobilizes the guilty person in his misdeed, identifies the agent with the act, and reduces the being of this agent to the having-done. But the misunderstood person protests against this simplification: one lie does not yet make a liar. The person infinitely exceeds the sin in which our rancor wants to imprison him. When we aim at a planet with the intention of hitting the target, it is necessary to take the movement of the planet into account, that is to say, the place that it will occupy in the sky when the rocket is supposed to reach it, and that is not its present place. Without this correction, we would be aiming at an empty place, at a place where there was indeed something at the moment of ignition and where already there is no longer anything. The rancorous person, fixing the offender in his immutable, incorrigible, and definitive essence as a guilty man, also sets out after an empty place. All the despair of *ressentiment* is contained in this powerlessness. *Ressentiment* does not even know whom to go after; the person whom it blames no longer exists!—All is thus dragged along in the general movement of becoming. The epoch that evolves irreversibly, the offender who is no longer the same but another person, and finally the offended himself—all of these advance along the route of time, with unequal speed, whether they like it or not. And just as the rancorous person is a sort of anachronism in full contemporaneousness, the rancor of this rancorous person can also be a local anachronism and an outdated element at the heart of the individual. For all the ingredients of this individual syncrasy that we call a psychism do not necessarily have the same cadence, nor do they necessarily march to the same step or with the same speed. All are not regulated by the same diapason, or at the same tempo. Personal life is a complex of lines that are relatively independent and each of which sometimes develops on its own terms. A man in the avant-garde of progress in the social sphere can be completely reactionary in his aesthetic prejudices. A lover of abstract painting can be completely outdated in his musical tastes and prefer Ambroise Thomas to Stravinsky. Similarly, little islands of inactivity—an unconsoled distress, an obsessive

remorse, an old and undigested rancor, the tenacious memory of an unfor-
given offense—can survive in the midst of a conscience that is wholly modern. The articulation and the pluralism of lines of conscience most often
save us the trouble of resembling the pope's mule that kept its kick in reserve for seven years and that itself wholly became this vengeful kick.[14] In
general, man is not this mule that is offended, humiliated, and passionately
obsessed with the fixed idea of revenge. The part of oneself that has stayed
vindictive and that resists the natural movement of history is generally a local portion of lived life. Rancor often resembles a lump that becoming has
not yet succeeded in dissolving. While our vital interests are moved according to new friendships and preoccupations of the hour, according to novel
terms in which problems henceforth pose themselves, a ghost has survived
in full modernity. A witness of time gone by, the antiquated phantom continues to wander in our memory. And this survival is all the more anti-vital
because it is the survival neither of a defunct love, nor of a ridiculously tenacious fidelity, nor of an out-of-season gratitude, but rather of a truly posthumous hatred. If the love that we have for a specter is a "bewitched love," then
rancor itself would be bewitched in two respects—first, because it too out-
lives its cause, and then because it is the memory of evil,[15] a heinous recollection and inverted gratitude, which is, on the contrary, *eumnémie* and a
good memory of kindness. Is not *ressentiment* a type of recognition in reverse? Love at least has not always been bewitched and becomes bewitched
only beyond the grave, once it is bewitched by magic spells of reminiscence.
Instead, hatred was already bewitched on the day of the affront, when everything justified it and when its actuality was indeed alive. What psycho-
analysis will exorcise this specter from long ago? Time obliges the old-
fashioned person not only to be a contemporary of the times of everyone,
not only to mark the same time as his epoch, but also to be a contemporary
of his own time and to adjust all the contents of his conscience to the same
"Now." Let evolution carry away our last fidelities, erase our last superstitions, and dispose of that which survives from an absolute past! Temporal
forgiveness dissolves the worries and migraines that linger in our present,
just as time of itself makes the regional dischronisms of chronology proper

14. [Jankélévitch is referring to a story called "The Pope's Mule" ("La Mule du Pape") from
Alphonse Daudet's *Lettres de mon moulin* (Letters from My Mill) about life in Provence, a work
that first appeared in 1866.]

15. In Russian, this is the name that we give to "rancor": *zlopamiatstvo*.

disappear. It mobilizes all fixed ideas, consoles sorrows that are incapable of being consoled, wards off obsessive remorse, and, in a word, thaws tenacious rancors. It liquidates by liquefying. The man who consents to becoming and renounces the delight of constant repetition makes fluid the advent of the future and lubricates the succession of the before and the after. He abounds in the direction of alteration that makes the other come to pass. For this man, slippery futurition will dissolve the pebbles of rancorous preterition that constantly tend to re-form themselves behind us.

III. Decay

The accelerando of futurition necessitates, by its very nature, the ritardando of preterition. The advent of the future and the suppression of remembrances are just one and the same process of becoming, considered, as before, to be right side out, or, as now, to be in reverse. As long as becoming is a continual creation turned toward the future, it counsels us simply to welcome something else, to think of something else, to open ourselves up to the alterity of the next day. A conscience without memory continually looks beyond as if nothing ever took place. But as long as becoming retains memories, alteration, slowed down by the weight of the past, implies the decay of this past, for the return to the status quo ante is impossible in any case. If becoming were futurition pure and simple, and incessant innovation, then frivolous forgetting would erase the recollection of the offense forthwith, at once, and as if by magic. Forgiveness (if we admit that this immediate forgiveness, that this instantaneous and continued forgetting merits being called "forgiveness") would thus intervene in the innocence of each new minute; or even better, forgiveness would be given with the offense, or the instant afterward, which amounts to the same thing. Such is the case of a *mens momentanea,* of a mind that is instantaneous and without memory, for which futurition is reduced to an *aeternum nunc* and a perpetual present. So, there is no longer even forgiveness, for forgiveness requires that a minimal delay open up between the offense and the absolution, that we have had the time, even if it were ten seconds, to hold a grudge against the sinner; it requires that infinitesimal rancor at least have the time to form; for *ressentiment,* a sentiment on top of a sentiment, a sentiment with an exponent, does not exist without temporalization. Without this temporalization, without this interval that perpetuates the injury, where would forgiveness find something to forgive? But the punctual, inconsistent "consciousness" of which we are speaking is the consciousness of a stupid protozoan that is stuck where it is on account of unconsciousness. Affronts and insults for this carefree consciousness are only will-o'-the-wisps, instantaneous fulgurations, and disappearing appearances. For lived time is not only innovative succession, it is, moreover, the conservatory and depository of memories. And memory, if it is not literally regressive, at least slows down and weighs down the *élan* of the progression. Without conservation, however, innovation would not even be innovative, for it is this mixture of innovation and conservation, the latter slowing down the former and the former pushing on the latter, that manufactures the relative renewal, the name of which is becoming. The new incessantly replaces the old. A present that is always other because it is always the same, a present continually different from the past and yet similar to this past, a present slowly transformed over the course of one thousand imperceptible modifications—this is what is suitable to being called evolution. This becoming, which is jointly futurition and preterition, has futurition itself as a consequence. What is more, the consequence of a progression and accumulation of memories is quite simply called progress. Progress is measured only in reference to experience. Progress represents, as it were, the difference between a pure futurition without counterbalance and a slowed-down futurition. The irreversible itself does not consist in turning its back to the past, for becoming always retains something from this past, but by continually evolving in the same direction. It is prohibited to come back backward; it is not forbidden to hold memories. The impossibility of becoming young again does not entail the necessity of being unfaithful or ungrateful. Insofar as becoming is futurition, its *élan* is slowed down by the weight of memories. But insofar as it is preterition, then it is the patrimony of memories, on the contrary, that is eaten away, nibbled away, and reduced by the *élan* of an innovative and madly extravagant futurition. Our sentiments demonstrate this: if the futurism of the project and of hope is retarded by backward-looking attachment, then attachment to the past by rancor and by remorse, by fidelity, or by regret and by gratitude disintegrates little by little with the effect of futurition. In rancor, there is something that clings on with a desperate fierceness, fighting inescapable becoming. In its turn, fragile gratitude is a type of paradoxical impossible undertaken by the grateful man despite the irreversible, and is sooner or later destined for nothingness. Fidelity is in the same situation. It is miraculous that the faithful person, the obstinate person stands up to the irresistible forces of disaffection and forgetting. Be it a heroic challenge or a mad protest, fidelity keeps its word against all odds. Or rather, it will keep its word . . . until there is a new order! A faithful oath or a rancorous oath, an oath of gratitude or an oath of vengeance, the powerless word that is given wages an unequal battle against all-powerful history, a battle that always finishes badly and always ends up in betrayal. At last, in regret, time's victory is no longer in the future but in the present; and the defeat of man is no longer a menace or a possibility but precisely a defeat. Here something has already escaped; here time has already performed its work! Starting now, presence escapes us, and this is what, in its melancholy way of speaking, the misfortune of nostalgia expresses.—Thus, futurition slowed down by preterition has the progressive decay of memories as a consequence. Successively erasing every trace of the past, and at each minute suffocating the memories that are reborn at each minute, a futurition without preterition would be nothing other than amnesia and continued forgetting; by ossifying becoming, preterition without any futurition would condemn man to mortal sclerosis. Combined, futurition and preterition join together to make forgetting progressive. Halfway between conservation without hope and alteration without memory, forgetting will then appear as a continuous degradation. Memories, instead of being abolished in one fell swoop, weaken little by little and fade before disappearing. This disappearance, which could have been instantaneous, dilutes itself with the passing years. Now it is no longer necessary to say disappearance, but rather discoloration or disaffection . . . Or, using other images: as the conscience, on the route of time, successively distances itself from its past, the echo of this past subsides more and more. It is more and more difficult to be faithful, and finally it is impossible! And forgiveness at last results at the same time from the survival of the past in the present and the incessant influx of novelties. The tenor of our modernity in rancor becomes a little weaker every day. Each day witnesses the dose of *ressentiment* that subsists in us diminish like something left over from old insults, and this occurs up until the day on which the rancorous point ends up by losing itself in the mass of the present-past by disappearing into the accumulation of innumerable memories. In this manner, a rancor that has become infinitesimal destroys itself by dint of running out; at the limit and with habit helping out, moribund rancor itself dies from hunger. As is the case with old anger and old pain, nothing more will subsist of old rancor than a vague memory, which is a phantom rancor or a shadow of anger. For the offended person becomes tired of holding a grudge against his offender! Time that erodes mountain chains and makes the pebbles on the beach smooth, time that levels all harshness and consoles all pain, soothing and healing time, is this not the vocation of decay? It appears as the dimension by which the past becomes less and less alive; it is the infallible comforter and the irresistible pacifier. That is to say in one way or another that futurition always has the last word. The erosion of rancor thus presupposes two opposite conditions: a residual past must linger in us in the form of memory, and the compelling movement that pulls us forward must always get the better of retarding traditions, when all is said and done. On the one hand, the traces of the event have to outlive the contingent event of aggression or sin, which causes relations between humans to veer off course. On the other hand, futurition has to make novelty come to pass incessantly, for a well-defined intention does not cease to orient becoming or to watch over the weakening of memory.—As with every qualitative mutation, this weakening is, moreover, irregular and intermittent; and in this, it rebels against scalar gradations. In the long run, time will have done its work; but it accomplishes this work piecemeal. The net result is that evolution will indeed have taken place in the direction of forgetting.—However, it does not take much for the memory to be further away and more vague day by day; no, loss of affection is not more complete today than yesterday, nor less complete than tomorrow! It is true that broadly speaking and after the event, time brings us forgetting and consolation, but it is not true that forgetting is proportional to the age of the memory or to the interval that has passed. It is not true that with each fraction of time there corresponds a proportional attenuation of rancor, for quality, sense, and intention cannot be divided up and, consequently, are incommensurable with the time that has passed or with the path covered. Quality is a totality that is altered qualitatively by always staying total. Decay is, therefore, only a metaphor for fastening down ideas. And just as the general truth about aging might seem to be refuted in detail by apparent periods of rejuvenation, or at least by stabilizations that are more or less long, or at least by a temporary slowing down of senescence, so the uncontestable truth about the loss of affection can find itself temporarily refuted by sudden acts of revenge from memory, by abrupt returns of sorrow, and by subtle outbursts of *ressentiment.* The reactivated preterit momentarily slows down the unyielding process of forgetting and provisionally interrupts the ineluctable consolation that, sooner or later, will console the inconsolable. It is in bereavement that is on its way to withering that

sincere tears reappear: such are these final high fevers that sometimes come
to retard the general process of convalescence. However, the temporal "forgiveness" that is more or less slowed down by resurgences of memory will
ineluctably have the last word. Rancor does not disappear *by dint of* losing
its fine edge, and nevertheless it *finishes up by* disappearing! Put in another
way, forgiveness results from an irregular but fatal diminuendo and from
an unequal but irresistible decrescendo! ... As time passes, the returns that
the flame makes are more and more rare, the points of *ressentiment* are less
acute. *Grosso modo*[16] the curve of rancorous chronology, with its zigzags,
stages, and turnarounds, tends toward the zero point of the horizontal; forgetting is a leveling off from below. Without a doubt, the graph of forgetting
would have the same profile as the graph of a pain that is irregularly but
progressively amortized. For the injured person, life fatally reclaims its
place, except of course when the organism that is too gravely affected can
no longer repair the consequences of the trauma that hit it. Better yet, if the
aptitude of the organism for restoring its health is necessarily limited, then
the elasticity of a soul that is pained or offended is practically infinite. Any
affront that we do not finish with in time by forgetting, or any sorrow that,
under the effect of habituation, does not empty itself little by little of its
fervor, becomes parrotry and drivel, the crocodile's affliction and the crocodile's fidelity. Of the old rancor that is hardened, lignified, and ossified,
there remains hardly more than mimicry without a soul. In such a way, the
inconsolable widow who is finally consoled continues twenty years later to
celebrate the liturgy of memory, and mechanically performs the gestures,
and mechanically pronounces the words of conjugal piety without even
thinking of the deceased. The fervor of the anniversary is on the path toward extinction, and one can anticipate that the survivors soon will cease
completely to commemorate it. The man of time, a finite creature, is made
neither for an eternal penalty, nor for an undying rancor; for such an eternity is really the hell of the damned; for such an inconceivable eternity
would actually be unbearable despair for us. In any case, the fact of progressive erasure, resulting from a futurition retarded by the preterit or by
a preterition turned back by the future, proves at least that the past does not
allow itself to be abolished without protesting. The progressive nature of
forgetting measures the tenacity of memory, just as the length of the agony

16. ["Roughly speaking."]

measures the resistance and vitality of the organism. It does not matter: retrospectively and in the future anterior, time will have gotten the better of our rancor.

IV. Integration

This decay, which is a retarded nihilization, can offer itself to us in a more positive light. For the past rarely disappears without leaving any trace; the work of time in fact consists of integrating or digesting the adventitious event. The adventitious event passes in latency and becomes, as Bergson has shown, an integrating element and a secret component of our present. If decay is a simple attenuation that is physical and passive, then assimilation, adaptation, and regeneration are vital properties. The organism, indeed, appears as a totality that is incessantly deformed and transformed, revised and retouched, altered by the petty accidents of existence. It is life that takes the upper hand by digesting antivital factors, and likewise the character and the person in general are totalities that are at each instant enriched, complicated, dilated, and impregnated by experience. Once assimilated, the fault that is committed and the offense undergone can become invisible ingredients of this experience. Is not the whole value of repenting only in that it makes the misdeed itself contribute to our spiritual enrichment? When the repentant, prodigal son returns to the fold, having finished the circuit of adventures and tribulations, no differential any longer separates him in appearance from the son who stays at home. Yet an invisible je ne sais quoi, a completely pneumatic complication that is the ordeal of suffering and temptation, distinguishes him forever. The one who returned and the one who never left are now both at the same point, but an indelible past separates them. This is why, according to the Gospel, there will be more space in heaven for a single repentant tax collector than for nine hundred thousand irreproachable hypocrites.[17] Just as the organism adapts to a strange body, so the offended person arrives at a *modus vivendi* with the offense. The offense that is rendered insensitive and painless, the offense that is transformed into an indifferent memory, the offense that is refrozen becomes an element of our personal past in the unconscious person. For-

17. [See the Parable of the Pharisee and the Tax Collector, Luke 18:10–17.]

giveness would thus resemble a mediation that integrates the antithesis into a higher synthesis. Is not dialectic conciliation literally "reconciliation," that is, pacification and cessation of all belligerence? So the consciousness passes its time digesting snubs and insults. The insulted consciousness really has a stomach of iron. Or, to use other images . . . the reconciled or repentant consciousness carries, in the form of a scar, the trace of old moral traumatisms—forgiven offenses and redeemed misdeeds. We will, then, be tempted to consider an undigested rancor or an inconsolable pain as pathological cases. Is it not the medical and soothing function of healing that is curbed here? It is not astonishing that integration is accomplished in time—for time is the natural dimension of mediation, for mediation is essentially temporal. This irreducible element of restorative temporality mediates just as much the expiation of one's own sins as the forgiveness accorded to the sins and offenses of others. Neither repentance, one's relation to oneself, nor forgiveness, my relation to the other, evades this delay. Atonement for the misdeed that was committed and forgiveness for an injury suffered both take time.

V. Neither Futurition, Nor Decay, Nor Synthesis Replaces Forgiveness

Do futurition, decay, and integrationist synthesis suffice to justify forgiveness? Can they serve merely as surrogates? First, as for futurition, to say that time is irreversible succession and continual innovation is to recognize only half of the truth and to pass over the other half in silence. This is to neglect the fact that time is also conservation and perpetuity, and in the end it is to make little of the mnemic property, which is the essential characteristic of every consciousness. Do not integration and the very decay that naturalism invokes in order to justify forgiveness suppose the persistence of vestiges and the permanence of memories? In this regard, the naturality of time would instead be an argument in favor of rancor!

Conversely, decay is the caricature of grace. Decay, when it appears as the forgetting of wounds that are received and affronts that are suffered, is not in the least a reason to forgive. Indeed, decay, a natural and physical fact above all, expresses the general orientation of vital processes, but it expresses these processes as long as they are headed in the end in the direction of death. For life itself, by virtue of a mysterious contradiction, is vital only by the death that denies it. This is because lived time is infinitely ambiguous; time is *natura anceps*.[18] Not only is it both futurition and conservation but futurition itself is both progress and retreat, since it is both development and aging at the same time. The living person does not cease to make himself real and to enrich himself by synthesis and apprenticeship—and in the same way he does not cease to consume what is possible to him and to come closer to nothingness. Day after day he sees his margin of hope dwindle in front of himself, until the final instant where, with the last future now actualized and having taken place, the person condemned to death finds himself nose to nose with despair. Or to say it better: being realizes itself in tending toward nonbeing! The singular paradox of temporal ambiguity! For a subject that is interior to itself, what has already been lived is still to be lived, and this indefinitely. But in the overconscious perspective of the witness and according to the objective chronology of calendars, what has already been lived is no longer to be lived, what has already been lived is nothing more than lived! For third parties, the portion of my life that has already been lived is removed by virtue of the irreversible expenditure on the average duration of the human life, which inscribes itself in a lapse of limited time. Such is the time of senescence: eternal at the time and for an englobed present, finished objectively and after the event, finished for the retrospective consciousness and the superconsciousness, marked off minute after minute by the ticktock of clocks, and gnawed away little by little by the insect of time! Temporal ambiguity can take another form and encourage optimism and pessimism at the same time. On the one hand, time is the natural dimension according to which sicknesses normally evolve toward their cure; the cure of fevers, the healing of wounds, and the regeneration of tissues attest to the medical and curative virtue of time. The seething of the first pain subsides thanks to this large temporal sedative. Baltasar Gracián contrasts the fecund slowness of "temporization" to haste, which generates stunted specimens.[19] But if time levels off that which protrudes in acute suffering and attenuates crises, then it also deadens the vital reactions of the organism. The leveling off that characterizes the cure of a fever also characterizes the cure of fatigue just as well. Becoming is, then, not only pain that is soothed but also, and ipso facto, biological energy that is blunted little by little: reflexes slow down and traumatisms are more and more difficult to

18. ["Dubious nature."]
19. *L'homme du cours*, maxim 55. *Le Discret*, chapter 3.

offset. Becoming is, then, not only restoration of form, it is also and in the same manner growing weariness, the next paralysis, stagnation, and, more or less in the long term, inevitable death. Do not, then, make too much haste to rejoice over the consoling virtues of time, for in the last analysis it is death that will have the last word; for in the long run everything settles itself out and falls into place little by little, except for death, which never works out. This equivocal time, this vital-mortal time, in the name of which one advises us to forgive and that is a double-edged sword, is every bit as much at work in the disparity of habitual effects; for if the habit in the moment in which we acquire it manifests the suppleness of the living organism and its effective power of adaptation, then the habit once acquired is nothing more than mechanization and stuttering. The man who grows accustomed augments his powers, but the man who is habituated grows sluggish and tends toward the inertia of matter. Such is the double effect of the temporal procession on our sentiments, and even more so on *ressentiment:* time discolors all the colors and tarnishes the flash of emotions, time amortizes joy just as it consoles pain, time puts gratitude to sleep just as it disarms rancor, the one and the other indistinctly. It dries our tears, but it also puts out the flame of passion. Love loses itself in the sands; enthusiasm is destined for ossification, for mineralization, for fossilization. Time thus conceived would imply a type of fatal entropy. This time is degradation rather than maturation, for if evolution prevails over involution during the first part of life, then in the end it is dissolution that has the last word. Decay, which we invoke in order to justify forgiveness, is thus a continued death diluted by the passing years, a series of little deaths before the big one, or in fact a "mortification." Can one preach forgiveness in the name of death and withering? Does forgiveness find its justification in our creaturely misery and in finitude in general? This would be to recognize that forgiveness, like forgetting, is a senile weakness and a poverty, a phenomenon of deficit, a headlong flight of consciousness, a letting go of memory and of the will . . . Forgetting is neither just a biological lack of concern, nor just a vital protection against impediments to living and importunate memories. It is another symptom of growing decrepitude; it is sinecure on the recto and negligence on the verso! This forgetful forgiveness is after all more amnesia than amnesty, more asthenia or atrophy than generosity, for it results from anesthesia and increasing apathy. It is not the good and long memory that is a void, rather it is forgetting, a privative phenomenon, that digs a hole in the fullness of memory! And consequently it is vivacious rancor that is tension and plenitude . . . Is fatigue a moral attitude?

Are lassitude and coldness ethical? To forgive out of lassitude, is this to forgive? Certainly not; lassitude is not ethical! Lassitude is shameful; lassitude is unworthy of the moral agent. The very idea that a will grows weary of willing in the long run is injurious for this will. The indefatigable will that never grows weary of willing, or of *holding a grudge* against the guilty person, such a will is antipodal to vague and forgetful desire, just as it is antipodal to ill will. Would time, the principle of forgetting, counsel us to forgive? But in this case here, time, the natural foundation of forgiveness, would also be a reason to show oneself as ungrateful and unfaithful, frivolous and versatile. We will perhaps distinguish good forgetting from bad forgetting . . . We will say: it is not the fact of forgetting itself that matters, rather it is the item that is forgotten that alone is decisive. Everything would depend on the nature of the past that we forget, just as, conversely, everything depends on the memory that we recollect. Depending on whether it concerns a good deed or a bad deed, the intentional quality of the memory changes completely. Forgetting an offense is called "forgiveness," whereas forgetting a good deed, when it is not egoism pure and simple, is called ingratitude or infidelity, lack of earnestness and of profundity, guilty frivolity and thoughtlessness. And reciprocally, a proper recollection of a misdeed is called rancor, whereas a proper recollection of a good deed is called recognition. Forgetting the misdeed and recollection of the good deed are both good, just as forgetting the good deed and remembering the misdeed are both an evil. Thus, a forgetting that is openness and receptiveness with an eye to the future must then be distinguished from a forgetting that is guilty negligence and mortal loss of affection. And the distance between the two types of forgetting is as large as the distance between selflessness and lack of interest.[20] It is true. But the asymmetry itself between the two types of forgetting stems from the transfiguring virtue of true forgiveness, and this transfiguring virtue has no relation to temporality. It is the chiasmus between misdeed and love that forms the essence of forgiveness! If the intention behind rancor is to render evil for evil and the intention behind gratitude is to render good for good, then it would be possible to consider forgiveness as a diametrical reversal of ingratitude, that is, as true *grace* that is right side out. For if ingratitude, so to speak, returns evil for good, then forgiveness, being

20. [*Désintéressement et désintérêt.*]

wholly the opposite, returns good for evil. Forgiveness goes beyond commutative justice, whereas ingratitude stays on this side of it. Under these circumstances, would forgiveness not resemble the type of biological amnesia that brings us the forgetting of old sufferings, old sicknesses, and bygone misfortunes and indeed protects the organism against bad memories? Far from it! The forgetting of offenses, when we truly forgive the offender, is not a simple, protective sinecure; the gratuitousness of generous remission here excludes all utilitarian finality. The chiasmus by virtue of which forgiveness denies or contradicts the offending intention thus owes nothing to the naturality of time.

The idea of integration, that is, of a synthesis, is not equivalent to transfiguring forgiveness any more than gradual decay is. We were saying that the forgetful person, off whom the offense glides without leaving the least trace, does not even know what he is supposed to forgive. The rancorous person who keeps the memory of evil in his gut knows what he has to forgive, and whom, but he does not will it. Does the person who swallows and stomachs the offense, who has an iron stomach, and who sins neither out of insufficiency nor out of surplus of memory at least forgive the offender? Certainly not; to stomach is not to forgive! To stomach and to assimilate call more for practical fitness, or for elasticity and utilitarian suppleness, than for generosity. The egoist knows the art of turning the insults that he receives to his advantage and turns snubs and humiliations into profitable lessons. Injuries themselves serve to enrich his experience. He knows how to use snubs in the way ascetics know how to use temptations and trials with an eye to spiritual formation. Who knows, for such champions of forgiving, maybe a snub that is received is an occasion for becoming more perfect! The one who turns the other cheek, not out of love of man as Jesus demanded, but in order to exercise his will and resistance to vindictive temptation, in order to soften his faculties of adaptation, in order to diversify the synthesis, and in order to integrate food that is particularly difficult to stomach into a totality that is always richer is a cunning and voracious man. This is not a generous man. We would do him a small favor by slapping him. His project is to exploit everything, to devour everything, and to lose nothing, not even the windfall of a slap in the face. Is this forgiving? No, this captivating and annexationist synthesis is not opened toward the other. Here, it is only a matter of me, of my profit, of my beautiful soul. Hypocrisy and complaisance, philauty and pleonexy are the true ulterior motives of closed forgiveness.

We would gladly call this simili-forgiveness "spiritual avarice," in the language of Saint Francis de Sales.[21]—There is still something worse. The synthesis that results from a mediation, if it really is a synthesis, takes into account the two extremes or the two contraries that the mediation has reconciled. Is compromise not the raison d'être itself of reconciliation and the very function of the middle term? The mediator, when he offers his services and puts himself between the adversaries to arbitrate their dispute, looks to integrate the unilateral nature of the thesis and the antithesis in a higher synthesis that stomachs both; it is thus that concessions have been made on both sides in the course of the negotiation. The injured person has to make do with his appeal to rights. The outcome of the two contrary forces, which for an optimist is at the same time both the one and the other, is for the pessimist neither the one nor the other (*neutra*). Integration, in this regard, is more impoverishment and diminution than enrichment; in this, it resembles the adaptation of a wounded or mutilated organism that settles into a type of modus vivendi with its infirmity. If he pulls through after the myocardial infarction, then the person who had the heart attack slowly adapts to his new state. After the stroke, it happens that the effusion of blood is reabsorbed in part and that the damages are offset relatively. The sick person will live, but with a diminished life, or rather he will struggle along by curtailing his lifestyle just like an army that is reduced to a defensive position and that cuts down its effective front in order to survive; for each time the recovery definitively ends in retreat. A trace, a minuscule scar, an irreversible modification that forever prevents the restoration of the status quo remains ... Like the organism, the wounded conscience offsets its insufficiency, as well as can be expected. The offended person stomachs his humiliation, but this is a laborious and difficult process of stomaching. With habituation aiding, he makes *as if* the injury was nothing and did not occur, but he does not make *that* it never took place. He attenuates the memory of it without annihilating its effectivity. The pain of humiliation is always there, but it has passed into latency, has become invisible, has changed into

---

21. *Oeuvres complètes* (Vivès, 1872), vol. 4, pp. 230–31 and 277–78. [See Saint Francis de Sales, *Treatise on the Love of God,* trans. Henry Benedit Mackey (Rockford, Ill.: Tan Books, 1995), 534: "Temporal covetousness, by which we greedily desire earthly treasures, is the root of all evil; but spiritual avarice, whereby one sighs incessantly after the pure gold of Divine Love, is the root of all good."]

an aftertaste. Such a forgiveness is far too complex, and it has far too many ulterior motives to be forgiveness pure and simple. And how would this not be strained by scruples and unconscious worries, whereas the function of synthesis is precisely to integrate through fusion the innuendos and understated rancors within a totality? Synthesis is not as much the goal of a moral life as it is the masterwork of a learned chemistry; and combinations that are too cunning would not be able to claim purity. If forgiveness can be reduced to an integration, then grace remains incomplete; some part of the offense will always remain. The offended person secretly continues to hold a grudge against the offender. An imperceptible mental restriction prevents the remission from being absolute and unadulterated. The rancor is held in check, dissimulated, buried in the depths, but it is not, strictly speaking, abolished. Maybe a subtle analyst, an ultrasensitive detector, a diviner armed with his rod would succeed in capturing the radiation that emanates from this subterranean rancor. Or, to use the language of the Stoics here, a drop of perfume diluted in the Pacific ocean is practically indiscernible. But the theorists of "total mixture" claim that the entire composition of this ocean is in effect modified by this drop. Without a doubt, for the nostrils of angels, the ocean has to be imperceptibly fragranced. Twenty years after the offense, perhaps such is the tenor of our rancorous present, such is the tenor of our resentful feelings. Instead of being true forgiveness, integration is a cryptic rancor, or better yet, an infinitesimal rancor, and a rancor that is undetectable and almost indiscernible, that is lost in the mass of the present. However, these negligible traces, which truly are barely measurable, suffice to make an approximating forgiveness and an incomplete liquidation out of forgiveness. Here is the impalpable *ressentiment* that men in general call forgiveness. Does the offended person who does not fully sacrifice his rancor, who does not wholly offer up his condemnation, who does not give up his rights truly forgive? For him, the regimen of very vague and very remote *ressentiment* has supplanted aggressive rancor just as rancor had supplanted angry belligerence. In this way, offended people sometimes resign themselves to undertaking neighborly relations with their former hangmen in spite of terrible memories; these people accept it, they hold out a hand of pacifist coexistence to the hangmen, but not without repugnance. But the heart, as we say, "is not there"! The heart of forgiveness. The heart, that is, the passionate adhesion, that is, the enthusiastic conviction, and the spontaneity, and the *élan* of joy . . . The heart of forgiveness, where is it? Alas! this forgiveness has no heart; this forgiveness without a heart, like a declaration of love without sincerity, is nothing other than resonant bronze and a resounding cymbal.[22]

VI. Unremitting Time Evades Definitive Conversion, the Gratuitous Gift, and the Relation to the Other

True forgiveness, we were saying, is an event, a gratuitous gift, and a personal relation with the other. In a continuous time, where is the event, what does the instantaneous resolution become? If forgiveness rests only on temporality, be it forgetting, decay, or integration, how many years of aging are necessary in order for forgiveness to be considered as established? After what point will the misdeed and the offense be forgiven? And why at such and such a moment rather than another? Decay, by itself, interminably accomplishes its work as memory grows fainter in the fog of the past and as the old lapse becomes blurred at the horizon in passing through all the gradations of scalar attenuation. Or, to use other images: unremitting time nibbles away at, and day after day consumes, the substance of the memory. *Greater and greater* becomes our lack of concern, and *less and less* passionate becomes our rancor. Less and less and greater and greater mean, that is to say, in all cases, little by little! Infinitely, of the first rancor, there remains nothing more than an infinitesimal rancor . . . But at what moment does the pianissimo diminish into silence, the hardly visible into the invisible, and the almost nothing[23] into the nothing? At what moment is the last thread of fidelity broken? At what moment has the event itself come to pass? Never, responded the Megarics—for the Megarics invoked the *acervus ruens,* denying the event and the transformation in general. Many famous sophisms were born of this aporia . . . Is the process going to drag out until the end of the centuries? Until centuries of centuries, if there were not death, then an echo of the old rancor would expire in silence. The glow of memory, if there were not death, would never finish illuminating the night of forgetting. But

22. 1 Corinthians 13:1. ["If I speak in the tongues of men and of angels, but have not love, I am a noisy gong or a clanging cymbal."]

23. [*Le presque-rien:* This is an important element of Jankélévitch's philosophy. See the three-volume work *Le Je-ne-sais-quoi et le presque-rien* (Paris: Presses Universitaires de France, 1957; and Paris: Éditions du Seuil, 1980).]

just as the decrescendo of rancor would not be able to prolong itself indefinitely and just as adversaries are pressed to eliminate their old disputes, the
law determines in an authoritarian manner the date of legal elimination for
their benefit. This arbitrary decree precipitates things, accelerates the interminable process, and with a single and assertive decision picks up the lazy
adagio of forgetting. Such is the raison d'être of prescriptive delay. Frivolous
people, who more or less already have a light heart, will have the *right* to
have a light heart twenty years after the crime; juridically, they will have
a light heart. It is legitimate to have a grudge against a criminal for twenty
years, but after the twenty-first year, one becomes rancorous! With full
rights and from one day to the next, the unforgivable is thus forgotten. What
had been unforgivable until May 1965 has abruptly ceased to be in June
1965. It is indeed necessary to set a date, is it not? And so official forgetting
begins tonight at midnight. What a mockery! If we have to have a waiting
period, why wait twenty years? why not right away? why not forgive in the
instant itself that immediately follows the affront? This is the case in which
one can say: now or never! Jesus urges the humiliated person and the person who is slapped to turn the other cheek, but not twenty years after the
slap, not after much thought, not after having slept off the affront and having sought to forget, but rather forthwith. Without a doubt, he thought that
temporization and the state of uncertainty would add nothing to the gratuitous gesture, and rather that forgiveness would offer something resembling the spontaneity of a supernatural reflex. Is forgiveness not a first
movement like undeliberated charity or like pity? So it is true that forgiveness is always a *fiat,* an event, and an act. The only decisive forgiveness is
the one that comes to pass in the suddenness of the instant. To leave it to
decay or the passing of the years is thus to drown the unexpected instant
and to evade the discontinuity of the conversion that forgiveness inaugurates. Indeed, when forgiveness is refused, then mere time does for itself,
very slowly and approximately, that which the offended person has not
been generous enough to do. But conversely, in one moment and in one
blink of the eye, forgiveness does that which naked time would need years
to accomplish, and, without a doubt, to leave unfinished.

Such are the two insufficiencies of a duration that is given over to itself.
On the one hand, raw time does not at all possess the conversionary and
transfiguring power of forgiveness. For all that, the man in mourning, consoled by the very ancientness of his old sorrow, has not metamorphosed his
sadness into joy, nor found positive reasons to be happy. Parched and eroded

by the effect of time and habit, the primary emotion quite simply has been cooled down, the source of the tears is dried up—nothing more! An indifference, perhaps tainted by melancholy, has taken the place of sorrow ... And likewise, the emotion of anger perpetuated by chronic *ressentiment* does not little by little change into an *élan* of love. With the passing of time, rancor has simply become an automatism without conviction. The high pathic temperature of anger cannot keep itself up. The fever has died, and just as irascible congestion had given way to rancor, so rancor gives way to apathy. Forgetting has thinned hostility into indifference; it has neither inverted it into love, nor converted it into love, because a decrescendo is not an inversion! The passage from more to less, traversing all the degrees of the comparative, would not know how to replace this complete change, this conversion from contradictory to contradictory that forgiveness supposes. Do the progressive relaxation and the convalescence that duration brings us have even the least relation with the intention of forgiving? Even if they lessen rancor to the extreme limit of subtlety, then decay and integration are never the advent of a new era and never found a new order. By themselves, they are incapable of inaugurating positive relations between an offended person and an offender intimately reconciled. The disintegration of an old, passionate complex that crumbles, decomposes, and falls to dust, such a wholly negative disintegration is in no way foundational. As with conversion, true forgiveness is by itself capable of building a new house for a new life.—On the other hand, time, of itself alone, is not a permanent guarantee against old *ressentiments* that are quelled and soothed little by little. The flame still smolders in the room where memory is, and it can reawaken the fire. What tells us that rancor will not be reborn from the cold cinders of forgetting, that the flame of anger will not wake up from the embers of rancor? No, nothing tells us this. Nothing tells us—to use another idiom—that the tumor of rancor will not be reformed or that the wound will not reopen. So, admit it right away: a rancorous person who is cured solely by the accumulation of the years is poorly cured and is prone to relapses. For forgetting, which the simple passing of time brings us, is a superficial remedy, a precarious and provisional solution, and the peace that we owe it instead resembles a truce. The one who withdraws his rancor under the general anesthesia of time, and who has, consequently, evaded the surgical operation of the instant and of conversion, such a person who has not recognized the decisive event will remain obsessed by a humiliating memory. The only healing that is definitive and complete is the one that the injured person, if he had the strength, would give to himself in a sudden decision taken once and for all. This decision would contrast with immanent temporality just as, according to Schelling, the sacrifice of Christ would contrast with the successive ordeals of Dionysus. The grace of the redemptive decision would not content itself with making a fever fall; it guards against fever, and it even excludes the possibility of fever. It does not simply put the final touch on rancor; it renders rancor impossible; it extirpates rancor down to the roots. It is up to us to see if man is capable of such a decision.

We have just verified that since forgiveness is an instantaneous event, it is necessary to admit that the continuous and immanent time of evolution, incubation, and maturation has nothing in common with the act of forgiving. No more is the gratuitous gift, which is the second characteristic of forgiveness, implied in a becoming where nothing comes to pass or appears. Forgiveness is forgiveness only because it freely can be refused or graciously conceded prematurely and without any heed to legal deadlines at all. Is an absolution that automatically and ineluctably intervenes when the term has arrived a forgiveness? No, a fatal forgiveness is not forgiveness, for this is not a gift, or rather, this is a gift that *gives* nothing. And besides, it gives nothing to *no one*. Here indeed is the third mark of forgiveness: the relation with someone. Not only does the negativity of forgetting not imply this relation, but it rather excludes it; the forgetful person, ceasing to have something against the offender, breaks off any relation with him. Forgiveness is an intention, and this intention is quite naturally directed at the Other, since it addresses itself to a sinner, and its raison d'être is to absolve, since it looks him in the eyes. Does naked time have an intention? Indeed, time is oriented; indeed, it goes somewhere. Time looks at the future, but it does not look at the other; it does not have eyes for the second person and it does not even make an exception. In this sense, time is rather blind. And solitary! For, the anonymous future is never either the personal correlate of or the loving partner in an immediate allocution. Likewise, time is indifferent to good and evil, is just as ready to serve evil as it is good, and is ethically neutral. Days and weeks flow in the same way for repentant people as for unrepentant people without there being any differential element that permits a distinction between the time of good people and the time of wicked people. In this, time resembles generous nature, of which we were saying that it loves everyone, which is to say that it loves no one, for a universal dilection, without a predilection that favors, is more of an indifference. To speak the language of Leibniz here: what naked time lacks is the *Potius quam,* or the *Rather-than,* or, said otherwise, the principle of choice and of preferential discernment. We showed how the time of forgetting, which is supposed to counsel forgiveness, would just as well counsel frivolity, superficiality, and fickle inconsistency to us, for there is forgetting and forgetting! Moreover, time counsels no matter what to no matter whom, pell-mell and indistinctly. And as it works for the most opposed parties, it likewise furnishes arguments and excellent reasons to everyone. This indifference, so perfectly foreign to any discrimination, is particularly ruthless in forgetting. From what people say, forgetful nature is without rancor, but its unconcern has no moral significance, for the unconcern of a renewal that absolutely does not take note of the past is just as much an absence of gratitude and fidelity. Innocent springtime glows for wicked people as well as for good people . . . Each year, trees blossom in Auschwitz just as they blossom everywhere, and grass is not disgusted to grow in these places of inexpressible horror. Springtime does not distinguish between our gardens and the accursed plain where four million offended died by iron and fire. "It is the beautiful springtime that makes time glow."[24] And time shines, shines, alas! as if nothing had happened. Beautiful springtime does not have a bad conscience. In all truthfulness, it does not have a conscience at all, neither a good one, nor a bad one . . . On the contrary, the forgetful man possesses a conscience that could remember, remain loyal, and hold the past in the present. The forgetful person possesses a memory and does not use it, or uses it only to recall the most insignificant incidents, for in the order of naturality without intention, derisive memory is the worthy counterpart of derisive forgetting.

VII. Naked Time Does Not Have Moral Significance

We were heading down the wrong path in general when we searched from within temporality for the justification for forgiveness; for the pure and naked time that we envisage as futurition and conservation is by itself a natural and unjustified fact and is incapable of justifying anything. At least, such is the case of raw and substantial time, with abstraction being made from every superadded specificity; such is the case with nude chronology,

---

24. [This refers to a musical piece—"C'est le joli printemps" ("It is the beautiful springtime")—composed in late 1942 by Francis Poulenc with the text written by the poet Maurice Fombeure.]

considered independently of every ethical and psychological addition. If we begin by investing unqualified temporality with all sorts of moral qualities, it is not surprising that we find them in it. But it is not the temporality of time that is redemptive, it is the virtues themselves with which we have invested it. In the time of expiation and penitence, for example, it is not the years themselves that redeem the criminal, rather it is the rigor of the expiative and penitential ordeal; it is not raw duration but the duration of suffering. For the apprentice of the penal apprenticeship, it is purgatory itself that is supposed to give a "purifying" value to the span of time. In this respect, from all evidence, four years of vacation on the Riviera will not have the same effect as four years of forced labor. Four years without another determination are then an indifferent delay; indifferent is the length of a delay of which we do not specify the content. And, in moral life, indeed, time is less important than the manner in which one passes or occupies time. And besides, if empty time does not have moral significance, time filled by expiation itself, even though able to have such a significance, renders forgiveness useless; for the one who expiates obviously does not have need that one forgive him!—More precisely yet, the lapse of time that we invoke in order to justify the prescription is a biological process but not a moral progress. Without a doubt, twenty years weigh more on the shoulders of an aging man than do twelve months, but how would this mass of inert time that has passed, or how could the purely quantitative accumulation of the past, be endowed with this mysterious power to absolve the criminal? That the repentant person possesses such a virtue in himself can be understood—for repenting implies a drama and a moral life: a moral life, that is to say, acts of contrition: a moral life, that is to say, burning regret accompanied by the wise proposal to do better in the future by courageously taking on the suffering. The repentant person turns and returns the memory of the misdeed and endeavors to redeem it. The time of repenting, in opposition to the twenty hollow years of the prescription, is thus a meditative and contemplative plenitude. What is operative in repenting is the sincerity of the regret and the intensive ardor of the resolution. Repenting is redemptive because it is, first, an active will of redemption. But is prescriptive time, the time of forgetting and decay, something other than a delay that is empty, negative, and above all passive? This time, without events, does not have a history, and as such its story cannot be recounted. Separated from every task as from every effort, reduced to the single, inert automatism of futurition, empty time is a lazy time, *argos chronos,* and, to express it better, a dead

time. Such is in certain cases and for the man of action the biological time
of germination, maturation, and growth; such is too up to a certain point the
therapeutic time of healing and recovery. Here it is still a question of a fecund time that demands to be guided by interventions of man, to be started
over again, or more simply not to be bothered, for the time-doctor needs one
to help it, or acknowledges that we accelerate it. Precautions are indeed
necessary to allow the medicine of becoming to work and to push aside the
obstacles that would hinder its action. However, and even in this case, the
role of man sometimes confines itself to not disrupting the process at all and
to not evading the successive phases at all. It happens that human participation in time, that our cooperation in its work, and that our collaboration
in its labor do not go beyond this. The laborer buries the seed in the ground,
and then he goes to rest. He waits for springtime to awaken it and for the tel-
luric forces to make it germinate and be fruitful. What is most essential is
that he puts his confidence in invincible time.[25] This is why we are told: Let
time be, time flows all alone, time works in our place! Nonetheless, the time
of farmers works only for those who already work. But it also happens that
man has nothing to do, for example, when time is reduced to the pure, in-
compressible thickness of weeks, months, and years: such is the case with
boredom or waiting. Here it is a question literally only of killing time; to kill
time or, better yet, to sleep it away if necessary, or to render it numb with
"pastimes." Here, it is a question only of patiently enduring the duration . . .
Is it patience that alone is necessary, that supposes infinitesimal tensions
and a nascent cooperation with temporal work? There is nothing left to do
but to allow the ineluctable work of futurition to complete itself, to allow the
clepsydra to empty itself, to allow the hands of the clock to turn, to pick off
the pages of the calendar. Wait for the sugar to melt and for the moment to
come . . . Wait for the coming years to come to pass! Time takes charge of all!
In contrast to the work that pushes a bit and reorients time in the preferred
direction, the man in the state of uncertainty is present qua passive spectator in the unfolding of the film. It thus suffices to consult chronology, which
will decide by itself if the adversaries are ready for reconciliation, if the hour

25. Mark 4:26–29. ["And he said, 'The kingdom of God is as if a man should scatter seed
upon the ground, and should sleep and rise night and day, and the seed should sprout and grow,
he knows not how. The earth produces of itself, first the blade, then the ear, then the full grain
in the ear. But when the grain is ripe, at once he puts in the sickle, because the harvest has
come.'"]

of forgiving has sounded. To forgive, for Sophists of bad faith, is to abandon oneself to the unfolding of hours and days; it is to leave it up to the process that inevitably will make next Sunday's expiration date or the fixed term for the prescription come to pass. A forgiveness that is conferred prematurely evokes a harvest that is untimely . . . Neither more nor less immoral! Fear forgiving too soon and not too late! And we, we would say the opposite: beware of forgiving too late! At least the repentant person gave himself the penalty of expiation. Unlike courageous repenting, forgiveness that is conferred by the calendar resembles a rather cowardly and facile consolation. The repentant person works to free himself, but here the offended person and the offender especially wait to be released. As for the offended person, he does not himself intervene in the irresistible and infallible operation of the years; we do not ask him for his opinion. Again, we insist: the blindness of raw time does not provide us with any means of distinguishing between the condemned person who has expiated his crime for twenty years and the cheater who hid in Monte Carlo for twenty years after his crime. The second criminal, having had the luck to escape capture and to make himself forgotten, quite simply played a good trick on justice. Nothing happened during these twenty years! A remission without pain—that is the convenience offered to happy cheaters. If they economize their time in purgatory, they will wake up free one beautiful morning without ever having had something of which to be acquitted.—Thus for the Sophists of the calendar and of the hourglass time in and of itself would possess I know not what medicinal virtue. And for us, it is rather pain that would be purifying. For them, as for us, and despite Schopenhauer, pain is not inherent in the essence of time. Pain is continued in duration, but in itself it is distinct from painful time. The relation of the attribute to the substantive indicates as much. Time is only sometimes painful because it can also be painless or even agreeable. Pain is always more or less temporal, but time itself is not necessarily painful; time is distinct enough from pain that it could rather be the remedy for it. Time is a *medicina doloris;* acting as a sedative and an analgesic, the morphine of time attenuates old pains and makes old sorrows sleep. But it does not follow that the temporal medicine of pain is, in one fell swoop, the moral medicine for sin: first, because the sin of the offender and the rancor of the offended are not "sicknesses" at all. Furthermore, if costly heartbreak is, as we think, the condition of true forgiveness, then the time that soothes the wound must render this forgiveness less true, less authentic, and less meritorious. There is almost nothing left to forgive, therefore nothing is really forgiven. Twenty years is a sufficient sedative that exempts us from all sacrifice. The temporal palliative, leveling the bumps and the rough patches of moral life, in sum serves only to spare us from suffering.

Man, qua moral being, fulfills his vocation in time, but as a biological being he has neither a vocation nor an intention and contents himself with becoming and aging, for aging is not intentional. To confuse biological evolution and psychological becoming with the moral life is, without a doubt, one of the most Machiavellian forms of ill will. Moral life is not a process but a drama punctuated with precious decisions. Moral progress advances only by the deliberate effort of a decision that is intermittent and spasmodic and in the tension of an indefatigable starting-over. The will, willing and willing again incessantly, does not rely in any measure on the inertia of the acquired movement, does not live on the laurels of accumulated merit. And thus, with each instant, moral progress begins again from zero. There is no other ethical *continuity* than this exhausting *continuation* of "relaunch" and resumption. Moral progress is thus laboriously *continued* rather than spontaneously *continual* or *continuous,* and it resembles a recreation rather than a growth. Abandonment to slippery continuity, in the current of duration and in the rocking chair of becoming, is not the moral life. And the gentleness of abandon in turn has nothing in common with the crisis of forgiveness. Ascesis, and not the rocking chair: such is the moral life. The time of moral life forbids sleepers to give in to letting themselves go in a life of immanence and expectation.

VIII. Time Cannot Get Rid of the Fact of Having Done

Raw becoming, without any other specification, is the mode of being of man as he is, but forgiveness is the gesture of man as he ought to be. In the measure in which it is a duty, that is, in as much as it is, if not always rationally justified, then at least supernaturally, paradoxically, and categorically required, forgiveness is of the order of value. And value, unless it is monetary or a style, *has worth* independently of any chronology. It has value, not a temporary *validity* like a passport, but an atemporal *value,* not by making exceptions for delay or for such and such circumstantial determinations, but absolutely, *haplōs,* that is to say, it is "worthwhile" purely and simply. It "has worth," that is all that there is to it, and without an adverb of degree, of manner, of duration, or of place. How would this normative gesture result from the succession of seasons and years? Matured by summers, formed by experience and habit, it is no more capable of forgiving the guilty person than it was on the day of the affront. This is the place for saying again: now or never!—But the atemporality of the law of forgiving comes into conflict with the atemporality of the misdeed to be forgiven. Here let us distinguish more clearly the personal offense from the moral misdeed properly speaking. The offense wrongs only the self-esteem and the self-interest of the offended person, and consequently even when justice is at issue, the rancor that the offense arouses in the offended person always has a character that is more or less selfish and passionate. We can understand that natural phenomena such as forgetting, decay, evolution, and aging take hold of natural passions such as *ressentiment* and susceptibility. It is useless to explain (though this erosion is not forgiveness) why this quick-tempered emotion has to weaken as time passes, become vindictive rancor and then an indifferent image. A perpetual anger is incompatible with the entropy of becoming and the status of the finished being.—We already find it even harder to understand that a cruel mourning can subside solely because of the effect of time. Each person is indeed unique and irreplaceable, and the loss of one of these irreplaceable persons is no better compensated twenty years after his disappearance than the day itself when it happened. The situation is the same whatever the moment of time happens to be. The void (at least this void) will not be filled. The "hapax" (at least in its incomparable haecceity) will not be replaced. The death of the irreplaceable would thus have to leave us inconsolable. Indeed, it is a fact that the inconsolable will not remain eternally distressed. In the long run, the inconsolable is consoled. We say "one has to live"—which is not a response, at least not a philosophical explanation. The as yet unconsoled man, who is consolable in the end, will find other beings to love . . . other beings, but not that same one! The one for whom he weeps, the one for whom he will cease to weep is lost forever. Approximating consolation, miserable compensation! In any case, the fact is there: the one who has the right to be inconsolable is well and truly consoled. The irreplaceable is, in fact, replaced. This mockery that is similar enough to the mockery of a love that is eternal at the time and provisional after the fact—what a beautiful subject for Pascal's irony! The oath of loyalty is always broken . . . yet it is no less sincere! The contradiction of the inconsolable-consoled has, in our misery, become so normal that an eternal sorrow, as painful twenty years later as on the first day, would easily pass for a pathological case.[26] The absolutist who feels in all of its rigor the despair for the irreplaceable-that-cannot-be-compensated has to be a type of sick person: he is sick about not being able to liquidate that which cannot be liquidated!—But the absurdity of temporal pacification is still more striking when the act to be forgiven is a sin, that is, when values are at stake. Sin is an attack on values, but as values themselves are invulnerable, indestructible, and atemporal, the attack is always in vain. After the insult, justice and truth remain just as before; the lying and injustice of man do not make them hot or cold. There is never any damage, not a scratch, and consequently no injuries to heal, no ruins to stand back up ... Values, which are outside of history, no more enter back in on a beautiful morning under the pretext that man has violated them. Being suprahistorical by essence, they do not become historical and thus datable on day D and at hour H of the misdeed. Afterward, just as before (and is there even an "after" and a "before"?), chronology remains without any relation to axiology and without any effect on it. With values finding themselves intact immediately after the attack, one of two things follows: either in this relation there is nothing to be forgiven, everything being forgiven in advance—for values have not become aware of anything; or (which amounts to the same) there is something unforgivable in the very fact of the attack. The attack on values thus confirms what we were saying about the act of forgiving: it is now or never!—One will say that values are atemporal—but the crime of the man who raises a hand against them is not, and the victims of the criminal even less so. This crime is an event that carries a date with it and that comes to pass one beautiful day on the calendar. The flux of becoming, insofar as its successive moments continually drive each other back into forgetting, exercises indeed an erosive action on the misdeed; it trims the circumference, it nibbles away at the contours. The victims of the infamy will not come back to life, but the material consequences are repairable, and in the same way the memories with which the crime leaves us are more and more vague. Physical repercussions and psychological effects do not cease to abate. In the long run, we were saying, the traces of an infamy become so insignificant that there are no longer either any apparatuses or any sensory organs subtle enough to detect them and measure them. The crime, forced back into a past that is further and fur-

26. Pierre Janet gives examples thereof in *L'Évolution de la mémoire et de la notion du temps* [The Evolution of Memory and of the Notion of Time] (Paris: A. Chahine, 1928).

ther away becomes almost doubtful and improbable.—But at the center of the physico-psychological envelope there is at the same time an ethical spark of the intention and a metaphysical knot that we could call the *quoddity* of the misdeed. The intention, which is very brief, can change, for it is an imperceptible shock and a fugitive shuddering of will. But time, properly speaking, *tempus ipsum,* has nothing to do with it. It is the man who of his own initiative evolves by conversion and a thoughtful will. On the other hand, the elusive movement of sin constitutes an event; for the initiative of liberty creates destiny. The Quoddity is that element of destiny that is inscribed in the metaphysical nucleus of the misdeed. With time, all that has been done can be undone; all that has been undone can be redone. But the fact-of-having-done (*fecisse*) is indefeasible. We can undo the thing done, but we cannot make it so that the thing that was done never happened, we cannot, as Cicero says, following Aristotle, make an *infectum* from a *factum.* Or, more simply, the effects of the misdeed can be repaired, just as every defect lends itself to repairing. But malevolence, that is, the fact of bad will in general, that is, the sole fact of having one time willed evil, that is, the sole fact of having had a bad intention, this is what is inexpiable, strictly speaking. Sin, par excellence, is this evil quality of intention, which, being impossible to locate in the action committed, comes to pass in the very occurrence of the misdeed. In the space of the flash of lightning and in the time of the blink of an eye, the ill-willed design has been conceived. Certainly the bad intention could have been as fleeting as a disappearing appearance, could have lasted as long as sparks last, flashing and extinguishing in the same instant . . . : the semelfactive instant is no less of an eternal instant, *aeternum nunc,* and it is already too much that it was possible! It is already too much to have had merely the intention! It is already too much merely to have thought about it! To commit a crime is an act that happens once in the chronicle, but the fact of having committed it will always last! Such is the paradox of *atemporal semelfactivity.* Thus, the fact of having-taken-place, which is the misdeed reduced to the pure advent of the event, is in itself eternal. Eternal or rather imperishable—for it is not atemporal at both ends. Culpability has indeed begun, although it does not have to finish. The commission of the misdeed happens in a history that previously knew nothing of it. Does not this temporal initiative that decides in favor of the atemporal, and that is infinitely surpassed by its own consequences, in itself sum up all the asymmetry of our freedom? So then the thing that was done has begun and will finish, instead of the fact of having done, once having begun, never finishing.

The thing done appears to disappear progressively by the effect of becoming, but the fact of having done makes itself eternal as a disappearing appearance. Little by little, the inert time of continuation erases *that which* has been done, but it has no hold over the *fact-that.* Through aging, that which has been done, *res facta,* becomes *practically* zero: so be it! But how would time ever make it that the *fecisse* was absolutely nothing and did not happen? But how does one go about it so that what happened never happened? It is of little importance that the crime of twenty years ago left an infinitesimal recollection in the memory of men. It is of little importance if, at the limit, this barely existent recollection, if this almost nonexistent recollection is indiscernible from forgetting, if the last echo of the crime has expired in silence, if the little flame of reminiscence has almost extinguished itself in the shadows; that is not the question! The number of years has nothing to do with the affair. Even if the crime were committed twenty years ago, the commission of the crime committed would not be any less horrible; simply the idea of having been able to commit it would not make it any less disgusting. Besides, on what would decay act? What would it find to wear away? The thing-done has a form, a volume, and a mass. On its morphology, we can understand that the years have a type of influence. Time precipitates the ruin of the form—or if not time itself (for it does not have any teeth for gnawing at things), at least the physical factors that act temporally and that dull, refine, and lessen the form, in the way bad weather levels the contours of the ground and the profile of mountains, or in the way the ocean gnaws at cliffs and smoothes pebbles. But the having-done! what influence over the "fact-of-having-done" will the accumulation of years be able to exert in order to make the ridges round, gnaw away the contours, exhaust and wear away the frame? Time necessarily leaves intact that which is devoid of all massiveness, or in other words that which is without consistency or resistance and finally without substantial existence. And for the same reasons, the quoddity of the misdeed, being "hard-wearing," is similarly incapable of being integrated and assimilated. It does not allow itself, in the manner of any new experience (the recollection of a voyage, for example), to be integrated or totalized in a higher synthesis. It is not digestible, and in turn it is not physically enriching. Subsequent good actions, following upon the bad one, are juxtaposed with it, but without absorbing it or without transfiguring it from the inside. The bad intention has become good for a long time, but the good one has not absorbed the *fact of* the bad one, just as it has not destroyed the *eternal* fact of having *one time* missed out on love. The good one and the bad one stay forever incomparable. And though this quoddity had liberty as its source and responsibility as its consequence, it remains in our history as a foreign body. All the burn and all that is incurable of remorse lie in the impossibility of integrating that which we cannot, however, renounce. If time does not chew on the quoddity of the misdeed, it is because it is impalpable and pneumatic, so to speak. The thing-done falls under the senses, but the fact of the having done is of the order *of sense,* since it is an eternal event that is triggered by an intention. The fact is labile because it is tangible. It disintegrates and falls into ruins insofar as it ages, like the temples of Greece. But the *fact of the fact,* but the fact with its exponent, but the fact to the second power, evades the corrosive action of duration.

In sum, what is the action of time on the fait accompli, on the intention of doing, and on the fact of having done? On the one hand, time erases the accomplished misdeed.[27] Or maybe it would be more exact to say that the misdeed that was committed becomes temporally blurred, which is to say, little by little, for time is nothing other than the indifferent, passive, and entirely docile dimension of all our experiences.—On the other hand, the intention, as we saw, is transformed without time's having anything to do with it. If time all by itself, if time without drama suffices to metamorphose a sinner, and if the intention, like wine, improves with age, then without a doubt it would be useless to take seriously the spontaneity of the conversion and the autonomy of the will. In maturing the ethical disposition, providential time would take charge of our improvement; the automatism of progress and of continuous perfection would release us from all penitence and from every moral crisis. However, it is man himself who lifts himself up out of the swamp by the sweat of his brow. It is man himself who saves himself by the deliberate, initial, and attentive effort of his will without looking to economize on the sufferings of remorse or on the sacrifices of repenting and of contrition. But time, the primary and natural given of lived experience, is incommensurable with the normative order of value; and value, for its part, is of a *wholly other order* than time. As we were saying, there is no common measure between chronology and axiology. In other words, "conversion" does not depend on the chronological circumstance; the date is here indifferent. What influence can age exercise on the value or antivalue of an intention? In order for temporality to have this transfiguring effect and these absolving virtues, it would be necessary for it itself to be a value capable of

27. [*Faute accompli.*]

recouping the antivalue of the ill-willed person and of transmuting malevolence into benevolence. But no one can explain whence it can draw this magical power, or how it can set about exorcising the guilt of the guilty person.—In the third place, the ethical inefficacity of temporality is heightened by a metaphysical powerlessness. We were asking why raw time would render the guilty person less guilty. Let us now ask why it would render the misdeed of the guilty person less serious, and a fortiori, why it would annul it. Time can attenuate or erase the misdeed that was committed, but not get rid of the commission of it. It neutralizes the *effects* of the misdeed, but it cannot destroy the *fact of* the misdeed. Time cannot make it so that what came to pass did not come to pass, for it would be contradictory that the same thing was at the same time done and not done; if, then, the having-done is not capable of being destroyed, then it is because the contradiction is not capable of being surmounted. In order to reconcile the contraries, a synthesis that is skillfully mediated, a wise compromise, or a good mixture suffices; but in order to unify contradictories, a miracle is necessary . . . We will have to research whether forgiveness is not just this very sudden miracle, this miraculous coincidence of position and negation. It is not sufficient to say that the having-done is *physically indestructible* or inexterminable; it is this destruction itself that is *logically impossible.* Consequently, to claim to make a tabula rasa of what was is very close to being an absurdity. As for that, we can *make as if,* but we cannot *make it that,* we can make it as if that which happened did not happen, but not that what happened did not happen. Gods themselves would not be able to do anything. The minor gods of mythology, specialists in marvelous details, unusual metamorphoses, and disappearances of all kinds, cannot do the impossible, that is to say, that which in no way *can be allowed.* As for humans, they neutralize the defeat by revenge; victory serves to make them forget the humiliation of the debacle and the shame of capitulation. The advocates of prescription admit among themselves that Auschwitz never existed; they do not speak of it anymore. But every now and then a secret remorse, attesting to the indestructibility of the "having-taken-place," reminds them of the point at which this fiction is fragile. The impossibility of destroying has the impotence of man as its verso. Considered from its positive side, it is nothing other than the necessity of the quoddity. The notion of the Imprescriptible, in general, refers us to this diptych of an impossibility and a necessity. The French Parlement proclaims that crimes against humanity are a priori imprescript*ible,* that is, *are not allowed* to be prescribed. Granting the fact that it is a question of an absolute principle, temporary prorogation of the prescriptive delay has to be considered as a miserably empirical measure; the moral dilemma would be just as acute thirty years after the expiration date as in the twentieth year. Strictly speaking and theoretically, every misdeed is imprescriptible, since every having-taken-place, from the moment in which it takes place onward, becomes eternal: the having-taken-place of the personal offense just like the having-taken-place of the moral misdeed, and that of peccadillos just like that of atrocious crimes. The attack against the humanness of man has something inexpiable where the quoddity lays itself bare. In cases that are literally "venial," the liquidation of the penal action can pass for beneficial approximation. On the other hand, the prescription of a colossal crime is a monstrous caricature of ordinary prescription and in fact makes manifest the absurdity of it.

When it is a question of a personal offense, we can say that time, of itself alone, is neither an efficacious forgiveness, nor a lasting forgiveness, that it lacks charity, that it implies neither the event, nor the relation of one heart to another, nor the gratuitous gift. We were contending that the empty continuation and the savage interval in no way replace repenting. But we were not able to deny, and we even presupposed, that the renunciation of hate and the conversion to love are still the supreme end. We were questioning only whether the long road of becoming was the straightest and most sincere path for arriving at peace. However, as soon as it is a question of a misdeed, to take time into consideration becomes injurious for scorned values. We were feeling doubts about the efficacity of evolution; now we are facing a moral dilemma. The idea that we can pass the eraser lightheartedly over an attack against values is in itself something of a sacrilege. And could one here even incriminate the "rancor" of rancorous people? Can we reproach the all too tenacious memory of those who refuse to make a complete break with all of this? Imprescriptibility is no longer in the psychological plan of memory. Loyalty to values, unfailing attachment to justice, and respect for the truth are not "memories." And the refusal to betray reasons for living in the name of a supposed right to life, such a refusal is no longer a rancor. No one, save by cynicism or coquetry, professes rancor out loud, or admits to being rancorous. And even the egoists who foster a shameful personal *ressentiment* and a shameful desire for vengeance against the offender at least take the trouble of justifying and sanctifying their passion in the name of principles; they confuse their rights with a real right or their cause with the just cause, and accuse their adversaries of injustice. But a crime against humanity is not my personal affair. To forgive, in this case, would not be to renounce one's rights but to betray *the* right. The person who "harbors rancor" against the criminals of such a crime literally *has the right:* the right and, what's more, the duty. Better yet: is holding the crime against the criminals really "holding a grudge" against whoever it may be? The loyal man who refuses to make peace and speak to his brother is not a sullen and more or less stubborn child. The sullen person will cease to be sullen when his sullenness has lasted for a sufficient time; he will cease his protest when the rancor has entirely melted. No, the serious and loyal man is not a capricious protestor. What one takes as rancor in him was rigor. Values themselves, indeed, do not have need of our rancor or of our rigor since no infamy, however monstrous it may be, would be able to reach them or make us doubt of their perpetuity. But the millions of exterminated people, they have need of our rigor. These exterminated people are not a motive for sullenness or for a quarrel. Rancor, a frivolous passion, puts the tortured person who bears a grudge against his torturer on the same level with the torturer against whom he bears the grudge. The tortured and the torturer, they are in short blurred. In this, rancor does not differ very much from coquetry. Far from being the suspension of all relations, it is rather the institution of a new mode of relations. Such are the very provisional relations that the people of the world establish between themselves when they are *on bad terms* with one another. The person with scabies is quarantined and without a doubt we judge that forty days amply suffice to rid him of the contagion of the scabies. Well, we ourselves are not on bad terms with torturers. Our "rigor" simply would like to express that there is *no relation* between their crimes and time, not even a relation of rancor. And there is then no reason for time, of itself alone, to render them less serious. In this respect, forty days and forty centuries have exactly the same weight. Time that levels the greatest misfortunes, time that smoothes, time that redeems proposes to us in vain the conveniences of disaffection: the years pass over the stationary situation, without soothing the disaffection.

IX. Do Not Ratify the Naturality of Disaffection

Or perhaps it is necessary to reason in more general terms. That remission goes in the spontaneous direction of natural evolution is in no way an argument in favor of remission; such an argument would rather be an objection.

And what an objection! In other terms, the naturality of forgiveness, if forgiveness were natural, would rather be a reason never to forgive. Since when has morality had the function of imitating nature or of reproducing traits of it? Because painting itself refuses to be purely photographic and to copy what is given but rather draws its inspiration from it, reshapes it, stylizes it, deforms it, or adds a supplementary vertebra to the female body, as Ingres did, it is all the more reason for moral life to begin with the derealization of reality. Realism itself, in art, is realist only because of this nascent idealization. And similarly, the "conformity to nature" of the Stoic sage has to be understood not in the sense of a conformism that is slavishly naturalistic, but rather as the search for a rational profundity hidden in what is perceptible. Better yet, it suffices for art to be unreal or surreal. Ethics, on the contrary, wants to be scandalously, paradoxically antireal. Its goal is not at all to transfigure what is perceptible, but to renounce pleasure; its function is not at all to ratify nature but rather to contradict it, to refute it, and to protest against it. The object of the renunciation, far from being an indifferent given upon which to elaborate, is a passionate temptation to be combated; this object is attractive and thus deceitful for it is supposed to seduce us in order to trick us. The vocation and the "categorical prohibitive" are the two aspects, the one positive and the other negative, of this absurd and supernatural exigence.—Justice, for example, is there not to confirm violence or to reinforce force, which in fact by themselves, already tend to prevail, but rather to give a supplement of strength to weakness, of which it has need in order to compensate for the physical disadvantage of weakness with a moral advantage, and, conversely, to disadvantage the physical advantage of strength. Justice disadvantages the unjustified advantage of some and provides advantages to the unjust disadvantage of the others. For one cannot have all the advantages at the same time! That would be asking too much! The one who already possesses the physical advantage of strength, of wealth, and of undeserved honors cannot claim in addition to increase his many advantages on account of a moral advantage. One cannot be a happy shark and be right also, or monopolize, in defiance of the alternative, that which is impossible to accumulate. One cannot at the same time obtain a chair in the Académie Française and refuse it, devote oneself to all the distinctions at once, or be rich and seem poor. Allow something for those who are poor and alone; at least allow them the very humble dignity of misery; do not contest their inalienable strength of weakness. Without justice, inequalities left to themselves would not stop growing. Everyone knows that money goes to the rich, happiness goes to the happy, who have no need of it, and is denied to the unhappy who would have so much of a need for it. Material superiority goes to the powerful to augment their power disproportionately and monstrously. In the end, good luck smiles on those who already have it; instead of replenishing the void of bad luck as it should, good luck is scandalously attracted by the abundance of luck! What would you say about justice if it gave itself over to the service of billionaires or if it flew to the aid of sharks and ogres? You would say that it was a laughable justice, a revolting deception, a horrible caricature, or better yet, a cynical injustice! Nietzsche, the defender not of orphans but of sharks, finds that the weak are still not weak enough, or that the brutes still are not strong enough. The brutes had need of being justified too! It is the last superiority that they were still lacking . . . Let us here respond to the advocate of the brutes. Justice is not made for favoring the one who already has all of the favors of nature. Justice is the compensatory mechanism, or, if one prefers, the allopathic remedy that neutralizes the contrary with its contrary; it takes the opposite course to the superiorities of the fact; it is just compensation and the just "chiasmus." Thus, it goes to the aid of the weak, helping the widow and the orphan, defending the humiliated and the offended, assisting the oppressed and the exploited, and arming the unarmed. Being the consolation of the afflicted and the rampart of the poor person, it protects the miserable person against the avalanche of miseries, for misfortunes, as they say, never come alone! Far from being in complete agreement with the inequality that is always growing and the lack of equilibrium that is incessantly aggravated, justice puts the breaks on the "more and more" of pleonexy, of compulsive desire, and of passionate frenzy; it reverses the tendency of feverish overstatement. Moderating justice impedes every crescendo and every accelerando, compensates every auction, and deflates every inflation; in the end, it stops the proliferation of abuses.—In the dimension of time, such is also the typically moral function of fidelity. If there is a temporal weightiness, and if becoming, as the factor of forgetting, designates to the person the direction of least resistance and the path of repugnant ease, then, on the contrary, the duty of fidelity would indicate to us the path of the greatest resistance, which is the most difficult and austere path of all. To swim with the current, to go where the wind blows, to allow oneself to be led by fashion, to consent to the declivity of time, is this not just conformism itself? The duty of fidelity refuses these temptations. It does not go in the direction of nature, but, as with all duties, it goes in the opposite direction, against the current, that is to say, upstream.

Thus, it is headed not only in the opposite direction from tropisms and from instinct, but also in the opposite direction from inclination. Or, more modestly (because no one is able to make becoming come back), the horizontal of fidelity holds back the consciousness that is ready to slide down the inclined plane of forgetting, and in this way it retards stupid disaffection. And just as justice stands in the way of the exaggerations of pleonexy, so fidelity thwarts frivolity and stops us halfway down the incline. Indeed, if we set innovative futurition in opposition to certain purely mechanical forms of verbal attachment and drivel, then it is fidelity that may seem inert. But it is no longer the same if we set cordial fidelity against the geotropism of forgetting and of ingratitude. When rancor is a simple spite and a wholly negative stubbornness, then forgiveness is a duty of charity; but when in reality the so-called "rancor" is an unshakable fidelity to values and to martyrs, then it is forgiveness that is a betrayal. We often hear that the rights of life, the general evolution of the historic situation, and the necessities of reconciliation should in the end prevail over outdated *ressentiments;* and we are criticized at the same time for the tiresome monotony of our stories and of our rancors. We are no longer, so it seems, "up to date." But first of all it is not so much love for one's neighbor that inspires the apostles of reconciliation, it is rather practical commodities; this is the perspective of attractive relations. Charity has nothing to do with it. They present as duty simply that which they wish to do and which they do out of egoism, cowardice, and frivolity. That is right, blame forgiveness. Can giving in to the impetus of general reconciliation, the communicative warmth of a superficial sympathy, and the unrefined good-naturedness of daily relations pass for a moral attitude? Similarly, the old torturer who has retired from torturing is without a doubt a placid citizen and a family man: the enormity of his crimes can no longer be seen on his face. As for the sympathy that this easygoing face can eventually inspire, it is impossible to find names other than stupidity, sordid vulgarity, or spirit of approximation. This type of fraternization would rather make us disgusted with forgiving. Indifferent people, unconcerned people, those who always think nothing happened and for whom not even the perspective of associating with torturers would be very disgusting, would do better not to invoke forgiveness and to spare us their sermons. One does not even see why they would talk of reconciliation when they were already reconciled with the criminal on the day after the crime, when they have never demanded an explanation from the assassins. On the other hand, can one seriously criticize loyal people for slowing down the course of history and for upsetting the relations of people among themselves? Let us respond that the litanies of rancor will not prevent anything and that the partisans of general liquidation can in any case be without anxieties. No matter what happens, forgetting will be the strongest, forgetting will have the last word in all cases. One day, sooner or later, the ocean of forgetting will submerge all, and our powerless despair will itself finish by giving in to the irresistible tidal wave of indifference or the rise of new interests and of new preoccupations. Like a wisp, triumphant modernity will sweep away the cult of the past and the piety of memories. For the present, that is, ambient every-dayness, besieges us in all aspects and does not cease to invite us to forget bygone things; this is the pressure of each minute. The present does not need us to remember it expressly since it is always there; the present has no need of anyone; the present itself takes care of its own defense without wait-ing for the counsel of lawyers. Forgetting does not, then, have as much need that we preach it, and it is indeed pointless to recommend it to people. There will always be many swimmers in the waters of Lethe. Men already have too much of a tendency to forget and they ask only for that. Why exhort them to follow the road that they have such a need to follow otherwise and that they will follow in any case? This would be to precipitate a fall that is already rendered inevitable by the gravity of instincts, to fortify this irresistible gravity by a moral acceleration, to subscribe to the brutal superiority of the present, and fly cowardly to the aid of victory. By nature man is indeed ego-istic and cowardly enough for moralists not to believe that they are obliged to "overdo it," to keep nudging, to help the coward find excuses and honor-able pretexts. And if forgiveness were this glorious pretext? The raison d'être of the moral imperative cannot be to be in agreement with the direc-tion of facility. Moreover, how would facility be good and normative? The conjunction of duty and desire would be an incredible godsend, and the merit of Kant is to have denounced the eudaimonism of this optimism or the doubtful status of this "harmony." It is not the present that needs our aid; it is rather the past. It is not present people who have need of our loyalty, it is the absent ones. Yes, it is the past that demands to be ceaselessly recalled, expressly recollected, and piously commemorated. The past, no longer ex-isting, needs that one honor it and that one be loyal to it; for if we ceased to think about it, then it would be completely annihilated. The past will not de-fend itself all alone! As the past is inactual, it is indeed necessary that we spontaneously take the initiative to go to it. It is, thus, the frivolity of some that renders necessary the fidelity of others; this fidelity is perhaps the remorse of the frivolous. But let the frivolous reassure themselves, for memories will never be as burdensome as interests. Moral fidelity to the past is, then, always of a protesting nature. This protest, which is essentially ethical, is itself a desperate challenge and sometimes provocative of the natural forces. The moral man, reduced to the defensive, protests solemnly against the inevitable triumph of forgetting. Against this all-powerful strength of becoming, what can the thinking reed[28] do if not protest: a Platonic protest, an impotent protest, which, however, is one of the forms of moral sublimity! For this loyalty is loyal to the point of the absurd and in spite of the absurd, paradoxically loyal to that which is anachronistic and useless . . . When universal disaffection wins us over in turn, when everything counsels the one who loves not to love, a solitary and absurd voice recommends unfailing loyalty to us. Remember. Do not forget. Do not be like vegetables, ruminating animals and mollusks that at each instant forget the preceding instant and never protest against anything. And conversely, when everything counsels us to erase, to liquidate, and to absolve, a voice in us protests, and this voice is the voice of rigor; and this voice orders us to continue to be the witness of invisible things and of innumerable things that have disappeared. This voice tells us that the real is not only made of things that are palpable and obvious—good business, beautiful travels, and good vacations . . . No, vacations are not all that there is! And in the end, it, this voice, speaks to us of the crimes without name that were perpetrated, the mere evocation of which fills us with horror and shame.

Thus, there is an imprudent manner of recommending forgiveness to us that rather is a means for making us disgusted with it. Time, far from justifying forgiveness, renders it suspect. The ensemble of the moral problem that forgiveness has to resolve is, indeed, situated outside of time; first, values, which are atemporal, then the sin, which began but which is atemporal *a parte post.* The sin can do nothing to values, and values, consequently, do not have need of being restored. The misdeed, once it is committed, in some respect juxtaposes its faulty atemporality with that of values without influencing it, and the conversion even of the faulty movement is accomplished outside of all evolution and in the instant of sincere remorse. And it is also the atemporality of gratuitous forgiveness that, outside of every progressive restoration, can alone sever the Gordian knot of faulty atemporality. This

28. [See *Pascal's Pensées,* intro. T. S. Eliot, trans. W. F. Trotter (New York: Dutton, 1958), 97 (§347).]

grace is not acquired little by little with passing time, and the number of years does not yield any right over it to the guilty person. Or, in other terms, the agony of the misdeed, prolonged as long as one wills, never will produce a result comparable to the instantaneous gesture of forgiveness; forgiveness is not a chronic mortification. Forgiveness, as we will see, again finds a direction if one gives oneself the trampoline of an unshakable, good memory that alone projects the offended above the offense, that alone confers on grace the *élan* and the spring of which it has need. The discontinuity of forgiveness is rendered possible by the fullness of memories. Nothing could be more evident: in order to forgive, it is necessary to remember. Rancor is the strangely contradictory condition of forgiveness; and conversely, forgetting renders it useless. For forgiveness jumps into the void, leaning on the past. In the dwindling of time, we have nowhere found the plenitude of fidelity that had given a sense to the sudden rupture, to the gracious gift, and to the relation with someone. Decay and forgetting are not events and they have no intention. Indeed, they end up by reducing rancor to zero, but they finish, and how slowly, where forgiveness had begun. Let us repeat it here: the heart is not there! As for the heart of forgiveness, we have not found it.

2   The Excuse: To Understand Is to Forgive

Confidence in intellection is in all respects more philosophical than is confidence in time and the virtues of forgetting, for at least intellection is an activity of the mind and it results from a personal effort of the human being, whereas time flows all alone, independent of our initiatives. Confidence in intellection presupposes a certain philosophy of evil, which is precisely intellectualism, and we rather would like to be able to say *intellectionism*—for if intellectualism is the philosophy of the intellect, then it is "intellectionism" that is the philosophy of penetrating intellection. This "intellectionism" itself bases its indulgence on the negation of sin. "Intellectionism" is a theory about misdeed, and the intellectionist has an opinion about the nature of the culpable act, whereas the forgetful person does not have any opinion about anything at all and moreover intrinsically does not look to account for his need for reconciliation; forgetting is not a philosophical theory, and those who preach forgetting do nothing other than use the fickleness and sloth of men, their amnesia and their superficiality. For what is forgetting if not a void and an absence? In short, forgetting, decay, and integration are three analogies, one psychological, the other physical, and the last one biological, that possibly allow for an interpretation of the thawing of rancor; but here every normative pretension would be usurped. Let us reconcile because history urges us to do it, because such are the exigencies of life and the necessities of good neighborliness, because duration soothes all *ressentiments,* because, because . . . But this because is not a *because:* it does not indicate the grounds for reconciliation; it simply gives an explanation of reconciliation. Let us do as time does, seeing as time invites us to do it, or so it seems. Time, indeed, passes without turning back . . . Now, this is not a "reason," and not even a physical cause, let alone, an analogy. To conform to the directive of the natural process, simply because it is natural, is a type of conformism; the general evolution of things is not necessarily justified from the point of view of the moral person. The one who forgives in the name of time, and in consideration of the age of the crime and because there supposedly is prescription, does not deny that the crime took place, and strictly speaking does not even pretend that the crime is forgivable or the sin venial; in short, he does not express his view on its intrinsic quality. He does not tell us anything about the gravity of the misdeed that is forgiven; he does not consider the degree of guilt of the guilty person. The intellective excuse, on the contrary, is the taking of a position on the wrongs of the culprit of whom a fault is reproached. It implies the moral appreciation of the act that it excuses; it penetrates deeply into the mechanism of intentions; it is an internal reading of these intentions. Those who preach forgetting do not say that the wicked person is not wicked, they simply say that enough is enough and that it is time to finish with the state of war. It is the intellectualists who deny the wickedness of the wicked person. And consequently, if age by itself is not a philosophical reason to forgive, then the nothingness of the sin itself surely is this reason.

I. There Is No Will of Evil

For the intellectualist, to forgive is to recognize implicitly the nothingness of evil, and in turn, one thing leading to another, the nonexistence of sin, the absurdity of rancor, and the uselessness itself of forgiveness. Actually, what is intellectualist is not so much to deny the substantiality of evil but rather to refuse the idea of an absolute wickedness inherent in the will of man. For if the source of evil is a counterprinciple, a transcendent hypostasis, or I do not know what diabolical arche, then the guilty person is no longer so responsible! There are then no longer very many reasons for holding a grudge against the one who is himself the victim of a corrupter. Here, personal rancor does not even find anyone on whom to put the blame! Instead, address the serpent who perverts the sinner, or Satan, who commanded his serpent to pervert the creature and plotted the whole machination. Paradoxically, this radical pessimism is a means for excusing the sinner by accusing the seducer who put the wrong idea in his head. The more that Satan is guilty, then the more that Adam is innocent! If the devil is the instigator of sin, then the sinner is only a dupe. But it is also true that *ressentiment* is displaced: man now holds a grudge against the devil himself. Can we say, however, that an abstract principle is the object of rancor, that the word *forgiveness* here has a meaning? In all cases, be it hypostasis or human malevolence, evil is denounced as an idol of "knowledge of the first sort," as an idol fabricated by dramatic Manicheanism and by the inveterate pathos of primitive thinking. The optimistic intellectualism of Socrates negates the very possibility of an ill will.[1] And just as the will cannot be evil, it cannot be, strictly speaking, good. For what is a will that cannot will evil? This is not a will at all! By abolishing the possibility of bi-willing, intellectualism thus abolishes the will in general. Sin, in its most characteristic aspect, which is the lie, constitutes the object of an insoluble aporia for Plato.—Once the mirage of sin is dissipated, rancor, no longer having anything on which to chew, dies of inanition. Transforming sin into a slip of the tongue, intellectualism takes the bread from the mouth of the rancorous person, the dry bread, the bitter bread of *ressentiment*. We no longer even know against whom to hold a grudge, nor what to want from the person against whom we hold the grudge. And how do we *hold a grudge* against a will that cannot even *will*?—Without a raison d'être for rancor, forgiveness in turn is without material. There is no longer an offense, an offended person, or an offender; there is no longer sin or sinner. As before when the rancorous person did not know against whom to hold a grudge or why, the generous person does not know whom to forgive or why, or which sinners to pardon and which sins to absolve. Golaud asks Mélisande: "Mélisande . . . do you forgive me, Mélisande?"—the innocent one responds, "Yes, yes, I forgive you . . . what is it necessary to forgive?"[2] Forgiveness from the heart, passionate forgiveness found its material in the positivity of the misdeed: perverse malevolence—here is the resented of *ressentiment* and the privileged forgivableness of a gracious forgiveness. If there are wicked people, then very well! Rancor, which is the direct relation of the offended person to the offense, and forgiveness, which has rancor to

---

1. *Lesser Hippias,* 373b: *os an kakourgē akōn suggnōmēn exein.* ["EUDICUS: Well, Socrates, I don't think Hippias will need us to plead with him. For that's not what he said earlier; he said that he wouldn't flee from any man's questioning. Right, Hippias? Isn't that what you said? HIPPIAS: I did. But Socrates always creates confusion in arguments, and seems to argue unfairly. SOCRATES: Oh excellent Hippias, I don't do that voluntarily, for then I'd be wise and awesome, according to your argument, but involuntarily. So please be lenient with me, for you say that one who acts unfairly involuntarily should be treated leniently." Trans. Nicholas D. Smith, in *Plato: Complete Works,* ed. John M. Cooper (Indianapolis: Hackett, 1997), 932.]

2. *Pelléas et Mélisande,* 5.2. [Debussy completed this opera in 1902, basing it on a play written by Maurice Maeterlinck in 1892. Jankélévitch cites this work quite often in his writings.]

overcome, will both find their role. Is the misdeed of the guilty person who is to be forgiven not a rancor to be overcome in itself? The positivity of the sin and the paradox of charity stand in solidarity in the spirit of Saint Paul. On the other hand, "forgiveness" that is founded on an excuse is reduced to the simple admission that there never was an offense and that the idea of fundamental wickedness is an entirely illusionary mirage. Such a forgiveness is an admission of deficiency! To forgive is, thus, paradoxically to recognize that there is nothing to forgive. The obstacle called misdeed was the contradictory condition of forgiveness. In obliterating the obstacle, we get rid of forgiveness itself. The subjective sentiment of having "forgiven" is rather a general effect, a type of approximate impression or, when viewed up close, an appearance that resolves itself in rational comprehension. What we add to it in generosity and gratuitousness is the simple product of a feverish imagination. Forgiveness is thus just as vain as sin itself; the drunkenness of forgiveness is a delirium that is just as absurd as the obsessive fear of the misdeed. Worse yet: since sin does not exist, then the one who forgives a nonexistent sin, in taking it to be a true sin, either plunges into error or effectively risks creating a type of sin by dint of believing in it; he resembles a veridical liar who tells the truth while taking it for a lie and with the intention of lying. To forgive a sin that does not exist would thus be a sin, and the sin of forgiving what is not a sin would even be the first of sins and the only sin! In order to avert the folly of forgiveness, intellectualism, as we see it, is not scared of contradicting itself a little. And if by chance sin already existed, then the forgiveness that absolves it would be a second sin. The sin of forgiving the sin is an additional sin that doubles and aggravates the first one, so that in forgiving the sin, you commit another one and stand in solidarity with the guilty person; you share with the guilty person the responsibility for an attack against values. Is this negligence not complicity? The Gospel subsequent to Jeremiah recommends to us to turn the other cheek. Is this not willing out of gaiety of heart to fabricate injustice there where it does not exist, or to aggravate the guilt of the guilty person for pleasure? The offended person spontaneously accepts doubling the humiliation without taking into consideration that if one slap does not yet make a sinner, then two slaps will perhaps suffice. More simply, radical intellectualism denies the very possibility of sin. Intellectualism is therefore the negation of all irrational supernaturality, be this supernaturality that of evil or that of love. The mirage of sin dissipates under analysis. The one who believes himself obliged to forgive is the dupe of the pathetic system of which the myth of the misdeed is at the center; he participates in the imaginary world of sin. Exaltation born of wickedness communicates itself to the magnanimous person who makes the gesture of absolving it; and the more that the wickedness is unforgivable, the more that forgiveness will be sublime. Intellectualism makes this accumulation of aberrations disappear. The partners in this little drama—the devil, the sinner, the rancorous person, and the magnanimous one—were playing imaginary roles: they all slip away at the same time. Since there is no radical malevolence, it is useless to waste one's time forgiving; the guilty person is simply poorly taught, incompletely informed, and we would be better off to instruct him; the expiation itself, of which *Gorgias*[3] speaks, has an ortho-pedagogical character. Why charity and not justice, asked Anatole France? Why forgiveness and not the simple truth?

II. An Excuse Is Neither an Event, nor a Relation with Others, nor a Gratuitous Gift

The intellective excuse does not unite in itself the three distinctive features of true forgiveness. It is neither an event, nor a personal relation with the Other, nor a gratuitous gift. A stranger to the event, the excuse loses its offense; a stranger to every real relation with another, it loses its offender, and, as a consequence, there is no offended person. The three correlates obviously stand in solidarity, such that if you take away one, they all fall at the same time. Without an offense, the offended person and the offender disappear arm in arm—for the offense does not exist in itself. Without an offender, there is no offended person . . . unless he has offended himself all alone! Without an offended person, there is no offender—for an offender who offends no one, that is, an offender who is an offender in title, is a pure abstraction, except if the offended person, in disdaining the injury, does not even feel touched by the offender. For a start, a comprehension that absolves is not a true event; for if it comes to pass or intervenes at a certain date in

3. [See *Gorgias,* trans. Donald J. Zeyl, in *Plato: Complete Works,* 821–25 (477a–480b), 825 (490a–b): "And if he or anyone else cares about unjust acts, he should voluntarily go to the place where he'll pay his due as soon as possible; he should go to the judge as though he were going to a doctor, anxious that the disease of injustice shouldn't be protracted and cause his soul to fester incurably."]

our personal history, then this is solely because the creature is weak, myopic, or even entirely blind, because the capacity of his understanding, to speak as Malebranche does, is horribly limited. The finitude and lack of clear-sightedness of the person make a discovery out of intellection, and out of the discovery they make a news item that comes at such and such a moment in the chronicle. This discovery is the point of insertion of our duration into the eternal truth of sense; or better yet, it is the tangent point of the temporal with the atemporal. It marks, so to speak, the advent of that which is atemporal. And so the true sense of human relations reveals itself to us one beautiful morning, but this sense itself is outside of time; and, in contrast, it is all the more atemporal insofar as it teaches us how superficial is the spite of the offender, how ephemeral and inconsistent are our recriminations, our angers, and our susceptibilities. The rancorous situation is comparable to a room of mirages, a skiagraphy as Plato would say, to a play of shadows and phantasms, the source of which is the exaggerated importance that the ego—offender or offended—attributes to its self-interest. Indeed, it is in the egocentric perspective of hangmen and their victims that it is necessary to interpret the passionate illusions born of philauty. To understand the sense is to recognize here that the offended has never been offended, that in short the sin never took place. If the offended person were more clear-minded, he would "forgive" at the very instant of the offense, at once and forthwith. Even better, he would have "forgiven" in advance (but can one still say "forgive"?) all the future sins of all the sinners; he would acquit the wrongdoer before the misdeed and without even taking the time to forgive, since the wrongs and sins to come have already all been forgiven. This is how one day the sage understands the affirmative positivity of all that is: the universal indulgence of a lucid vision responds to the universal transparency of a world rid of sin. We would not know how to consider this clear-minded reading as either an effective act or a creative conversion; this is why we called it Discovery instead of Invention, for it is the ineffective discovery of an eternal positivity. The excuse misjudges the sudden instant of forgiveness not only by discovering an atemporal sense that existed before our discovery, but by discovering this sense at the end of a discursive labor; intellectual intuition is temporally prepared. For men in general are so slow that they understand a long time after the misdeed, and little by little. And sometimes they even have to rehabilitate an unjustly condemned man after the fact, and too late. This posthumous reparation for a judiciary error, is it forgiveness? Time is needed for quelling anger and the vindictive reflex, for overcoming rancor, and for dominating instinctive naturality. As with every other effort, the effort of intellection takes time: here, understanding supposes trial and error and touch-ups, a laborious focus, a sustained attention and a well-considered analysis of the misdeed. Indeed, time as we have shown has no influence on the gravity of the misdeed. It is not time that makes us understand, whatever the case may be; time is simply the dimension of the intellectual effort and it measures the duration of it. This time of incubation is inefficacious and insufficient without the intuition that crowns the continuation of the interval. And yet intellection implies a process of laborious deepening that the instant of forgiveness excludes. In this immanent process, it is up to us to verify that the painful event is dissolved.

Intellection does not imply a true personal relation with the other any more that it is an event in itself. First, from the point of view of the offender there is no *allocution,* and, consequently, no *interlocutor.* The "other" in flesh and bones, the partner in forgiveness is nonexistent, as it were. It is not in his honor—in yours! nor out of love for him—but for you! that we go beyond the irascible or rancorous relation; it is in the name of an impersonal and anonymous truth. The guilty person would be able not to exist if need be. The guilty person is not guilty, since guilt is the myth of an excited imagination.—The guilty person is only sick or insane; between that point and loving him, there exists an abyss that justice in itself does not at all ask us to traverse. For the one who loves everyone does not love anyone; there is nothing there except disengagement and smiling tolerance. With regard to the perspective of the partner, our disinterestedness—admitting that the partner has a face and an ipseity—is indiscernible from indifference, *praōs exeis pros ton loidorounta,* claims Epictetus's *Handbook:*[4] you will use gentleness with the one who offends you, because he is mistaken . . . But this gentleness toward a guilty person in error has nothing in common with transitive love; it is pure negativity. Like violence, which is its opposite, gentleness is on the other hand a simple external comportment. Gentleness by itself has no

4. *Encheiridion,* §42. ["When someone acts badly toward you or speaks badly of you, remember that he does or says it in the belief that it is appropriate for him to do so. Accordingly he cannot follow what appears to him, so that if things appear badly to him, he is harmed in as much as he has been deceived. For if someone thinks that a true conjunctive proposition is false, the conjunction is not harmed but rather the one who is deceived. Starting from these considerations you will be gentle with the person who abuses you. For you must say on each occasion, 'That's how it seemed to him.'" *Handbook of Epictetus,* trans. and ed. Nicholas P. White (Indianapolis: Hackett, 1983), 25–26.]

intention; it can express contempt just as much as love, for disdain is precisely a way of not doing violence. To be gentle with the offender? It is in this way, comments Guyau, that we "forgive" the stone that strikes us. And to comment on the commentator, we can add that our anger toward the offender is just as absurd as that of Xerxes toward the Hellespont. It is the same as carrying a grudge against the blow that strikes you.—From the point of view of the offended person, humility would obviously be absurd. A liquidation to which he has consented in the name of truth is much easier, more painless, and less costly than the agonizing sacrifice called Forgiveness. Costly for self-esteem and for self-interest, cruel toward honor and toward the very dignity even of the one who forgives, forgiveness excludes all compensation and all payback; and in this it is sacrifice, period. Intellection, on the other hand, is without pain. Here we are speaking only of the pain inherent in the relations of man with his fellow men: violent people, wicked people, and torturers. Pain, as irrational effectivity and lived affectivity, is indeed of a wholly other order than intellection. A tiresome effort is sometimes necessary in order to understand. But abstracting from this effort, intellectual comprehension is without either relation to or common measure with the event that affects the nervous system and the whole of psychosomatic life. No wound to stitch up. Assured analgesic. Thus, to understand and to suffer are incommensurable. So understanding does no evil. And not only does understanding do no evil but understanding moreover does not cost anything. In this forgiveness self-esteem is in no manner engaged; intellection is not even meritorious, strictly speaking, since the evidence of the truth asserts itself by itself wholly on the basis of good faith.—At last, from the point of view of the offense: our conflict, redeployed into the impersonal cadre of human affairs, clearly allows its insignificance and nullity to come to light. Our Lilliputian rancors, reinserted into general determinism, become as negligible as a bit of grit in the eye of a highway worker somewhere in France; my grievances are no more than an element or component in the chain of causes and effects. The offense has been diluted in the interior of the general order . . . Now it now longer suffices to say, as we were saying of clemency, that the offense has become microscopic and that the offender is no longer even visible to the naked eye; now it no longer suffices to say, in the manner of disdainful men, that the injury is minuscule and in a way imperceptible. Haughty clemency, with its somewhat condescending noble-mindedness, does not deny that the injury took place;

it denies only that the affront can reach it or that it can even detect it. On the other hand, although clemency is above offenders and sinners, it is still with them in a relation of domination. It does not really want to abuse its superiority, to employ only a part of its strength, and not do all that it can; but this is only a tactic and a form of cold war. Intellection is even beyond clemency. It is the person granting clemency, and not the sage, who scorns injuries, for scorn is still too passionate for the one who has nothing to scorn and who takes into consideration the partitive truth of each error and refuses existence only to nonexistent phantasms. For the magnanimous person, offenses slide off without hurting, but the wise person himself is not capable of being offended. In clemency, there is an offender although there is no offended person. In intellective wisdom, there is neither offended person nor offender. And as for the offense, it is not even contemptible, negligible, and infrasensible; it is purely and simply nonexistent, which is to say, null and void. Let us say it again here: intellective "forgiveness" is the cognizance of the fact that in short there never was an offense, an offended person, or an offender.—Few words are now needed for concluding that the intellective excuse, being neither an event, nor a relation with the other, is also not a gratuitous gift. To recognize the nothingness of sin is not to give a gift, or even less to give alms to the sinner, since there is no sinner; it is quite simply to recognize the truth. To absolve the ignorant or sick person is not to pardon him, for he has no need of our grace, he has no need of our charity. It is quite simply to give him justice.

To understand is to forgive? *"To understand is"* . . . would imply that forgiveness is not only the result or obligatory consequence of, but the necessary and automatic effect of, comprehension. Better yet: to understand would be, ipso facto and immediately, to forgive, as if one and the other amounted to the same . . . Can forgiveness be deduced from knowledge? To make forgiveness into a conclusion would be to suppress the liberty of forgiving, and along with liberty, the uncertain event and charitable gratuity. Just as a will ceases to will if it can will only the Good, if it wants the Good naturally and in virtue of physical laws, so forgiveness ceases to "forgive" if it flows from intellection in the same way that the secretion of gastric juices flows from the ingestion of food. For the Good is that which we are able not to will! And likewise, forgiveness is that which we are able to refuse . . . In what respect would a freedom that is free solely and unilaterally to choose the Good, a freedom without alternative, a liberty denuded of its bi-willing and of its bi-ability, a freedom incapable of choosing one or the other, in what respect would it be free? Furthermore, if there were nothing hazardous, in what respect would it be forgiveness?

III. The Total Excuse: To Understand Is to Forgive

Reasonable comprehension renders the impulsive grace of forgiveness useless. But if this comprehension itself did in a certain fashion imply a gracious gift, an event, and the relation with someone, then it would not be pacifying either. Lived comprehension is perhaps what distinguishes Spinoza from Socratic intellectualism. In the early dialogues of Plato, it is only a matter of refuting by way of didactics the contradictions of an erroneous discourse and of enriching the nescience, of filling this void, and of replacing this nothingness; and especially it is about denouncing the nothingness of the misdeed since ignorance or amatheia is the only sin. Socrates, although persecuted, is tempted neither to hold a grudge against nor to forgive his persecutors: he only shows by refutation that the guilty person is an ignorant person. He does not say to Anytus and Meletus, who condemned him to death, "I forgive you." He only says, with full objectivity and without addressing anyone in particular: *oudeis hekōn hamartanei,* "no one does evil knowingly."[5] That is all there is to it: these people apparently do evil but they do not know that they do it; the science of their nescience, that is to say, the conscience, is authorized to absolve them. The superficial and partially unconscious science that we call "lie" is thwarted by a more profound science. In this regard, Epictetus is closer to Spinoza than Socrates. From the bottom of his misery and dereliction, the slave-philosopher speaks for the offended and the humiliated, his brothers, rather than for his offenders. The problem that he resolves is his personal problem: how to stay happy during the most extreme misfortune? how to stay free while in the most humiliating servitude? The thawing of the rancorous situation, which was not in question at the time of Socrates, now overrides the problem of error. Spinoza himself is the contemporary of an epoch that begins to be acquainted with hatred

5. [See Plato's *Apology*, trans. G. M. A. Grube, 25d–26b, in *Plato's Complete Works*. See also the *Protagoras,* trans. Stanley Lombardo and Karen Bell, 358d: "Now, no one goes willingly toward the bad or what he believes to be the bad"; and the *Meno,* trans. Grube, 77d: "Do you think, Meno, that anyone, knowing that bad things are bad, nevertheless desires them?"]

and all the varieties of *ressentiment;* after Spinoza, modern man will experiment with forms of gratuitous hatred that Plato, the enemy of violence, and Spinoza himself had not suspected. The diabolical art of making people suffer and of torturing, the Machiavellian will to humiliate and to offend, and novel wickedness have become a type of national talent among certain peoples who are specially gifted in this regard. It is also necessary to say that knowledge of ipseity, and the precise aim that permits hitting it at its weak points or in its most vulnerable center, have all been immensely perfected since the epoch of Callicles. For him alone, the refined art of the injurious word, an eminently modern specialty, would already pose in all its acuity the difficult problem of forgiveness—of a forgiveness that is often beyond our strength. We would not know how to claim seriously that Spinoza was a humiliated person and an offended person in this sense. Robert Misrahi states strongly that if Spinoza had lived at the time of the massive exterminations, then there would not have been Spinozism.[6] Spinoza, survivor of Auschwitz, would not have been able to say *"Humanas actiones non ridere, non lugere, neque detestari, sed intelligere."*[7] From this point on, to understand is no longer to forgive. Or better yet, we can no longer understand; there is no longer anything to understand. For the chasms of pure wickedness are incomprehensible. But in the end, Spinoza in his way had something to forgive.

To understand is to forgive. All the ambiguity of an intellective excuse is

6. ["Responses to the Papers by V. Jankélévitch and S. Zac" in] *La Conscience juive face à l'Histoire: Le Pardon* [(Proceedings of the Congrès juif mondial), ed. Eliane Amado Lévy-Valensì and Jean Halperin (Paris: Presses Universitaires de France, 1965), 285–86. Misrahi states: "I only want to ask if we do well by employing Spinoza in our profound question on [what to do about] Germany. And this is to say that I fear, indeed, that Spinoza is not capable of being used [in the debate] for the excellent reason that—and I am certain, even if this hypothesis is absurd—that Spinoza would think otherwise after such an event, that there would not have been the same philosophy of Spinoza after the catastrophe, after Nazism. This is why we shouldn't invoke Spinoza for this affair." It should be noted that Misrahi is responding to Sylvain Zac's paper on sin and forgiveness in Spinoza. The other paper at this session was Jankélévitch's own "Introduction to the Theme of Forgiveness," in which Jankélévitch was working out many of the themes of *Forgiveness.*]

7. *Tractatus Politicus,* 1.4. ["I have laboured carefully not to mock, lament, or execrate, but to understand human actions." *Baruch de Spinoza's Political Treatise,* ed. and intro. by R. H. M. Elwes, trans. A. H. Gosset (London: G. Bell and Son, 1883). Throughout the second foreword to his book *Athens and Jerusalem,* Leon Shestov mentions this passage from Spinoza. See Leon Shestov, *Athens and Jerusalem,* trans. Bernard Martin (Athens: Ohio University Press, 1966).]

reflected in the double sense of this equation. First, "to understand is to forgive" means that there is no other forgiveness than knowledge. Comprehension takes the place of forgiveness and renders forgiveness useless. In other words, it is forgiveness in general, it is the *venia* itself, that is reduced to an intellective movement. But we can also interpret the formula in the opposite sense: it is no longer intellection that absorbs forgiveness (*intellegere, id est ignoscere*), it is forgiveness that flows from intellection (*intelligere ergo ignoscere*). Now, for the first point: to understand is to forgive in a cold manner; intellection, instituting an abstract fraternity among men, recognizes and respects the relative truth of each being and the equal promotion of all beings. But such a forgiveness does not have a second person; it concerns the anonymous universality of "third" persons; it does not address itself to *you*. It is not engaged like true forgiveness in an immediate relation with the person opposite from it, but it is impartial in the manner of the transcendental instance that Aristotle calls *dikaion empsuchon*. For in order to *decide between* antagonistic truths, it is necessary not *to participate in* any one of them.—However, intellection, like forgiveness, can imply a real communication with the offender and a real transfiguration of the offended person. First, an equitable form of forgiving, a form of forgiving that entails renouncing the optic privilege of the first person, the autistic point of view of philauty, and in a word the egocentrism of the me-for-myself, lacks neither warmth nor even generosity. Indeed, the interlocutor of the allocution is no longer called the Other,[8] *Alter,* the partner in the immediate tête-à-tête, but the Other, the Other who is a legion, the Other multiplied infinitely. In spite of his anonymity, this Other of a thousand heads, this hydra of the not-I in the plural, indeed represents, around the I, *alterity* par excellence. In spite of its indetermination, this Neighbor who is so far away is for the offended and hurt ego a permanent invitation to deflate the tumor of self-esteem and the hypertrophy of passionate susceptibility, to dismiss every pettiness. Renouncing the exceptionality of the egoistic point of view, the man who forgives through understanding or by dint of comprehension, in his modesty, finds the strength to recognize, if there is the room, the issue of the rights of the offender and the issue of the well-foundedness of the offense. In his lucidity, he draws on courage to treat the other as himself, in treating himself as another. The law of reciprocity, which asks us not to be unilaterally in one single party, and, in the case at hand, in the camp of the me, but to be at the

8. [*L'Autre.* The three subsequent instances of "the Other" are translations of "*Autrui.*"]

same time in one's own camp and that of the other by surveying the two truths, this law is called Justice. Justice and also Reason. For justice is reasonable as reason is just. For it is from reason that justice receives the principle of omnilaterality, and with it the resolution of all rancors. In sum, rancor was a misunderstanding founded on a miscomprehension. The false relations and false situations that flow from it, favoring the first person to the detriment of other monads, instituted an imaginary order, a warlike and frenzied order. Comprehension resolves misunderstandings born of miscomprehension, or in other words, dissolves the lumps of rancor that were altering the fluidity and the transparency of human relations; in liquidating or liquefying the false relations frozen by sulkiness, it reestablishes the binding force of pacifistic communication among men. It is not for Spinoza but rather for Leibniz that forgiveness becomes foreign to every alterocentric intention. Wishing that the limited monad would reconcile itself as much as possible with the point of view of general harmony, Leibniz would also accept saying that "To understand is to forgive." But since he admits necessary evil and since this evil is a least amount of evil, sin finds itself more minimized than eliminated. Now, if the negativity of evil is a least positivity, then forgiveness in its turn risks being no more than a least rancor. In a certain measure, optic accommodation, diminishing the gravity of the misdeed, has the same effects that time does. Someone's sin is organized into the general plan of the universe of which it is an ingredient for all eternity. With the elements of universal economy linked to each other, the singular misdeed must be understood serially like all the rest. Leibniz does not say that sin is nonexistent; he says only that sin fits well into the painting; the harmony of the universe is saved, but the sinner is abandoned to his own fate. In this "contemplationist" vision, it is *scopy*—telescopy, microscopy— that is important above all, and not personal felicity. Less concerned about the beauty of the fresco, Spinoza is much more helpful for the individual.[9]— To understand implies not only a communication with the human race but an interior transformation of the subject who understands. To understand is not only to become a friend of men but to become a friend of oneself. "To understand is to forgive," as we saw, signifies not only that intellection is intellectual, but that intellection is soothing: intellection reduces anger as aspirin reduces a fever. Whether it is a matter of indignation or irritation,

9. See the beautiful book by Georges Friedmann, *Leibniz et Spinoza*, 1946. [Reprint: Paris: Gallimard, 1975.]

of rancor or shame, lucid knowledge is in all things the great sedative; it soothes suffering, takes the heat off tenacious sulkiness, decongests the inflammation of anger, and "relaxes" the aggressive and strained man. With a view to this interior recovery, this total transformation, Socratic Refutation (*elenchos*) has become insufficient. Man has need of an efficacious method and, if we are permitted to say, of an art of persuading, and sometimes even of a type of starvation diet that alone is capable of making him wise. To reattach injustice to its causes, to reintegrate the misdeed into a universal necessity where it becomes intelligible, to dissipate the areas of shadow and the opacities that the mirage of wicked liberty project into the world is not an enterprise that is purely speculative. The truth that intellection wants to reestablish is that of an amicable world in which man will cease to curse his brother and will live in peace of mind and of heart. In that, intellection implies an effort and relates to the future. Serenity is not completely finished and wholly given as it was with Socrates; serenity is not acquired; it is to be conquered. It is this passage from prosecution to serenity, it is this process of the *recovery of one's serenity* that distinguishes inalterable Socratic serenity from Spinozistic wisdom. In order to recover serenity, the offended, angry person has to withstand a fight that Socrates had not known. The soothing transfiguration of enmity by the effect of a better understanding is also the conversion of hatred into its contrary. And thus, it is not surprising that such a conversion is accomplished in joy.

IV. The Partitive Excuse: The Ambiguity of Intentions and the Guilty-Innocent Person

Up to this point, we have spoken of the total excuse, the one that, in advance, eliminates sin in general and that aims at a universal absolution that is indiscernible from forgiveness. Although it is not forgiveness, it *conforms to* forgiveness; it takes the place of it and produces practically the same result; only its reasons differ. Or rather, it distinguishes itself from forgiveness in that it has motives and forgiveness is unmotivated. But an excuse is not always Spinozistic! More often than not, it is partitive and relative, and it has as its function to excuse mixed, complex, and impure beings, whose intentions are always equivocal and cannot therefore be appreciated in a univalent manner. The partitive excuse no longer rests on the metaphysical negation of evil, of wickedness, and of sin, as does the total excuse; the very idea of a reduction of responsibility by mitigating circumstances presupposes the possibility of being guilty or malevolent. Do not the "circumstances" remain peripheric with respect to the center of the bad will? This possible responsibility, nuanced by circumstances, permits the gradual introduction of innumerable degrees (levels and gradations) of intentional culpability. The being is more or less discharged of the charges that burden it. In fact, the partitive excuse excuses the guilty person not because evil is nonexistent in general, but because every intention is complex. The intermediate nature of the intellective excuse reflects the fundamental ambiguity of intentions. Moral thought has always been aware of this ambiguity. The first sin, the sin of sins, the very one of which Genesis tells us is in reality an innocent curiosity prior to ill will, for its object is precisely to know the distinction between evil and good. The one who is going to commit evil does not yet know what evil is; he will know it only after having tasted of the fruit; he knows only a prohibition and is, thus, guilty of simple disobedience. He does not even know the sin par excellence, which is called the lie. But in another respect, the man tempted by opening his eyes would not be tempted if he did not have a presentiment of the flavor and the savor of *dignoscentia;* he is tempted by the advantages of the mind, of which an appetizing fruit is the symbol. Consequently, he possesses a precognition of the distinction that he wants to cognize. Likewise, this fruit appears to him in the form of an enviable fruit. Moreover, the reptile is there in order to give the sales pitch, to validate the tempting object, and to extol its attraction. The original impetus of the prelapsed Adam is, thus, not as indifferent as we thought. Even before his eyes are opened, he takes advantage of the loss of innocence; he knows that God forbids him to give in, he already knows all that there is to know; the fruit itself no longer has anything to teach him. Or, rather, as we can say neither that he does not know, nor that he knows, it is necessary to think that he guesses. The first sinner, in the instant of his initiation, is both guilty and not guilty. In as much as he is guilty, God ruthlessly chases him from the garden of felicity forever and without possible amnesty; the entire course of history will not be enough to buy back this infinite misdeed; the inexcusable sinner can only be punished . . . , or miraculously given grace. But in as much as he is innocent, guilty only of acting carelessly, and thus excusable, a temporary period in purgatory must suffice. Or, better yet, it is necessary to send him to school in order to teach him obedience. It often happens that in the assessment of an intention, we have trouble choosing between the sin of ignorance and the sin of malevolence, and therefore between the excuse and

the alternative of condemnation or forgiveness. The oscillation is very perceptible in the Gospels. The Gospel of Luke, and this Gospel alone, attributes
a word that is somewhat "Socratic" to the crucified Jesus: "Father, forgive
them for they know not what they do," *Pater, aphes autois ou gar oidasin ti
poiousin.*[10] Indeed, if the *aphiēmi* is of the order of supernatural forgiveness,
and of a forgiveness that is even more supernatural in that it is demanded
of God, then the *ouk oidasin* itself is clearly *cognitive;* they do not know what
they do (they do not know that they have put the son of God on the cross).
Thus, if they knew, they would not do it; if they had known, they would
not have done it. Consequently, divine forgiveness is not so necessary . . .
It would be better to teach them! Like the ignorant and narrow-minded
people who made Socrates drink hemlock, the sinners who insult and cru-
cify Christ are poor lunatics and are all in all more to be pitied than cursed.
The Acts of the Apostles,[11] where Peter says to the people, "It is out of ignorance that you have done it," *kata agnoian epraxate,* seems to confirm this.
However, no one has made sin of bad intention less of a Socratic idea than
Saint Paul!—The same oscillation appears in the way that Christian theologians judge the lack of comprehension of which they accuse the Jewish
people. At one moment they condemn the necessarily inexpiable "crime" of
the people, supposedly "deicide"; and in the next moment, Pascal above all,
they incriminate the blindness and stubbornness of the believers of the old
faith: this superficial group of people was expecting a glorious Messiah,
clothed in the most visible and the most tangible attributes of royalty . . .
They were thus guilty of puerility and frivolity more than perfidy! It was
only childishness and peccadillos. The synagogue was not lucid enough to
recognize the *true* Messiah? The synagogue must have been seeing things
. . . It is thus not so wicked! It is rather a dupe . . . and one is not eternally
cursed simply for having seen things. What is lacking in stubborn people, in
short, is an opening of their eyes. It would have been necessary to teach
them, as Plato instructed them, to mistrust carnal appearances, to read the
pneumatic meaning behind the grammatic literalness, to see the humble,
cryptic beauty behind the sensible forms. And we know that for Plato this
secret vision, this esoteric reading of signs, was linked to the exercise of
irony. The absentminded people did not know that the tortured victim of

10. Luke 23:34. ["And Jesus said, 'Father forgive them; for they know not what they do.'"]
11. *Praxeis apostolēn* 3:17. ["And know brethren, I know that you acted in ignorance, as did
also your rulers."]

Golgotha was the Messiah; if they had known it, without a doubt they too would not have spilled that blood. But at the same time that one reproaches the Jews for not having recognized the Messiah, we accuse them of not having *wanted* to recognize him: in reality they recognized him, but on purpose made out to misjudge him. Out of wickedness. From ill will. Is it necessary to think that blindness and the will to be blind endlessly refer to one another, as in the *proairesis*[12] of Aristotle, and that inexcusable responsibility and excusable irresponsibility correspond to two different levels of intention? If the Jewish people are blind, then let us excuse them. And if they are malevolent, then have twenty centuries of implacable rancor not been sufficient for the religion of forgiveness in order to forgive those whom they accuse? Forgiveness, after all, serves for this or it serves for nothing at all. How many centuries of persecutions are still necessary for it?—Such is in all cases the infinite amphibole of moral appreciation. Philanthropy and misanthropy, optimism and pessimism, are equally true, or, which amounts to the same, equally false. The guilty-innocent person is also an innocent-guilty person. The sincere-liar is no less sincere than he is a liar. In him there is, in the partitive sense, "some good" and "some evil." Is he good? Is he wicked? Contradictorily, he is without a doubt the two together; the overturning of the Against for the For immediately calls for the overturning of this overturning, that is, a return of the For for the Against. The paradoxical reciprocity of this going and coming authorizes no univocal judgment about the guilty-innocent person. The guilty-innocent person is neither at an intermediate point between culpability and innocence, nor at an equal distance from the one or the other, which is to say, statically neutral. No, the guilty-innocent person is at the same time innocent and guilty, more innocent than guilty and more guilty than innocent.

V. Indulgence: More Stupid Than Wicked. More Wicked Than Stupid.

In the equivocation of the For and the Against, which is the equivocation of the human being in general, intellective indulgence sides with the For and

---

12. [*Proairesis:* this can be rendered in English as "decision" or "rational choice." See Aristotle, *Nicomachean Ethics*, trans. Terence Irwin, 2nd ed. (Indianapolis: Hackett, 1999), 1094a: "Every craft and every line of inquiry, and likewise every action and decision, seems to seek some good." Book 3, chapter 2 concerns "decision."]

gives credit to the "good heart," to the happy nature, and to the original in-nocence of man. It insists on the optimism of pessimism; it chooses against pessimism *tout court* and against the pessimism of optimism; it tips the scales of equivocation to a favorable side. It immobilizes the oscillations and alternating overturnings of our evaluation. This fixation is the excuse: the guilty person is acquitted by the benefit of the doubt. Man, alarmed by am-bivalence, is always tempted to simplify and to treat the equivocal in a univ-ocal manner. He takes sides and introduces a preferential disequilibrium into the isostheny[13] of severity and of indulgence. The partitive excuse con-sists either in unilaterally taking into account only the innocence of the guilty-innocent person, or in emphasizing innocence without suppressing, for all that, the complexity of the *natura anceps,* without completely erasing the other face of "two-faced Janus." In the first case, the intention is consid-ered purely and simply as a good, unambiguous intention. In the second case, the good intention becomes something dominating in the interior of a context of guilty innocence, a context where culpability is relegated to the second level. With an appropriate editing job, the excuse interprets innocent culpability in the favorable sense, which is that of indulgence. This tenden-tious presentation constitutes the very art of appeal—and we know that "everything can be appealed." To blow out of proportion the good that forms the favorable half of the ambiguous melange and of the hybrid named in-tention, to gather together skillfully all the facts of nature so as to disburden the accused, by neglecting or minimizing the accusatory elements, to obtain for the price of an insidious accentuation or of an imperceptible nudge in the right direction the very light deformation that will throw the equivocal off balance in favor of innocence and will incline toward acquittal—such are the ABCs of the excuse. This art of page production, of stage production, of value production is at one and the same time sincere and in bad faith, since it is half true: veridical in what it says, and dishonest in what it keeps silent. In this regard, Optimism is the chef-d'oeuvre of the art of excusing. In general, are optimism and pessimism not two contradictory, and yet equally justified (that is to say, equally false), readings of the same text? two unilat-eral readings, where, in reading almost the same things, all the good "bad faith" of the readers is expressed? Leibnizian "theodicy," for example, is the

---

13. ["Equipollence" or "equality of force." See Sextus Empiricus, *Selections from the Major Writings on Scepticism, Man, and God,* ed. Philip P. Hallie, trans. Sanford G. Etheridge (Indi-anapolis: Hackett, 1985), 34.]

plea of a lawyer in favor of God; it is an arrangement of all the good reasons
that the creature can have for admiring the creation, of all the motives for
contentment that a good conscience can find; it is a justification for apparent injustice. Conversely, in its closing speech, pessimistic antitheodicy as-
sembles together all the arguments susceptible of shaking our confidence
in the harmony of the universe. By turning evil into good, by projecting
the light of hope onto imperfections, optimism decides in favor of general
indulgent ambiguity. If no cause is absolutely pure, then none is absolutely
indefensible either. If no good fortune is without admixture, then no situation
is absolutely without hope, and likewise, in the end, no person is absolutely
ill-intentioned; no guilty person is wicked through and through, from head
to toe, and to the bottom of his toenails. In the intentional complex that
we attribute to the guilty-innocent person, the accent is thus on the innocence of the guilty person. According to the pleas of the Excuse, the guilty-
innocent person is less guilty than innocent, assuredly guilty in his acts, but
innocent in his intentions; for when the act accuses, the intention often excuses ... "*More* stupid than wicked," we sometimes say ... Yet a little wicked
all the same! But not as wicked as stupid; but especially stupid! The sole fact
that stupidity is the only way of being innocent for many people already
would prove the impurity of selflessness, the misery of our condition. For a
man who is stupid *and* wicked at the same time would really be excessively
deprived; it would be excessive bad luck to have all misfortunes at the same
time! Is it said that in a regime of alternatives stupidity will be the ransom
of innocence? A decidedly poor excuse, and for the use of a very poor man!
The wicked-stupid person, who is still more stupid than wicked, is to be especially pitied; all in all, he merits our pity! The guilt of this pitiable, wicked
person is not contested; it is an accepted fact. But it is understandable for
the one who takes the complexity of the situation into account; it becomes
venial when we take into consideration all the elements of the problem.
"Mitigating circumstances," as their name indicates, *mitigate* or lighten the
responsibility of the guilty person without eliminating the *commissio pec-
cati,* which is to say, the fact that the misdeed has been committed, and a fortiori without eliminating the very principle of responsibility, since on the
contrary they suppose this responsibility. *All things considered,* the misdeed
is benign. Does such a line of reasoning not evoke the optimism of the
"theodicy," of this theodicy that is in its own way a philosophy of the *balance
sheet*? In the general accounting of evils and goods, the sum of goods, in
total, prevails over evil, credits over debits; so the balance sheet turns out

positive. Let us remember that for the optimist the world is not perfect but is simply "optimal," in the relative superlative, the best possible. Providence has done its best, given the circumstances, which is to say above all given the incompatibles. For anyone who sees the universe from on high, God merits mitigating circumstances ... It is to this perfection mixed with imperfection, to this consonance seasoned with dissonances, to this complex that the Leibnizian Excuse in a word gave the name of Harmony. All the philosophies that take into account the complexity of a man by renouncing the chimera of a Sovereign Good without admixture, and that have regard as does Aristotle for the circumstantial determinations of the act, will recognize themselves in this idea of the good mixture and of modest, common virtue.

From another point of view, optimistic indulgence for a guilty-innocent person, who is more innocent than guilty, appears like an intermediary, an intermediary between the myth of the guilty person who is purely guilty and the pessimistic idea of the innocent-guilty person who is more guilty than innocent. Or, in other terms, the lucidity of indulgence is, so to speak, a mean between an infra-lucid severity, which is anger and blind prosecution, and a super-lucid severity, which is rigor and which is a prelude to forgiveness. Let us remember here that the lucid indulgence that has surpassed the primitive stage of passionate condemnation rehabilitates condemned people to some extent. They are *more stupid than wicked.* But immediately after this affirmation, the opposite affirmation comes to dislodge the preceding one and to revise the revision. In spite of it all, they are, alas! still more wicked than stupid. If they are stupid, let us excuse them. If they are wicked, let us punish them ... or let God forgive them! The wicked person who is only wicked, the innocent person who is more stupid than wicked, and the guilty person who is more wicked than stupid thus correspond to three forms of moral intellection. Indulgence for the innocent-person-who-is-more-stupid-than-wicked (and even more crazy than wicked) situates itself beyond severity for the purely wicked person and on this side of rigor for the guilty-person-who-is-more-wicked-than-stupid. Or, conversely, on this side of indulgence, there is primitive, obvious, and immediate evidence of the guilt of the guilty person. This rough, visible evidence sticks out a mile for the carnal man, but it is, so to speak, obvious only for a type of "knowledge of the first sort," which is to say, for a knowledge that is deformed by the perspective of the first person, for a knowledge that is blinded by anger and passion, for a knowledge that hardly knows and that is closer to "doxa" than to science. The bad action has a bad agent for its cause: in short, such is elementary etiology, a classical etiology, rooted in the grammatical substantialization of language and adapted to the exigencies of society. Grammar relates the attributes to the subject, whose precedence it affirms. In order to apply these sanctions, society needs to fix a responsible person who is both the author of the act and the subject in the nominative. Guilty causality, for this substantialist simplicism, is perfectly nonreciprocal and unambiguous. The imputation obeys the primitive tendency, the passionate law of "frenzy." The will is incriminated outright and the person is held to be undividedly guilty. It is true that judges look to disentangle the psychology of intentions, to nuance imputation and incrimination. In doing this, they refine to some extent the precision of their aim; the accusation tends to be articulated and to become more detailed. This judiciary psychology, however, remains as subtle as the psychology of the guardians of peace.—At the extreme opposite, severity for an innocent-guilty person who is more guilty than innocent, *more wicked than stupid,* more of a liar than sincere, such a severity is not, as with severity for the guilty-guilty person, a simplistic and unilateral severity; it is a severity that has known the complexity of intentions, the ambivalence and the relative innocence of the guilty person, and mitigating circumstances of which the first severity had not the least idea. In opposition to antecedent severity, which is severe a priori, consequent severity has put its trust in the guilty-innocent person, has given the hardened sinner every chance, and it is only in the face of evidence of an inveterate and incorrigible bad will that it exclaims, with death in the soul, like the Eagle emblem on the helmet, "I consider you as a witness that this man is wicked."[14] This severity, tempered by experience, is thus the height of despondency and disillusionment.—Thus, in "to understand is to forgive" the *is* foresees absolution. We postulate, in an optimistic fashion, that the deepening of the misdeed obligatorily will reveal the good sides of the intention. We posit as obvious that the heart has remained good. Now, nothing says that the more we are lucid about the culprit, then the more we have to be indulgent about the misdeed. After the indulgent analysis that discovers mitigating or undermining circumstances and the good intention of the bad intention, here comes the hyperanalysis, the severe analysis, that discovers the bad intention of the good intention and the aggravating circumstances.

14. [The reference here is to a line from the poem "L'Aigle du casque," from Victor Hugo's collection *La Légende des siècles,* first published in 1859 (Paris: Gallimard, 1950).]

After the indulgent minutiae, here are the accusative minutiae. The mitigating details help us to excuse, but the damning details make us more rigorous . . . From this point on, to understand is to become uncompromising!
Ruthless lucidity deciphers sordid philauty beneath philanthropy, and beneath virtue villainous motives, the inadmissible interests of hypocrisy and
the thousand little calculations of the interested and petty ego. For there is
a misanthropic microscopy that in its turn reads infinitesimal things. Thus,
the two understandings vie with each other, the pleas and closing speech,
rivaling each other in lucidity; the version from the public ministry is as
overwhelming as the one from the lawyer is soothing. And finally, if indulgence is often more comprehensive than rigor is with regard to the Other,
then it is not the same with regard to oneself: It is rigor that is lucid and scru-
pulous, and indulgence that is complaisant and approximating. The second
reading, the aggravating reading, has a third reading in store. The third reading, as we shall see, is that of forgiveness. Men are even *more unfortunate
than wicked*—a reading that is symmetrical to its contrary in equivocity:
they are even *more wicked than unfortunate.* Beyond the analytic decompo-
sitions dear to indulgence, we shall show that forgiveness, by restoring simplicity to the guilty ipseity, holds its hand out to the first severity. It accuses
like the latter and absolves like the former; it accuses in order to absolve! If
understanding in excusing is not to have any need of forgiving, then understanding in accusing never forgives either, but has more to forgive.

VI. The Middle Depth: Mitigating Circumstances

Between the two severities, the indulgent excuse thus discovers the inter-
mediarity of the man who is complex, innocent and guilty, but above all innocent. And it is not a simple tolerance with respect to evil, but a veritable
exoneration and a rational rehabilitation of the suspect. Beyond appearance,
it encounters the first truth, the one that corresponds to the depth of the first
degree, to the first complexity, and to the first exponent of consciousness;
for the first truth is also a truth to the second power. Indulgence represents
the first depth beneath the superficial plan of primitive severity. But conversely, compared with the second depth, compared with the truth that is
more than deep, compared with the one that makes the malevolent intention reappear under the alibi of psychology, indulgence is much more of a
superficial profundity, as we shall see. The investigation of the misdeed

finds itself impeded. Indulgence stops halfway down before meeting the new and cruel truth, which is truth to the third power. With its middle depth, the indulgence that is half-deep is thus at the same time less severe than that passionate severity of origins and less rigorous than the ethical rigor of the disabused man. But especially it is its relative depth that distinguishes it from vindictive reflexes. Intellection, not content with scrutinizing the motivations, intentions, and cryptic motivating forces of the act, reveals the invisible factors in it, for palpable effects have impalpable causes, for the manifest act obeys a causality that is not manifest. Intellection discovers, thus, a type of esoteric truth; under the dramatic appearances of sin, it weaves the web of an unapparent etiology. This unapparent etiology is also a delicate etiology; it rests on a critical analysis of guilt that is detailed and meticulous. Instead of mixing everything together, it distinguishes; this etiology disentangles the threads that totalitarian accusation and summary condemnation do not care to unravel. It assumes consideration for, and expertise about, the misdeed. In the end, it demonstrates the paradoxically mutual character of guilty causality; the cause is also the effect of its own effects, the effects are also the cause of their own cause. By dint of understanding everything, we finish by discovering that hangmen are the true victims of their victims and that, all in all, the wrongs were "shared"! Besides, with all conditions being equal, severity, a judgment of the whole, is on average more approximating than is indulgence. On average, indulgence is more nuanced and meticulous than severity; it takes into account more numerous and complex circumstances, society, and heredity; it cites the determinism of antecedents, and in that, it is more psychological. Psychology, in its turn, by multiplying nuances and citing mitigating circumstances, renders the accuser indulgent and furnishes not only reasons but also pretexts for the excuse. Mitigating circumstances and mitigated responsibility constitute the specialty of the psychologist; they represent the perimeter of excusability around the quoddity. Better still: all the "circumstances," whatever their nature may be, are to a greater or lesser degree *mitigating;* they more or less mitigate the misdeed that they "detail," they contribute to nuancing the basic and brutal fact of having done. Having killed, stolen, lied, having committed this or that—such is the undivided quoddity of the commission, and this ineradicable quoddity admits neither of gradations nor of mitigation. Having done . . . but how? The one who does not know the How of the misdeed knows nothing. The one who knows the effectivity of the commission and only this effectivity, this person does not know the subtle message

of guilt; he does not know the message of nuance and of qualitative specificity. The science of the misdeed begins with categorial determinations and
notably those that are expressed in the adverb of manner and that qualify
the intentional disposition of the guilty person. Partitive indulgence no
longer asks itself if the agent has done it or has not done it ("*an . . . annon*"),
if he is physically guilty or not guilty; it no longer questions itself about
the alternative of all-or-nothing, about the disjunction of the for-or-against,
about the polarity of the yes-or-no. Its own problem is the innumerable degrees of more-or-less, that is, the degrees of How Many, and especially the innumerable varieties and modalities of the How. After the dualism of the *option,* which instructs us to decide between Good and Evil, between day and
night, and which adds: "Take it or leave it," there is the pluralism of *choice;*
after the effect of Manichean relief, and after the dramatic antithesis of light
and shadow, there is the impressionistic palette of a thousand colors of innumerable tonalities and gradations. In opposition to Stoic rigorism, indulgence chooses transitional nuances and the most delicate of tints; it inserts
all the colors of the prism between white and black. The judge is no longer
summoned to "take" or to "leave," nor to adopt "one of two things." We can
take or leave at the same time, take this and leave that, mix and make selections. Mitigating nuances dull the sharp edge of the judicial and police-
related ultimatum: "guilty-or-not-guilty." They render the contours of the act
fluid and hazy; they drag out and tie up the misdeed in a circumstantial
context where guilty causality becomes equivocal and reciprocal. Thus, in appearance a more intimate and finer truth is constituted, a truth that we enjoy believing to be more true because it is comprehensive and omnilateral,
and because it considers, as does Leibniz's God, all the aspects of all situations, because it takes into consideration the most durable duration. The
philosophy of nuance and excuse multiplies the alterations by considering
heredity, ethology, physiology, and sociology, which is to say, by considering,
at the same time, the past, the organism, and the milieu. The guilty person
is a man viewed from afar, judged by approximation, accused unanimously,
and globally condemned: the guilty-innocent person, the guilty excusable
person, is the same man viewed from up close, having taken into account all
the circumstantial factors, and at the price of a focus that, for the indulgent
person, is the condition of the proper perspective and of the best vantage
point. The excuse has left the rectilinear path of rigor for the sinuous me-
anderings of indulgence.

And here is one last aspect of indulgent commonality: situated between antecedent severity, which immobilizes the sinner in his sin, and consequent severity, which globally accuses unforgivable liberty, indulgence refuses to consider the isolated misdeed and the faintness of an instant apart from other factors. The criminal never coincides entirely with his crime, the sinner never wholly expresses himself in his sin, and the agent is never entirely contained by the reprehensible act. And a detached lie still does not make a liar. Hence, indulgence refuses to identify the guilty person with his misdeed and to imprison him in a definitive definition! Nothing is ever closed, terminated, irremediable; and we are never eternally damned or destined to hell for one misdeed. Throughout his life, the person continues to express himself and to renew himself beyond the misdeed, and he has never uttered his last word. Indulgence envisages the global future of the person and holds open his future chances for amendment. Indulgence has faith in time in its entirety and in the unforeseeable surprises that it brings about for us. Pessimism, which is pointillistic and atomistic, detaches the misdeed from the entire temporal context, and an optimistic hope, an open hope puts it back in place.

In opposition to the primitivity of condemnation and to disabused pessimism, progressivist optimism can be considered as the bias of modernity. Michelet, in the *Bible de l'humanité*,[15] shows us in magnificent terms civilized Hellenism following upon the ruthless barbarism of talion, taming the monsters of violence and ogre-like behavior, renouncing every vendetta, and everywhere embracing the cause of man. From Socratic intellection to the indulgence of the Cyrenaic Hegesias,[16] to the almost Christian gentleness of Marcus Aurelius, the Greek Excuse did not cease to tend toward the limit of forgiveness ... without, however, ever being confused with it. Indeed, in order to forgive the misdeed, forgiveness does not ask the misdeed to be mitigated by circumstances. Obviously, this does not mean that it searches out aggravating circumstances, but aggravation does not scare it. The fact of having condemned the misdeed does not at all prevent

15. [Jules Michelet, *Bible de l'humanité* (Paris: Éditions complexe, 1999). A reedition of a classic French book on the mythology and stories of early civilized cultures, originally published in 1864 in Paris by Librairie F. Chamerot.]

16. [Hegesias (early fourth century–late third century BCE), one of the later adherents of the Cyrenaic school, was both a hedonist and an extreme pessimist. Following the school's view, he held that physical pleasure of the moment was the highest good to which one could aspire. He was skeptical about altruism and friendship. The story is that he was banished from Alexandria in Egypt for publicly advocating suicide.]

forgiveness from forgiving: quite the contrary. Forgiveness is not "indulgent," far from it. It is quite severe, or at least, has been.

VII. To Excuse Is to Forgive: Lived Adherence

However, in yet another way, the optimistic indulgence that excuses the misdeed by understanding it already concedes a kind of forgiveness; in its own way, indulgence is very much of a humble amiability. Let us here distinguish between the effort over oneself, the generator of an intimate transformation, and openness toward the Other. In its own way, is the effort to understand not as costly and meritorious as the gesture of forgiveness? First, intellection, just like attention or reflection, is rendered difficult by our somatic finitude, by our weakness, and by the obstacle of one's own naturality. And actually man is not a pure spirit at all, nor a sage; man is not, as Spinoza said, an *automa spirituale*,[17] or, as we would prefer to say, a "rational automaton." Man is a psycho-somatic amphibian, that is to say, a symbiosis of soma and psyche, which is to say, a mixed being. The sloth and inertia of the flesh, blind reflexes, and recalcitrant instinct, which are all generators of distractions and dissipation, already would suffice to explain the difficulty of intellectual work. But here it is a question of still more difficult work: just as the sentiment of duty fights against the heaviness of egoism in us, against the resistance of the concupiscible part, and against the attraction of pleasure, so the impersonal and objective comprehension of an event in which the freedom of the other is engaged arouses a passionate interest and a fierce resistance of self-esteem in the vindictive person and the rancorous person. Egoity, in its rancorous partiality, is naturally interested in not understanding the guilty person. Are anger and *ressentiment* not modes of lived participation in the drama of sin? Like forgiveness, although in a less acute form, the effort of intellection implies the moment of the costly sacrifice, of cruel heartbreak, and sometimes even of heroic renunciation. It requires that the offended person throw away his own susceptibilities. And if it is not a question of an offense, but rather of sin, then what does one do to hold in check

---

17. [See Baruch Spinoza, *On the Improvement of the Understanding*, trans. R. H. M. Elwes (New York: Dover, 1955), 32 (§85): "though the ancients so far as I know, never formed the conception put forward here that the soul acts according to fixed laws, and is as it were an immaterial automaton [*et quasi aliquod automaton spirituale*]."]

the wholly natural indignation that we feel in the face of the infamy, or to surmount the insurmountable aversion reflex that the guilty person inspires in us? And then, once this negative work is accomplished, what does one do to understand the venial character and the "excusability" of a misdeed, or to admit that passionate motives are capable of mitigating the gravity of the crime? Here, a veritable ascesis or a type of cathartic of comprehension seems necessary. Where will intellection find the strength to defeat the opposing forces? There is no "victory" in general without one force physically prevailing over another. Victory supposes an obstacle and a battle; likewise, the idea of victory is not an entirely rational concept. Of course the truth that intellection claims does not favor obstacles; truth is victorious in advance, without ever having to vanquish, and the idea of a "triumphant" truth is nothing other than an anthropomorphic allegory; truth would stay true even if no one recognized it, even if all men were in agreement among themselves in misjudging it. We are free to speak of the elimination of eternal truths, but then we must imagine I do not know what metaphysical catastrophe that belongs to the realm of "impossible suppositions" and that therefore is an unthinkable absurdity. Atemporally and for all eternity, the true is *index sui et falsi!*[18] But the comprehension of this truth itself knows the eclipses and vicissitudes of defeat. Effectively to assure its mastery and its preponderance over angry or rancorous violence, to affirm its empire over its own concupiscence, comprehension has to take possession of the one who understands; the necessity arises for it to dominate his instinctive life, for it to occupy the terrain in some fashion. The indulgent person allows himself to be penetrated entirely by intellection. The problem of authority-over-oneself, *egkrateia,* that is so important in Greek wisdom expresses this need of a taking-hold and of a taking possession. For authority over oneself is the virtue of a mind that again has become master in its own house; authority over oneself is a serenity conquered by a hard-fought struggle and that gives us control of passionate forces. In *egkrateia* is there not *kratos,*[19] which is strength mastering violence? The victory of rationality cannot be assured, in sum, by rational means. In order for intelligence to be able to

---

18. ["That truth is its own standard": See Spinoza, *Ethics* (New York: Dover, 1955), book 2, paragraph 43, note. Cf. Spinoza, Epistola 76, in *Spinoza Opera* (Heidelberg: Verlag Carl Gebhardt, 1925), 4:320: *"Est enim verum index sui."*]

19. [*Egkrateia* means "temperance" or "self-control," while *kratos* means "power" or "strength."]

prevail over passion, it is necessary that it impassion itself; it is necessary that intelligence itself become passion a little. Singular paradox! Intelligence has to be impassioned in order to dispassion the passion . . . For passion alone has a hold on passion. Descartes's *Passions of the Soul* knew something about this passionate homeopathy.[20]—On the other hand, the effort over oneself implies the passage to effectivity. If the excuse is really an excuse and not this simple passive, and Platonic observation that the guilty-innocent is, all in all, innocent, if indulgence is really indulgence and not the simple, polite recognition of a misunderstood excusability, then outside of and in addition to comprehensive vision, an active adhesion of man to comprehension is necessary. And this adhesion is of a wholly other order than this comprehension; without it, we would not be able to surmount the obstacle of naturality. A comprehension that is purely speculative would stay powerless. The misdeed is a drama, and a dramatic event calls for a drastic solution . . . To understand, we say, is to forgive, or at the very least, to understand is to excuse. But if we can forgive without understanding, we can just as well understand without forgiving, which proves that to understand is one thing and to forgive is another. It sometimes happens that we understand without in fact becoming indulgent with respect to the misdeed, without in fact making peace with the guilty person. The excuse does not flow automatically and in every case from comprehension, but it is as one might say "synthetic" in comparison with the act of understanding. "To understand *is* to forgive" thus expresses not a perfectly reversible identity but a relation of capricious and uncertain consequence. In order to forgive and even in order to excuse once one has understood, it is necessary that a supplement of energy be added to comprehension, a supplement without which comprehension would stay eternally powerless and Platonic, and, therefore, would be nothing other than a pious approbation. For a man who lacks this supplementary *élan* stays a witness and an indifferent spectator to the reasons for forgiving or excusing, instead of *himself* forgiving or excusing, instead of entering in person onto the path of forgiving. There is then an efficient, efficacious, and effective impetus that alone determines the passage from

20. [René Descartes, *The Passions of the Soul*, in *The Philosophical Writings of Descartes*, vol. 1, trans. John Cottingham, Robert Stroothoff, and Dugald Murdoch (Cambridge: Cambridge University Press, 1985), part 1, §45: "Our passions, too, cannot be directly aroused or suppressed by the action of our will, but only indirectly through the representation of things which are usually joined with the passion we wish to have and opposed to the passions we wish to reject."]

intellection to excuse. On another level, it is in this way that the deliberation and the confrontation of motives would never activate the assertive and courageous fiat of decision without a gratuitous impetus that alone is capable of shielding us from abulia and perpetual hesitation. This impetus, without which the debate eternally would turn in circles and which suddenly tips the scale in favor of a motive, is the will itself, the decisive and thoughtful will. Every option worthy of this name is at the same time an adoption, for if academic preference is unlikely to have any repercussions, then the option is an effective taking of a position; the option takes sides. "Video meliora proboque, deteriora sequor,"[21] says the poet. "Video proboque"... But as for *sequi,* as for adopting, "deteriora sequor"! I salute and I pass; or better yet, I applaud without budging. After a grand tip of the hat to the immortal truths, the insufficiently good will, which is only a bad will in disguise, returns to its rancors and its self-esteem. Let us fear that intellection, if it limits itself to recognizing the complexity of the act, may be a *probo* without *sequor*! This is why Plato asks the prisoners in the cave not to cry "Bravo" to the philosopher who has come to explain to them what is shadow and what is truth, but rather to turn themselves toward the sun "with their entire souls," and to go and to step into the light of day in person. Stand up and walk! Is this not what Plato calls *epistrophē* or conversion? The most intellectual indulgence already supposes this ontic conversion—or it is not even indulgence! And the excuse itself, however impersonal it may be, is not a theoretical problem but an event made for coming to pass. It is a matter not of blessing the guilty person but of absolving him! In this respect, indulgence is in the same situation as courage and justice. The analysis of danger does not give birth to courage, but rather to fear and cowardice. There is no courage without this *additional milligram* that is the vertigo of the adventurous leap and the effective affront. Justice, which asks us to abandon the egocentric point of view and the partial unilaterality of self-interest, does not itself exist without drastic renunciation. It is difficult to prefer everyone's interest to one's personal interest when such a preference is really taken seriously and passes into effectivity. Even the exchange and distribution of equal parts are efficacious gestures and militant acts that are not analytically implied in the speculative recognition of an impersonal

21. ["I see, approving,/Things that are good, and yet I follow worse ones." Ovid, *Metamorphoses,* trans. Rolfe Humphries (Bloomington: Indiana University Press, 1967), 154 (book 7, ll. 20–21).]

truth. Justice requires that we join gesture to word and action to notion, that we do as we say. Is justice not an imperative and an invitation to do, and to do for the sake of the good? Likewise, judgment is more than axiological; it is also "judiciary"; it condemns or it acquits. Better yet, when justice is not an impassioned desire for transforming the order of things, it reduces to a simple, notional *Video proboque;* a justice that is not love of justice and hatred of injustice is not even justice. Such, indeed, is the case for the intellective excuse. Wholly naked comprehension does not have the strength to make us change our attitude with respect to the guilty person. All alone, it does not induce us to abandon the accusation, it will not make us effectively renounce our grievances. It resembles these eloquent preachers who make us change our opinions but not our behavior, or who do not give us the desire to reform our existence. This is why Bergson, in *The Two Sources of Morality and Religion,*[22] speaks of emotional powers. The example of the life of the hero or of the life of the saint is alone stirring, alone liberating, and alone absolutely persuasive. Alone it gives us the desire to resemble and to imitate, and to live charity not in words but in acts. We know that such was the meaning of the preaching of Tolstoy. It is no less true for comprehension. A comprehension given over to itself convinces without intimately persuading. But a truly comprehensive comprehension, a comprehension activated by its supplement of energy and its "additional milligram," ends up at love. This comprehension that opens onto indulgence and this excuse that converts us to charity, are they not almost indiscernible from forgiveness?

VIII. To Excuse Is to Forgive: Opening to the Other

Intellection not only implies the effort over oneself and the adventurous leap, but still more, as with forgiveness, it is already the opening to and toward others. The one who wants to understand, in wanting to do so, avoids condemning immediately, and is thus a priori carried to benevolence. Indeed, love alone, a movement that is vitally interested and passionately engaged, furnishes us with the additional milligram and the supplementary impetus without which intellection would never open onto effectivity. Love alone has the force to persuade us to sacrifice our grievances. The sacrifice

22. [Henri Bergson, *The Two Sources of Morality and Religion,* trans. R. A. Audra and C. Breraton (Notre Dame: University of Notre Dame Press, 1977), 40–51.]

of self-esteem is easy only when we do it out of love for someone, love for the other being incomparably more dynamic than *amor sui.* The negativity of renunciation and the positivity of love are, thus, two aspects of one and the same heterocentric movement. Here, concerning the partitive excuse, it is necessary for us to reiterate what has been said about the total and impersonal excuse. It is a common truth that there is no intuition without a minimum of sympathy, that sympathy is more or less the consequence of intellection. And reciprocally, it is hardly less true that sympathy is very often gnostic to some degree. Is love (in order to begin with this reciprocal proposition) a means to knowledge? Certainly the loving intention is not expressly an intention of knowing, or even of understanding, for the intention to become acquainted is more of an indiscreet curiosity than true love, and love is more of a respect for a mystery than a desire to know. Strictly speaking, and in the analytic, theoretical, and abstract sense that the word "knowledge of" has for the scientist, the lover "knows" nothing of the beloved. In the sense in which the zoologist knows the structure of coelenterates, no, the lover does not know what he loves. And so much the better, for the less he is informed, then the less he will be discouraged . . . And not only is love voluntarily ignorant, but it renders the one who feels it blind and partial; each person knows that it engenders prejudices and passionate biases. In this respect, it is rather hatred that would render men lucid . . . But we can respond that the lucidity of hatred has nothing in common with clear-mindedness. For this hateful light is a garish light. For this hateful knowledge is made of disjointed notes and epigrams without connection, and the intuition that would perceive the unity therein is absent. The wicked person, like a gossip columnist or a hateful journalist, knows gossip, trivial details, and trivial events; he multiplies the exterior views and his knowledge is dust and a rain of darts . . . But he cares little about the ipseity, about the simplicity of the essence. In a wholly other sense that is ever so much deeper, the lover, and he alone, possesses the intimate and penetrating gnosis of his second person. He knows without knowing that he knows, or what he knows. Like Mélisande, who does not know what she knows,[23] and knows what she does not know, the lover knows with an innocent and supra-lucid knowledge that is similar to "learned ignorance."[24] Like Platonic Eros, which is rich and poor

23. *Pelléas et Mélisande,* act 2.

24. [*Docte ignorance:* see *Nicholas of Cusa on Learned Ignorance: A Translation and an Appraisal of De Docta Ignorantia,* trans. Jasper Hopkins (Minneapolis: A. J. Banning Press, 1985).]

at the same time,[25] he knows by not knowing and he does not know by knowing. He desires that which, in a way, he already possesses. We may now say: "To forgive is to understand"! Certainly forgiveness, as we shall see, is more drastic gesture than cognitive relation, more offering than knowledge, more sacrifice and heroic decision than discursive knowledge. Forgiveness is an act of courage and a generous proposition of peace. For intellection, there is nothing to forgive, but there are a multitude of delicate mechanisms, of cogs and springs to dismantle, of motives, of previous histories and of influences to understand. And conversely, for forgiveness, there is everything to forgive, and there is almost nothing to understand . . . Almost nothing, and yet I do not know what simple and indivisible thing: we understand this global presence of the guilty person in front of us, this malevolence that is never an object but that is rather an intentional quality and an undecomposable movement; and we understand it by intuitive comprehension. Forgiveness, which renders wickedness venial, discovers in the wicked intention a dimension of profundity. To forgive, indeed, is to understand a little bit!—But conversely, could we say yes or no that to understand is to forgive? To understand is either to exonerate an innocent person, recognizing that there was nothing to forgive, or to become sometimes more indulgent and sometimes more severe with respect to the accused depending on the circumstances. And yet comprehension sometimes prepares us to love and to forgive. If love understands a fortiori what it loves (for that which is capable of the most is capable of the least), comprehension loves with less reason that which it comprehends. Love, by dint of loving, finishes by understanding, and by dint of understanding, finishes by loving. By virtue of a veritable circular causality, sympathy is at the same time the consequence and the condition of intellection. One sympathizes by dint of understanding, but in order to understand, it is already necessary to sympathize, the two at the same time; intellection, effect and cause of love, is wholly penetrated by love. In the word *suggnōmē*[26] the Greeks unify at the same time the judg-

---

25. [See Plato's *Symposium*, trans. Alexander Nehemas and Paul Woodruff, in *Plato: Complete Works*, 486 (203c–204a): "As the son of Poros and Penia . . . he [Love] is always poor . . . having his mother's nature, [he is] always living with Need. But on his father's side he is a schemer after the beautiful and the good; he is brave, impetuous, and intense, an awesome hunter . . . Love is never completely without resources, nor is he ever rich."]

26. [*Suggnōmē*: In his commentary on *suggnōmē* or "pardon" in Aristotle's *Nicomachean Ethics*, Terence Irwin writes, "This is derived from gnōmē, 'mind' or 'judgment.' It is the exer-

ment of the *eugnōmones,* which is to say, the critical judgment—*gnōmē kritikē tou epieikous orthē,* says the *Nicomachean Ethics*[27]—and the sympathetic agreement with the Other that suggests the prefix *sun* and that makes us think of *gnōsomenoi kai suggnōsomenoi* of Alcibiades' speech.[28] Certainly *gnōnai* and *suggignōskein* have gnosis, which is knowledge, in common. But *suggignōskein,* being the act of coming around to the opinion of the partner, of giving him one's consent, of siding with his point of view, already implies a community, even though this community is cognitive. Besides, the community about which Alcibiades, himself a little drunk, discourses with his guests is an initiatory, orgiastic, and Dionysian community in which the exaltation of bacchanalians holds more importance than does knowledge. But "sygnomic" intellection is neither only an assimilation, nor only the leveling of an unevenness. It is not only "with," it is also "in the interior." The one who understands is neither merely opposite, nor merely on the exterior, as is the spectator of a spectacle or the subject of a speculative cognition, but he is also inside; he penetrates into the depths of the reprehensible act. He is inside and outside at the same time. In a singular paradox, he englobes and is englobed at the same moment. Insofar as he is outside, he knows the misdeed as an object; insofar as he is inside, he participates ontically in the drama of the guilty person. *Intus-legere.*[29] Intellection is a reading, but this reading reads in the interior and from the interior. The enveloped reader and the enveloping sin penetrate one another in a lived sort of intimacy that blurs the contours of cognitive objectivity. It is, thus, useless to look for the moment at which intellection becomes love, since it is continually loving,

cise of judgment and consideration that finds in an action circumstances (as we say, 'special considerations') that exempt the agent from blame USUALLY attached to that type of action. In the discussion of VOLUNTARY action, suggnōmē is translated as 'pardon' . . . In 1143a19–24 [see note 26 below], Aristotle plays on the etymological connection with gnōmē; 'consideration is needed'" (341).]

27. Aristotle, *Nicomachean Ethics,* book 6, chapter 11, §1. [The text reads: "The (state) called consideration [*suggnōmē*] makes people, as we say, considerate and makes them have consideration; it is the correct judgment [*gnōmē*] of the decent person. A sign of this is our saying that the decent person more than others is considerate, and that he is decent to be considerate about some things. Considerateness is the correct judgment that judges what is decent; and correct consideration judges what is true." Aristotle, *Nicomachean Ethics,* 95 (1143a19–24). See also note 25 above.]

28. Plato, *Symposium,* 218a–b.

29. [*Intus-legere:* the word "intellect" comes from this expression which means "to read within," signifying a thorough or deep or penetrating comprehension of something.]

and it is no less useless, therefore, to ask oneself if intellection loses all clear-mindedness in turning toward love, or, conversely, if love loses all of its loving fervor when its eyes are opened in order to know and to understand.—But it happens that the englobing-englobed is more and more englobed and less and less englobing. By virtue of a sort of absolutist tendency that is also a passionate temptation and which Bergson maybe would have called frenzy, sympathy born of intellection immediately goes to extremes. Indulgence does not stay indulgent for a long time! For we cannot assign any limit to the sympathy that makes the I come out to meet the you, or that makes us go out to meet the second person. We do not make allowances for it. We cannot say to this sympathy: go up to this point, but no further! *Alas!* you will not go beyond! Obeying the vertiginous auction, and the "frenzied" and, so to speak, totalitarian crescendo that govern all our inclinations, indulgence transforms itself at once into sympathy, and even beyond sympathy, into love and personalized dilection. In one fell swoop, it slips down the incline of amorous hyperbole. The indulgent person forgives by dint of excusing. The excuse passes "to the limit," or better yet, to the absolute, and it engages the total person in the comprehensive act. The excuse, going beyond the simple, negative recognition of the innocence of an innocent person, the excuse that has become infinite, the excuse that has become forgiveness, is henceforth indiscernible from gracious *venia.* Thus a lawyer finishes by marrying the accused that he has just got acquitted. The accused did not commit the crime that we imputed to her, or the crime was, if not justified, at least understandable, explicable, excusable, and mitigated in a thousand ways by the context of the circumstances . . . But this is still not a reason for marrying! But to go from there to marrying her! Between the pleading and the marriage, there is a vertiginous step to surmount. Yet one surmounts it. By dint of fighting for the accused, by dint of putting oneself in the place of the accused, the defender ends up identifying with him. The one who refutes the accusation is carried to side with the camp of the accused person in front of us, to rejoin his party, to embrace his interests, to take up his cause, to sign on under his flag. The one who understands the crime himself becomes the criminal thus understood. In person, he lives the drama of the misdeed that he absolves, and as if he himself had committed it, for he too becomes capable of the misdeed. He admits implicitly his community of essence with the guilty person; he recognizes his co-responsibility of guilt and innocence. Who will throw the first stone at the sinner? However, decency, reserve, the intellectual *epochē*,[30] and scruples would oblige us to take into account the unfavorable elements that we have neglected and the setting in parentheses of which permitted us to excuse the guilty person. Philanthropy does not give us the right to forget that innocence-guilt is an ambiguous mixture where evil figures for almost half ... But indulgence does not observe the measure that the amphibole of intentions commands it to. It exceeds the seriousness of intermediateness. It does not stay halfway between white and black, at an equal distance from purity and irremediable impurity; it hastens to whitewash the gray intention completely. In this manner, it substitutes a prejudice of sympathy for the prejudice of antipathy, the unilaterality of favor for the unilaterality of rancor, which is reverse unilaterality; it replaces one partiality by another. After having renounced self-esteem in the name of an impersonal truth, indulgence renounces impersonal truth in the name of personal love. Philauty, which, by a circular reflection of the I on itself, comes back to the first person from the first person, makes room for a disinterestedness that is in the third person; and disinterestedness, in its turn, allows itself to be supplanted by transitive love, which is a relation of allocution of the first person with the second person. The excuse diluted egocentric passion into an impersonal truth. Forgiveness concentrates the passionate unilaterality anew, but this time in favor of and for the benefit of the second person. Put differently, the indulgent person renounces the unilateral point of view of the ego for the omnilateral view of the Other, that is, for a rationally corrected point of view. But the indulgent person who has become a lover adopts, and acquires anew, a point of view, a privileged point of view that is no longer that of the I, or of others in general, but that of the *other,* that of the You. Justice, evaporating into unjust and unreasonable love, renders equality unequal for the benefit of the sinner. Has the sinner not become the object of a predilection that is paradoxically and scandalously preferential? After the vulgar injustice of egoism, here is backward injustice, one that is not on this side of but rather beyond justice, one that is not less than just, but more than just! Thus

---

30. [*Epochē*: the suspension of judgment. See Sextus Empiricus, *Outlines of Pyrrhonism,* in *Selections from the Major Writings on Scepticism, Man, and God,* book 1, chapter 12 ("The End of Scepticism"), 41: "In doing so, he met with contradicting alternatives of equal force. Since he could not decide between them, he withheld judgment. Upon his suspension of judgment there followed, by chance, mental tranquility."]

"unjust" humility, if we consider it as turned-around self-esteem, belittles itself more than justice would require of it, *pleon deontos* would refuse itself the right to exist. For in the order of grace, the first person absurdly has only duties without rights, by opposition to the second person who unjustly has only rights without duties. The truth of modesty would be halfway between this on-this-side-of and this beyond. And likewise, justice would be equidistant from egoistic injustice and ecstatic "injustice." But it is difficult to keep oneself in equilibrium on this delicate point of *juste milieu* or of median justice. Natural injustice and supernatural injustice, the lies of rancor and the saintly error of forgiving envelope from all sides the thin truth of the excuse.

IX. To Understand Is Only to Excuse. On the Inexcusable.

We are tempted to conclude that to excuse is to forgive. However, let us be precise that if excuse leads to forgiveness, then it is without a doubt for "all the less reason" and with the addition of supplemental energy. Intellection by itself would not suffice to give it the *élan* of which it has need in order really to pardon the guilty person. Thus, the excuse forgives only by surpassing itself and by going too far. But, on the contrary, in the measure in which it is purely intellective, it does not go far enough; in the measure in which it lags behind forgiveness strictly speaking, it lacks generosity. This excuse, which is moderately indulgent if we compare it with rancor and moderately severe if we compare it with forgiveness, lets go and does not let go;—it all depends on the point of view; it pulls back as it pushes ahead. If, in a movement that is spontaneous as well as precipitated, indulgence is prompted to go to the limit on the straight line of absolution, it also corrects itself, resists the temptation of universal forgiveness, and slams the breaks on the enthusiasm of reconciliation. Here, rigor appears as the verso of indulgence; in virtue of this rigor, intellection decrees the stoppage of the linear movement that would guide us in one fell swoop toward general absolution. In short, this "sygnomic" forgiveness of which the Greeks talked, and that Aristotle defined as *krisis orthē*, a correct discerning of what is equitable, hardly has a gift for impulsive generosity, is hardly prepared for universal embraces. *Krisis* rather seems to announce that we will not forgive everyone for everything indiscriminately, that selective "criteria" will be applied. The indulgent rigor that is just as much rigorous indulgence is in no way disposed to concede blindly the accolade of forgetting and of general fraternization.

Sygnomic and critical forgiveness, deliberating the grand amnesty that we expect from it, asks "to see."

To understand, we were saying, is not necessarily to forgive. In any case, to understand is to excuse. But for that very reason, to understand is *only* to excuse. It is only to excuse and nothing but that . . . In this restriction of the "only," the amphibole of severe indulgence is one more time expressed: what the partitive excuse excuses immediately evokes what it does not excuse, what it leaves outside; and it is an excuse only on this condition . . . Unless, of course, one wants to speak again of the total excuse; for in denying evil in its entirety, it precisely does not leave anything outside, and thus comes close to forgiveness. The partitive excuse, on the other hand, excuses by accusing, spares in condemning, affirms in refusing, and this it does by definition. In the excuse, the positive and the negative are in solidarity. Yet, forward and backward, it is still the same excuse. Let us here remember several statements of the obvious. The partitive excuse is an excuse only because it does not excuse everything, for if it excused everything, not, in the manner of Spinozistic wisdom, by dissipating the mirage of sin, or in the manner of supernatural forgiveness, but in the manner of general and idle indulgence, it would not be intellective either. It would not have need of understanding. It would acquit everyone in advance, without giving itself the trouble of analyzing the misdeed or of comparing the guilty individuals. For the one who excuses everything excuses nothing. First of all, the excuse excuses only what is excusable. As for the inexcusable, restrictive indulgence abandons it to the rigor of laws. It is forgiveness that takes charge of the inexcusable, for the inexcusable can be forgivable even though it is not excusable. The excusable is, a fortiori, forgivable, but it is does not need for us to forgive it since the rational excuse suffices to demonstrate its innocence: we would be using our graces on it purely in vain. On the other hand, the inexcusable, not finding advocates to defend it, has need of forgiveness. If, then, all is not excusable for the excuse, everything is forgivable for forgiveness, all . . . save, of course, the unforgivable, admitting that an unforgivable exists, that is, a crime that is meta-empirically impossible to forgive. There is nothing gratuitous, nothing gracious, nothing supernatural in the fact of excusing the excusable, any more than there is merit in loving the lovable: nothing shocking, nothing provoking, nothing scandalous. In every sense of justice, an excuse is due to the excusable; to excuse is simply to pay one's debt, to render to the guilty person who is recognized as innocent what is due to him, and to give it to him outside of all graciousness. At least, the guilty person who is not guilty has the right to what is due to him, does he not? Besides, he only reclaims justice; for one may very well say that this is the least of things! The person who is excusable is excused both all alone and with full justification; or, to express it better, he is wholly excused and the judge establishes only that it did not take place: only records the absence of all guilt and the nothingness of every misdemeanor, only draws up the affidavit of innocence, and only recognizes that there has been no misdeed. There is no miracle in that! Thus, the excuse erases the suddenness of the surprise. The one who simply renders justice to the innocent person perhaps creates the effect of surprise, but that is because people are thick and shortsighted. In reality, the innocent person was already innocent before the recognition of his innocence; the excuse is thus not a true event, and it comes to pass only in appearance. This excuse, that is so justified when it is a matter of an innocent person who has need neither of grace nor of forgiveness, this excuse that is so reasonable is a "hypothetical" excuse, that is, conditional and accompanied by reservations. The excuse is a forgiveness "with conditions." But a conditional forgiveness precisely is not forgiveness ... The excuse excuses in return for the objective excusability of the misdeed, with a quietus that is accompanied by preambles and considerations that serve to justify the indulgence. The excusing of the excusable and the love of the lovable parallel each other. The love of the lovable loves only beings who are worthy of love (because they are intelligent, artistic, remarkably gifted, and so on), and in these lovable beings it loves only the qualities that are the most worthy of esteem, the most eminent and the most precious, to the exclusion of flaws. If the excuse and the love of what is lovable rather represent the order of justice, then the unmerited forgiveness that we grant to the guilty person, and the unjustified, unmotivated love that we bring to an enemy represent the paradoxical order of charity. The Scriptures speak of this to us. Here, the scandal of forgiveness and the folly of love have it in common that their object is someone that does not "merit" it. Also, forgiveness does not forgive *because of;* forgiveness pays no attention to justifying itself and giving reasons, for as concerns reasons, it has none. On the other hand, the excuse, being ideologically motivated, announces its very reasons and its "grounds": here a "because" obligatorily responds to a "why." And not only does the excuse say "why," but it itself is the motive or the mitigating circumstance. Such is how the guilty person spontaneously produces "excuses" to aid others in forgiving him. More generally, excusability is the objective cause of the excuse, whereas the initiative of forgiveness is itself the centrifugal and considerate cause of the "forgivability." The fact that an act is excusable already justifies an excuse—but it is the wellspring itself of forgiveness, but it is the gushing fountains of forgiveness, without any other motivation, that render the inexcusable misdeed forgivable. This paradoxical inversion of the because makes forgiveness into a *causa sui* . . . But meta-empirical aseity[31] and meta-empirical immotivation are totally foreign to the empirical etiology of the excuse. In short, the excuse obeys the most trivial and the most classical causality. The excusable that it absolves already was explicable and justifiable. Being a type of sygnomic justice, the excuse excuses only what is excusable, and in turn it condemns what is inexcusable.—Let us show that the excuse excuses only certain guilty persons, only certain misdeeds, and in these misdeeds, only certain aspects of the act. First of all, it does not excuse everyone. In this, it is in opposition to total intellection and to forgiveness. Notably, forgiveness knows only one thing: that which is universally human without discriminations of any type, ecumenicity without a "*distinguo*" or disjoint categories. Forgiveness does not have knowledge of what Saint Paul calls *prosōpolēpsia;*[32] it makes sense neither of the *character,* nor of the *quatenus.*[33] It forgives the man insofar as he is a man, and not with regard to this or that. The philanthropic cosmopolitanism of the Stoics, Stoic totalitarianism, radicalism, and maximalism that postulate the equality of misdeeds are, in the end, equally foreign in another order of ideas to the articulated regime of the excuse. On the other hand, the *gnōmē kritikē* is very much in the spirit of Aristotelian pluralism: the severe-indulgent person, or indulgent-rigorous person, distinguishes between individual cases and makes sense of the category. He absolves this person here, condemns that one there, and discriminates between the excusable and the inexcusable. Thus, it is far from the case that the excuse says *amen* indiscriminately to everyone. It can lay the blame on the guilty person if

31. [*Aséité:* derived from Latin, meaning "from oneself." Traditionally, this has been a property ascribed to God, since God was seen as the only being that could exist absolutely independently and as the only being that could give existence to itself or whose existence could be ascribed to itself.]

32. [*Prosopolepsia:* "partiality" that arises due to one's power, status, or wealth. See James 2:1: "My brethren, do not hold your faith in our glorious Lord Jesus Christ with an attitude of personal favoritism." Romans 2:11: "For there is no partiality with God."]

33. [*Quatenus:* "to what extent."]

there is room, when justice requires it, or simply when the truth of this guilty person is less than ours.—And just as it distinguishes this one here from that one there, it also distinguishes and hierarchizes the this and the that. Here again, at the same time, the excuse strongly denies the law of the all-or-nothing, which treats all sins as mortal sins, and the universal charity of forgiveness, which, without discerning, considers them all as venial. The forgiveness of love, in its limitless generosity, indiscriminately forgives no matter what, as it forgives no matter whom. It forgives everyone for everything and does not linger behind in order to distinguish between serious misdeeds and trivial misdeeds. The excuse, on the other hand, excuses only certain carefully chosen acts. It excuses or does not excuse, *according to . . .* Is forgiveness not foreign to the "according to"?—Not only does the excuse excuse only certain acts, but these acts themselves, these excusable acts, it excuses them more or less. Do the "circumstances" of comprehension not serve to *mitigate* the gravity, the intensity, and the brightness of the misdeed? Lessening or diminishing guilt, the excuse acts in the direction of a decrescendo and the reduction of pain. On this point, as with the preceding ones, it is impossible to confuse the excuse with the maximalism of love, and impossible to assimilate it to the expansionism of forgiveness. Just as love tends to invade every aspect of life, to occupy all of the space and the entire duration into which it spreads, so forgiveness always forgives to the very hilt: one does not forgive just a little or halfway. Forgiveness is like love; a love that loves with reservations or with one single ulterior motive is not love; and so a forgiveness that forgives up to a certain point, but not beyond, is not forgiveness. Now it is necessary to place ourselves in the opposite point of view from the one that had been adopted before. It is the excuse that says: "Up to this point!" The relation between excuse and forgiveness is the same, in this respect, as the one between a professional responsibility that is limited in space and time, and a necessarily infinite moral responsibility. In analyzing the misdeed, the excuse isolates irreducible elements in it that no mitigating circumstance dissolves; it removes this inexcusable residue from absolution like someone who cuts out the spoiled sections of a fruit before eating it. This restrictive clause that removes a portion of the misdeed from the excuse is the excusing accusation in every excuse. Likewise, we can call it the organ-obstacle, even though the organ-obstacle has less of a hyperbolic meaning here than in the case of forgiveness. The partitive excuse is, thus, also a graded excuse: it doles out and measures its graces with severity, it parsimoniously rations guilty persons, it proportions its indulgence to the excusability of the act. Like justice, it weighs and feels the weight of retributions and punishments. Likewise, all degrees of excusing are conceivable, from partial indulgence to complete acquittal, or even to not having taken place pure and simple.—In the end, the excuse is a progressive focusing; certainly the truth that it establishes precedes this focusing, but intellection itself proceeds little by little and in steps as it penetrates into the mechanism of the misdeed. Also, in this, the excuse is contrasted with the sudden character of forgiveness, for forgiveness, as it forgives to the hilt and infinitely, also forgives in one fell swoop, without going deeper, without any focus.—Can we at least say that this excuse, which is so laborious and so limiting, has an enduring effect? Indeed, the excuse is not the ephemeral and always revocable caprice of a soul that is temporarily tender. Permanent like truth and valid at every moment, the rational excuse has nothing in common with outbursts of emotion or with the straw fires of pity. And neither does it resemble this progressive effacement that results from forgetting and from the accumulation of years. However much intellection is gradual, it dissipates the error once and for all, and definitively. The affair is settled for good. It is thus that Socratic refutation—the *elenchos*—denouncing contradictions, brings light into the shadows of error, and it does not do this temporarily, like a provisional palliative, but for good and without accepting delay. However, if truth once recognized is atemporal in itself, then the man who understands it can misunderstand it or ununderstand it after having understood it, and thus subsequently can again become the toy of passions. However much these bouts of drunkenness, these fits of anger, these purely morbid relapses do not affect the truth, we are forced to recognize that intellection itself can be put into question again. On the other hand, the excuse, which is conditional and rationally motivated, never undertook to bless and to absolve in advance all the future wrongdoings of the sinner. Forgiveness, in its tireless patience, its unshakable confidence, and its indefatigable generosity, is put to the test by the most inexpiable crimes. Mortal injury can neither disgust it, nor discourage it. But the excuse does not extend unlimited credit to the person whom it once absolved. It waits to see whether or not to reconsider, in each circumstance, the subsequent qualifications of the guilty person. Each individual case is examined separately.

Intellection does not imply true forgiveness any more than temporal forgetting does. It climbs over the misdeed that decidedly was not a misdeed, and thus consecrates the return to the prelapsed status quo ante. The historic man relies on time to wear away the memory of a misdeed that is quite real but that becomes more and more phantom-like; as for intellection, it simply demonstrates that if the excuse is total, then the misdeed has never been committed. Forgiveness, as we shall see, does not deny that the misdeed has been effectively committed, but it behaves *as if* it had not been committed. Intellection *discovers* that the guilty event (in totality or in part) is null and void, and consequently it does away with the advent and with the event; and for its part, this is not an arbitrary and gratuitous decree—for it has good reasons for that. Forgiveness, on the other hand, *decides* to consider the event as null and as not having come to pass, even though it certainly did, alas! come to pass; and come to pass it did only too much! And in spite of everything, forgiveness decrees generously, heroically, despite the absurdity, and against all evidence, that what took place did not take place. Furthermore, while temporal forgetting obtains the effacement of the guilty act by descending downstream in the current of becoming and by resigning itself to the direction of this becoming, intellection annuls the event of the sin (or a part of this event) by going back upstream in one fell swoop and by making becoming come back, or rather by revealing that the incriminated becoming never became. It is perhaps proper to call this postponement, which is on this side of contingent novelty, or which is on this side of the free initiative of a bad will, *the excuse.* To excuse is to annul, more or less, what accuses.[34] Similar to a nonplace that purely and simply crosses out the having-taken-place, the excuse is thus negative; it neither introduces a truly new era, nor is a prelude to a new youth or a new chastity. The innocence that the acquittal makes manifest and the liberty that we extend to the accused are not gracious gifts. The one and the other reappear, thanks to the rather late recognition of a right that was unjustly misunderstood, and thanks to the always too slow observation of a truth that has been contested for much too long. For it is the timeless permanence of the true that is here rationally justified beyond judiciary errors and impulsive passions. Better late than never: the scandalous denial of justice is rectified in the end . . . We indeed owe that to the accused, and in his turn he does not owe us any recognition for this observation. Forgiveness, very well! Forgiveness inaugurates

---

34. The Russian language clearly distinguishes between *izvinénié,* which disburdens us of the misdeed (*vina*), and *prochtchénié,* which says good-bye to the former life.

a *vita nuova*. It marks the accession of the former person to a resuscitated existence and itself is the celebration of this second birth. But the excuse, which levels unjust accusations and smoothes out the false protrusions of sin and which puts things back into place, makes conservative justice reign in place of creative charity. Likewise, it does not bring with it the joy of innovation. Where is it, this heart of forgiveness that changes hate into love?

X. Good Riddance

A few words will suffice to rule out, since it is not particularly philosophical, the third substitute of forgiveness, what we might call "general liquidation." Owing to the effects of time, the sin that came to pass became practically indiscernible from an event that did not come to pass. Thanks to intellection, we understood that the sin that came to pass, at least in its incriminated form, actually never did come to pass. Forgiveness, as we shall see, declares the sin null and as not having come to pass although it knows that it did come to pass, and whatever it costs. Pure and simple liquidation is a forgiveness without a sacrifice, an excuse without lucidity. At first, the offender, forestalling his offended, spontaneously excuses himself inasmuch as he is certain to obtain that for which he asks. He does not wait until the offended person finds mitigating circumstances for him; he does not doubt absolution. He utters the magic word for this and makes the ritual gesture; the reverence and salutation, which, like an open-sesame, will mobilize anew social relations, will loosen the tension, and will permit the partners to carry on regardless. This formulation is not a true reparation, but an elliptic and symbolic compensation. Like a spell, it miraculously disburdens the guilty person of all indemnity and takes the place of explanation or of contrition. As if by magic, the word erases the irregular act. As for the offended person, he decides expeditiously that the sin is null and has not come to pass, that is all there is to it! The one who liquidates hardly dares to confront the wrongs of the Other courageously in order to forgive them, and this outside of all anesthesia as outside of every euphemism. But even more, he does not care to recognize the nothingness of the sin, he does not take the trouble to denounce the nonexistence of evil. Forgiveness acts "as if," at the price of superhuman effort; and the person who liquidates, on the other hand, acts "as if" out of thoughtlessness. To liquidate is to agree to pass over the misdeed and not to hold it against the guilty person. The injury will be considered as never having been committed, nor does liquidation identify itself with progressive forgetting and with the gradual disaffection that result from time. Little by little, time dulls the force of our rancor; but if we were counting on duration alone to eliminate the offense, then an infinite time would be necessary, for natural evolution generally has the majestic slowness of an adagio. Without the intervention of man, organic processes would complete themselves interminably, relying heavily on imperceptible mutations. Just as time left to itself would never end up by erasing the memory of the misdeed, so the hurried, nervous, and impatient man helps chronology by working overtime. The resolution to finish up permits us to accelerate infinitely the interminable process; or, better yet, it gives us the capability to accomplish in one instant that which would take years and years ... Is instantaneousness not the "limit" of an infinite speed? In passing suddenly "to the limit," we forestall the decay of memory without having to wait for the end of centuries. The sudden passage to the limit is this final precipitation, this thundering acceleration of the time of decay. Such is the final prestissimo, such is the stretto that pushes along the last measures of a piece of music that is a bit botched.

Incontestably, in the passage to the limit, we find two of the essential characteristics of forgiveness: gratuitousness and suddenness. A very modest grace is already implied in the demand of the guilty person, for the offender begs the offended person to grant him what the offended person theoretically has the right to refuse, what no offended person is obliged to concede, *stricto sensu;* the guilty person solicits clemency from the one whom he addresses. Now, what about the offended person? To give time off to his rancor and his vengeful projects, to liquidate what is due to him and his rights, is indeed to accept a certain sort of sacrifice, even if this sacrifice costs nothing. To consider the insolvent debtor rid of what remains of his debt, to forgive him of the outstanding balance, and all this in exchange for nothing, in that is, indeed, a gracious and disinterested gift. This gracious discount, even when it discounts only part of the debt or the penalty, always remains total in one form or another; it knows nothing of the correct proportioning, the price scales, and the tariffs of the excuse. And no more than cordial forgiveness wastes its time in nuancing graces or proportioning them to merit does liquidation waste its time in multiplying "*distinguos*" and reservations or in splitting hairs. The affair is classified, the file destroyed, and the past is turned into ashes; and we cease completely to speak of it. The liquidator does not choose between the things to liquidate any more than the ascetic of the *Phaedo*, liquidating corporal life, takes care to sort out or to classify sensible things;[35] he does not wait to distinguish the primary from the secondary qualities, rejecting these here and keeping those there, and eliminating only the scraps . . . No! *Ea chairein:*[36] he throws the whole package overboard, without even giving himself the trouble of inventorying it or even opening it. On the other hand, this putting into parentheses is a sudden decision and an event. However much it inaugurates a carefree era, nevertheless it is no less the advent of a new life, for it comes to pass at a given moment. The person breaks with the past in one fell swoop without waiting for forgetting and disregards the rancors that were keeping him prisoner. The expedient and barely philosophical gesture of sending someone packing can thus paradoxically be the dawn of a renewal. This gesture is the signal of thawing. The rancorous person bids adieu to the season of sulkiness and enmity, acknowledges being finished with it once and for all, and makes a complete break with bygone things. He interrupts the escalation, or better yet—for vertiginous escalation is rather a circular movement!—he evades the infernal circle. Having decided to suspend the auction of vendettas and to elude the crescendo of the wild bid, the rancorous person, freed from his rancor, starts up a new emulation, an emulation of peace. It is indeed necessary that a man of good will decide first to take leave of the vicious circle unilaterally, arbitrarily, and with a thoughtful plan!

However, this final accelerando is the contrary of a philosophical attitude. In it we again find gratuitousness and instantaneousness, but not the relation with another person that is so characteristic of forgiveness. Under these conditions can we even speak of gratuitousness? Is a "gratuitous" gesture that does not have a partner even gratuitous? The one who burns the archives of his memory and of his loyalty and throws his rancors and superstitions, his scruples and concerns, his remorse and his oaths into the fire, and dances around the fire, such a person does not have the intention

---

35. [See *Phaedo*, trans. G. M. A. Grube, in *Plato: Complete Works*, 58 (66d–67a): "It really has been shown to us that, if we are ever to have pure knowledge, we must escape from the body and observe things in themselves with the soul by itself . . . While we live, we shall be closest to knowledge if we refrain as much as possible from association with the body and do not join with it more than we must; if we are not infected with its nature but purify ourselves from it . . ."]

36. [Ea chairein: Acts 23:26: "Peace be with you," a Greek salutation.]

of giving a gift to anyone. He has the intention of living in peace, rid of his troubling problems and delicate memories. Likewise, this intention does not imply anything other than egoism, sloth, frivolity, and even cowardice. The frivolous person says good evening and good night to his concerns; he cries out, To hell with the offense and rancor! First, let us not speak of it any more! but especially let us not speak anymore of it! It is this alone that is of importance to the frivolous person; if he treats the offense as a misunderstanding, then it certainly is not out of love for yesterday's enemy . . . ! *Ean chairein,* send it on its way, forget it, give it a rest—here is the beginning of the great thaw. Alas! to forget it, to send it on its way, to turn the page, this is not to have a relation with someone; it is rather to break with all relations. Along with worries and old nightmares, the neighbor is cast overboard. The whole package at the same time. We dismiss his presence in our thoughts all the way down to the memory of it. Does this disdainful and even somewhat contemptuous abstention have anything in common with forgiveness? Good riddance! says the frivolous person, without a doubt, after having chased the inopportune phantoms from his mind. Good riddance? No, this is just not how we deal with the most legitimate *ressentiments* and the most sacred memories. The philosophy of "*forget about it*" is not a philosophy. *How to be rid of something* is not a moral problem. First of all, the misdeed is not a "predicament." The misdeed is not a "bother." The misdeed is not a "discomfort." To say "good night" to sin is not an attitude toward sin.—The philosophy of good riddance is a caricature of forgiveness. Besides, it looks neither to convert the guilty person nor to excuse him. If the hurried person, dispensing altogether with the time of pacification, pronounces acquittal, then it is not because he discovered the lack of guilt of the so-called guilty person; he simply decided to be finished with it as soon as possible and to anticipate the liquidation of the abnormal situation. This hasty decision is rather a capitulation and a complete release than a positive, reasoned, or rational act. To disregard injustice blindly and hurriedly is to renounce truth and to give up what is within one's rights. The expeditious, negligent, and rather casual gesture of the impatient person who throws his grievances overboard is above all an approximative act, and it reveals nothing other than the thoughtlessness and superficiality of the person who resigns himself to it. We cannot, then, call this pragmatism without rigor, of which the essential object is to evade the difficulties of moral assessment, *intellection* . . . The one who liquidates, liquidates pell-mell and in any fashion. If well-

founded indulgence has a moral significance, then the precipitous abandonment of every accusation certainly does not have one. For this type of
abandonment, the *aphiēmi*[37] of the Greeks without a doubt would be more
appropriate than *suggignōsko,* for the decision to send one on one's way is
neither "sygnomic" nor in general "gnomic." Compared with the gesture of
dismissing, compared with this *ean chairein,* indulgence, however indulgent it may be, is still too philosophical. The Scriptures say: Do not judge;
and, with an imperceptible irony, Christ challenges the one who believes
himself to be pure to cast the first stone at the one whom he judges to be
impure.[38] But in this indulgence, there are many thoughts: humility, soul-
searching, pity for the misery of the human condition in general, the mental reservation that everyone is more or less guilty and that, consequently,
no one has the right to establish himself as the judge of anyone. Even the
moral relativism that says, To each his own truth, and that feigns to believe
that nothing has importance again implies a whole philosophy of values.
Addressing a different problem than forgiveness, the *Phaedo,* too, asks us, as
we know, to give the sensible its notice of dismissal. But this negation is itself loaded with meaning. Like an astronaut, the philosopher casts off the
load so as to climb higher more easily and so as to elevate himself up to the
Ideas. He gets rid of all carnal impediments that retard his ascension. In the
Phaedo, the *apallagē*[39] thus has a dialectic and anagogic sense.

If there is no other path to forgiving than that of good riddance, then let
there rather be *ressentiment*! For in this case, it is *ressentiment* that would
imply seriousness and profundity. At least in *ressentiment* the heart is committed, and this is why it is a prelude to cordial forgiveness. In opposition
to the doctrinairians of good-riddance, rancor represents the difficult, un-
comfortable, and ungracious attitude above all; in opposition to the indulgence that is injurious to values, it is rigor that will appear respectful of
human dignity; rancor expresses the essentially ethical rigor of the one
who deprives himself of the commodities of reconciliation, and who, in the
name of a more stringent justice, prolongs the regime of enmity.—Besides,
rancor, fixing our attention on such and such a past act, on such and such a

37. [*Aphiemi:* Greek for "forgiveness." See Matthew 6:12–15; Matthew 9:2–6; Mark 2:5–10;
Luke 5:20–24.]

38. [John 8:3.]

39. [*Apallagē:* liberation; healing, curing.]

particularly shocking misdeed, counters the isostheny, of acts and events, that would result from a general emptying of all the judgments of value. Rancor contributes to save hierarchies and moral distinctions from adiaphora. The solution by which one throws things into the fire is also the renunciation of recollection, of fidelity, of permanence, of all that by which men differentiate themselves from oysters and jellyfish. Can the quietus that we grant to guilty people by means of this good-riddance have the slightest moral significance?—In addition, finally, this accelerated liquidation is in the same situation as all the other natural and pathological processes that we wanted to push along or whose successive stages we wanted to evade; a fever that is too quickly cured is a fever that is poorly cured. Precarious is the forgetting, precarious is the peace that we regain in five minutes after we have thrown all our papers into the fire. For having wanted to economize on the process of convalescence, the quickly restored sick person remains exposed to all the relapses and offensive renewals of the rancorous fever. Who says that on the day after our hasty reconciliation we will not regret our sacrificed hatred? To say good night to rancor does not at all solve the problem once and for all or does not put a final end to the hostilities . . . Let us rather fear that the hostilities will spring back to life! If the negligent person has not, like the indulgent person, based the excuse on rational explanation, if he has not, like the charitable person, traversed the agonizing ordeal of forgiveness and undergone the red-hot iron of cruel renunciation, then the peace treaty will be put back in question very quickly. Only pure disinterested love will never put its sacrifice back in question, and thus only it founds a definitive peace.—The furnace of universal absolution is, thus, not purifying and simplifying, as is the pyre of forgiveness. Provisionally, it inaugurates acts resembling forgiveness, having the same effects as forgiveness and the same appearance as forgiveness. Ever since we began speaking of substitutes for forgiveness—temporality, the intellective excuse, instantaneous liquidation—we have not stopped dealing with conformable appearance: to liquidate is to make a semblance of forgiving. The "semblance" is obviously related to exterior conformity: just as simili-duty imitates only the appearance of duty, just as simili-charity imitates only the external manifestations of authentic charity (pantomime and alms), so liquidation imitates all that which is *capable of imitation,* which is to say, visible and negative, about forgiveness; initially, the mimicry of behaviors, the gesture of absolving, the archives of rancor delivered into the fire, and the files reduced to ashes. But this mimicry has neither intimacy nor living positivity. But these bonfires have no heart. From the divorce that throws the outside and the inside into disharmony is born all the relative misunderstandings of simili-forgiveness. Simili-forgiveness does not have a heart any more than temporality or the excuse does. Thus, we ask for a third time: the heart of forgiveness, what have we done with it?

3 Mad Forgiveness: "Acumen Veniae"

We were saying that the motivated excuse excuses only the excusable. Unmotivated forgiving forgives the inexcusable; in that lies its proper function. For the inexcusable is in fact not unforgivable; and the incomprehensible is not unforgivable, either! When a crime can neither be justified, nor explained, nor even understood, when, with everything that could be explained having been explained, the atrocity of this crime and the overwhelming evidence of this responsibility are obvious before everyone's eyes, when the atrocity has neither mitigating circumstances, nor excuses of any sort, and when hope of regeneration has to be abandoned, then there is no longer anything else to do but to forgive. It is, in desperation, the supreme recourse and the ultimate grace; it is, in the last instance, the only thing and the unique thing that there remains to do. Here we attain the eschatological confines of the irrational. Even better, the inexcusable itself is material only for forgiveness, precisely because it is inexcusable. For if we can excuse it, then the *unjust* hyperbole of forgiveness would not be so necessary; forgiveness would be reduced to a formality and an empty protocol. Such is also the case, for Pascal, with faith, this faith that is paradoxical and that believes despite absurdity. One asks us to believe in the indemonstrable only and precisely because it is impossible to demonstrate. If religion were demonstrable, and if the proofs for Christianity were convincing, and if the existence of God were manifest, then the folly of faith would be no more necessary than the folly of forgiveness. It would not be necessary to believe this insane thing: that a future of pain or of joy is reserved for the soul after death. Thus the author of a treatise on geometry or of an ethics *more geometrico demonstrata*[1] asks us not to "believe" in the apodictic link-

---

1. [Spinoza's *Ethics*.]

ing of his theories and his corollaries. One solicits our good will only when the theses are doubtful, uncertain, or even implausible and contradictory. This is why "reasons" for forgiving are hardly more admissible, in extreme circumstances, than "reasons" for believing. If we forgive it is because we do not have reasons; and if we had reasons, then it is the excuse, and not forgiveness, that is competent. Reasons for forgiveness abolish the raison d'être of forgiveness. And it is the same situation if we try to see things from the guilty person's point of view; the "right to forgiveness" is a contradiction and nonsense that is hardly less absurd than a "right to grace." Forgiveness is gratuitous like love, even though it itself neither is love nor inevitably changes into love. But it happens that we end up by loving the one whom we forgive. A man who is disappointed in the malevolence of his partner finds in his tribulations themselves an occasion to become impassioned. And conversely, we more easily forgive someone whom we already love. The grace of forgiveness, in sum, is rather that of charity in general.

I. Impure Forgiveness

At the interior of forgiveness, strictly speaking, three transitional cases that would lead us toward the hyperbolic limit of pure forgiveness can still be distinguished. Here is the first. With complete lucidity, we can forgive a person confirmed as guilty, a guilty person recognized as guilty and, consequently, as inexcusable, and we can forgive him without either decay, mitigating circumstances, or the willingness to liquidate the accusation having any part in it: like a very tiny calculation, a minuscule amount of speculation, however, an infinitesimal afterthought can creep into this apparently gratuitous forgiveness. In the same way, Pascal, making a plea for his indemonstrable faith, addresses nonbelievers in the utilitarian and probabilistic language of the wager. Incapable of convincing them by probative arguments, he at least tries to persuade them by the calculation of chances. He points them toward the beyond by employing a hazardous and straightforwardly plausible reasoning, which, taking into account the margin of uncertainty, justifies only probable conjectures. But the drastic and militant reasons by which we claim to sway miscreants to bet on the beyond are still *reasons*. These reasons, by making resonate the chord of mercenary interest, act on the gambler thanks to the power of suggestion of a holy rhetoric. What this may mean is (if we distance ourselves from Pascal now): God

is not so much indemonstrable as he is provisionally undemonstrated . . .
Demonstrated—maybe he will be demonstrated one day. Believe, mean-
while! The words "probability" and "probable," *probabilis,* themselves invite
this risky speculation since they designate what is susceptible of one day being proven, *probari.* In its turn, forgiveness might be only a very chancy excuse. Today, it adventurously forgives that which maybe it would excuse
very legitimately tomorrow and with full justification, if it could wait. If the
gambler makes a reasonable bet, today's charity can become tomorrow's justice. But conversely, forgiveness too accepts the risk of absolving here and
now an accused who is at least suspect, without being certain that the accused will merit this absolution. Forgive, then, if you accept running the
risk! This forgiveness is in reality an intellectualist excuse after the fact, a
motivated excuse for which the motivation is particularly adventurous and
risky; it is boldness alone that gives it the appearance of gratuitousness. In
this case, grace has its reasons, however fragile they may be, and this is thus
not grace! The one who absolves a guilty person has confidence in this guilty
person, and he hopes that the future will justify his confidence, that his calculations will prove to be exact . . . But this is a calculation! Who knows if
such and such an unknown circumstance will not justify a forgiveness
which, for the instant, is unjustified, illegitimate, and unreasonable, but
which tomorrow will be reasonable, legitimate, and justified? Maybe after
all the wicked person is not so wicked, or the guilty person is not so guilty?
Maybe the liar is not so much a liar, for there are plausible ways of inter-
preting a lie as actually good; and if a lie is a lie, then a lie does not always
make a liar. Maybe some excuse that is still unsuspected will one day render
forgiveness superfluous . . . Maybe, maybe . . . This "maybe" is the maybe of
hope and of Elpidian possibility, the maybe of intellectualist optimism. To
forgive is to extend credit to an innocent person who has all the appearances
of a guilty person; and this is to excuse out of anticipation, and for the love
of innocence that is hoped for, discounted, and presumed, one that later will
be revealed or verified. Let us recall that in the unfathomable depth of the
intention there is something for all tastes. In the infinite ambiguity of intention, there is plenty to justify optimism as well as misanthropy. Becoming takes it upon itself to actualize first one and then the other. The optimist
interprets in a favorable sense that which we were calling the *intentional
equivocation,* which is an equivocation for which time will develop all that
is possible. He wagers that the bipossibility and the contingency of the future will declare themselves in favor of innocence in the end. One never

knows . . . One chance suffices in order for the guilty-innocent person to be revealed as innocent; we have to reserve preciously and explore carefully this unique chance. But it also happens that the intellectualist excuse, disguised as forgiveness, professes an optimism that is somewhat forced and hides the sad truth from itself. This desperate truth, however, is not without glimpsing. And this truth is that there is no excuse; it is that the crime is inexcusable, that the criminal of this crime is incurably wicked and that no hidden circumstance that is still to be discovered mitigates his culpability, that the freedom of this ill will is wholly responsible, and that there is, thus, an evil of malevolence. After that, forgive if you can! To forgive? this is, however, all that there remains to do . . . But no! Intellectual conformism prefers to deceive itself and to invoke the benefit of presumed excusability for the guilty person. Indeed, those are the truths of the Bibliothèque Rose.[2] They express, above all, the phobia of liberty and consequently exempt the reasonable man from placing himself at once in the wholly-other-order so that he may have to run the wild adventure of forgiveness.

Another genre of speculation, entailing other risks, can creep into the interior of even the most gratuitous forgiveness. This speculation is the hope of ameliorating the criminal by the very effect of his gratitude toward the one who has pardoned him. Here, we approach even closer to the limit of pure forgiveness; for it is henceforth accepted as a fact that the guilty person is very guilty; the guilty person is no longer presumed fundamentally innocent. Earlier, we admitted not to be able to know a situation that is infinitely complex; we lacked elements that were perhaps likely to justify the revision of the process. For every condemnation remains cursory to some degree. We were explaining that severity is in general more simplistic than indulgence. It sufficed, then, to wait patiently for history, thanks alone to the spontaneous unfolding of its becoming, to make elements appear that were capable of rehabilitating the condemned. At present, the tribunal of history becomes useless. It is no longer temporality, or in other terms, the natural movement of futurition, that exposes the virtual excusability of a misdeed; it is the very act of forgiveness that determines the amendment of the guilty person or that hurries the conversion of this guilty person. At the moment in which forgiveness was going to forgive, the guilty person was indeed guilty; but the redemptive, purifying, and absolving action of generosity transfigures the guilty-guilty person into a guilty-innocent person, and then

2. [The Bibliothèque Rose: a series of children's books from the French publisher Hachette.]

into an innocent person. The infinite complexity and ambiguity of intentions, as we saw, justified indulgence toward patent malevolence and legitimated the belief in latent benevolence. In the same way, perhaps this complexity facilitates the amendment of the guilty person who is transfigured by forgiveness. If an invisible good will hides behind the bad will, then the role of forgiveness is to develop this infinitesimal good will, this esoteric benevolence enveloped in an exoteric malevolence, and to encourage the benevolence of the malevolence. But we can also think that the gesture of pardoning releases a type of miraculous mutation in the sinner who is touched by this grace. Thus, the idea of a good will in germination would have for a goal only to evade the discontinuity of the molting. Here, to forgive is no longer to recognize by anticipation a nonevident but yet given innocence; to forgive is to consecrate the sinner's accession to a new life. Henceforth, forgiveness is no longer the passive and quietist speculation of the gambler who buys a lottery ticket and leaves it up to his own good fortune and to the wheel of fortune, without himself acting on this wheel save by the superstitious magic of a Platonic wish. For the guilty person who is reputed to be guilty, forgiveness is not even the speculation of a gambler who reasons according to calculations of the probabilities and the law of the big numbers, or even the calculation of a providential speculator, who, in order to place the most on a sure bet, buys or sells on the stock exchange after a study of the market . . . It is none of this! Speculation no longer speculates about an independent chance; speculation itself creates a destiny by speculating. Redemptive forgiveness implies a transformative will and itself claims to have an influence on the guilty person by the power of its radiance alone. And it is thus a militant expectation and not a fatalistic hope; and it supposes an act of confidence and not a slothful waiting. The accuser who abandons the accusation in order to transform the guilty person engages his own responsibility in an actively conducted adventure. He does not take the risk of supposing the one who has a guilty air to be innocent; he himself works at redeeming the guilty person, not by punishing him, but in a paradoxical way by disarming him by dint of gentleness.—However, what prevents this purifying forgiveness from being pure itself? That which prevents it from being pure is precisely that it forgives *in order: in order to* purify. Naturally, there is no evil in that. The hope of enriching one's brother is among the most honorable of hopes, a disinterested hope, a hope that has nothing mercenary about it and in which we would look in vain for an iota of self-interest. And besides, by no means does such a forgiveness provoke infallibly and in all cases, as if by automatic release, the conversion of the pardoned, redeemed . . . and miraculously cured criminal. That would be too much to hope for! because if it were really so, then forgiveness would be a legal, obligatory, and universal institution, and as such the refusal to forgive the crime would be the crime. In this case, a rigorous justice would become something like the crime of nonassistance to a soul in danger . . . To be able to save a sinner on a sure bet by forgiving him, and yet to prefer to punish him as likewise he "merits," to be able to save him and to refuse to save him, is indeed a type of spiritual murder. If, by an infallible mechanism, forgiveness would activate the redemption of the guilty person, then it would not be necessary to ask for forgiveness, never necessary to implore the forgiveness of one's victim or of one's judges, or to supplicate in order to obtain grace. In a word, there would not be forgiveness. For what would exigible forgiveness be, if not a right, pure and simple? In fact, the one who opens the prisons and who unconditionally frees all the prisoners takes a risk: is this a good risk? We can thus save many souls and we can equally endanger all the citizens. It is this perilous imprudence, this mad and maybe mortal adventure, this incertitude that, in a word and at the limit, is supposed to render the forgiveness that converts indiscernible from forgiveness *tout court,* which is to say, from pure grace. The philanthropic eschatology of the libertarians, as we know, puts all of its hope in the revolutionary contagion of general absolution: to burn all the files, to give amnesty to all the scoundrels, to liberate all the gangsters, to embrace the gentlemen torturers, to give doctorates *honoris causa* to the metaphysicians of the Gestapo and the ex-commandant of *Gross-Paris,* to transform the courts into cinemas and prisons into skating rinks—this is the true, final judgment and the very object of the final wager; this final judgment, at the same time as it seems to put an end to history, would bring us back to the Golden Age or to a type of paradise lost. So, we ask again, what is impure in this promise of a paradise lost by the mistake of justice and found again by the grace of unmerited and purifying forgiveness? Let us respond: the promise itself! What is impure is the ulterior awareness of a connection between the remission of the punishment and the conversion of the guilty person; what is impure is the express and somewhat discreet intention of saving an immortal soul by forgiving. How would the rectifier of souls, having suddenly realized the purifying effects of forgiveness, not squint toward this relation? Forgiveness, under these conditions, is no longer the resolution to surmount the misdeed by love for mankind; forgiveness itself is no longer the conversion of rancor into charity. Forgiveness has become the hypothetical medium of another thing. In the proselytizing frame of mind, forgiveness implies a long-range calculation, an intelligent maneuver, or even better, a pedagogic strategy; and it indeed hopes to be paid in return, and not to have forgiven in vain or for nothing. It expects that the guilty person will be keen on meriting his grace afterward, that the guilty person will make it a point of honor to justify the imprudent confidence of which he was the object. The recuperation of this lost person will be the best recompense for our temerity. The optimist, betting on the perfectibility of man, hopes that the absolution will not be for naught. This forgiveness, a little too providential, engages us, if we can say it, in long-term investments. It is thus difficult to see in it something other than a well-intended generosity and an interested disinterestedness. In every speculation that is too well intended for the salvation of the sinner, we then distinguish a very subtle *concupiscence spirituelle.* In truth, forgiveness has become a type of gift destined to put pressure on wicked people, a method for buying the conversion of guilty people by forcing them to take your hand. Who would resist this generous bribe? It is necessary to admit that forgiveness, just like nonresistance to evil, is often a strategy. Instead of opposing force with force, nonviolent people in refusing combat disarm violence by the gentle force of charity. In a language that is somewhat militaristic, Spinoza proposes this ruse to us: *odium amore expugnare.*[3] For an *odium reciprocum*[4] does not assure victory. In Liszt's *Battle of the Huns,* this is the way gentle force itself became a weapon and prevails over barbaric violence. To forgive in this sense is to suppose that the problem is resolved in order to resolve it afterward; it is to suppose that the guilty person is innocent, in effect to render him innocent by the very supposition itself, and to this end recklessly to forestall the guilty person with a type of anticipatory suggestion. The magnanimous person will, then, meet the guilty person halfway. Such forgiveness, such a liberating liberty, leads to a redemptive movement in the other person. Can we say that the gratuitous gesture of the

3. *Ethics,* book 4, §46 f. ["P46: He who lives according to the guidance of reason strives, as far as he can, to repay the other's hate, danger, and disdain toward him, with love, or nobility . . . Schol.—He who wishes to avenge wrongs by hating in return surely lives miserably. On the other hand, one who is eager to overcome hate by love strives joyously and confidently . . ." Spinoza, *Ethics,* in *A Spinoza Reader,* trans. Edwin Curley (Princeton: Princeton University Press, 1994), 225.]

4. [*Odium reciprocum:* along these lines, see *Ethics,* book 4, §46 f., in *A Spinoza Reader,* 225: "P46: Now hate is increased by being returned . . ."]

first person causes gratitude to be born in the second person? What prevents us from saying it is the lack of innocence of this tactical forgiveness. The gratuitous gesture pardons the guilty person in order to lead him to gratitude. He himself is not in a state of grace.

Finally, there are hybrid cases, mixed forms in which the excuse is combined with forgiveness, not because it will discover later that forgiveness was an excuse, as in the speculation of the first type, but because the excuse and forgiveness are given at the same time. Mitigating circumstances aid in reinforcing our gratuitous decision to absolve the guilty person. We will respond, it is true, that a half forgiveness is not forgiveness at all and that forgiveness is all or it is nothing. In this respect, forgiveness is like confidence and love; a small amount of mistrust suffices to annihilate this confidence without limits; one tiny suspicion, one alone—and there will remain nothing more of this confidence that is vast and deep like the sea. One atom of interestedness suffices to annihilate the most pure disinterestedness. A few infinitesimal traces of self-interest, or merely of justified esteem, a suspicion of explicative causality—and love has ceased to be a purism, in the maximal and superlative sense of the word. In the same way that grace ceases to be grace with even the least amount of grayness that comes to dull its whiteness, so forgiveness ceases to be forgiveness if even a milligram of reasonable motivation comes to justify it. The absolutely initial, gratuitous, and supernatural spontaneity of absolution is thus tarnished by the excusability of the misdeed. Indeed, a purity that is tarnished is destroyed. However, although pure forgiveness is theoretically undivided and unmerited, it happens that it comes to ask for justificatory pretexts. So we call *gratuity* the disproportion that shines forth between the immensity of the absolution and the insignificance of the pretext. Thus the generous man sometimes clings to a semblance of mitigating excuse or excusing circumstance, immeasurably exaggerates the justificatory occasion, or even invents it whole, so as to be in accordance with rational logic. Love, solicited to say *why* it loves (as if it were necessary that there be a *why*!), looks into itself and naturally finds for itself, right away, some *becauses*. The creator, interrogated by journalists about the mystery of creation, reconstructs a retrospective causality—for he finds it more fitting to write his poems for this or that reason. And likewise, impulsive forgiveness gives itself an explicative etiology and some reasonable motives for indulgence after the fact; retrospectively, it finds reasons for excusing what it was wholly disposed to forgive without reason. For no thinking being either willingly admits to an unmotivated and undeliberated decision or renounces the exercise of reasoning . . . In the continuation of everyday life, it is most often these approximative admixtures of rationality and generosity that take the place of forgiveness. The unmotivated decision is hence enveloped in a perimeter of good reasons that are more or less retrospective.

II. Consciousness of Forgiveness and the Discourse on Forgiveness

It is thus necessary for us to restate about pure forgiveness, *venia pura,* that which can be applied just as well to pure love, as glimpsed and aimed at by Fénelon, to the pure despair of pure remorse, to the "pure" perception of Bergson, and finally to wholly pure innocence: pure forgiveness is an event that has perhaps never occurred in the history of man; pure forgiveness is a limit that is barely psychological, a peak state that is hardly lived. The isolated summit of forgiveness, *acumen veniae,* is barely existent, or, which amounts to the same, *almost* nonexistent! In fact, with the elements of the mental complex running into one another, the delicate, extreme point of pure forgiveness is crushed and is hidden in the thick continuation of the interval. At first, the conscience of the great, thinking metazoan cannot prevent itself from becoming conscious of itself, from reflecting on itself, or from contemplating its own image in a mirror; thus, the indiscreet and overly curious conscience gauges itself and measures itself like an object in all of its dimensions. Just as the weight of egoism holds back the centrifugal acts of the loving intention, so a type of fatal heaviness condemns the most disinterested forgiveness to lose its innocence. The changing of one's mind, in flowing back toward the ego, turns us away from this Other at whom we were aiming; heterocentric love is nothing more than a circumlocution of philauty. And likewise, when we are brushed by an ulterior motive of vanity, of self-interest, or of mercenary interest, the gracious efference of forgiveness withdraws into itself. Complaisance, which is to say, the secondary pleasure that one takes in one's own pleasure, supplants the primary pleasure. *Ressentiment,* which is to say, the secondary sentiment that we feel on the occasion of sentiment, replaces the simple, primary sentiment. What is re-sented shines forth in all its extension around what is sensed, as around a central point. So the intention with exponent, the intention to the second power, which is the intention of the intention, is substituted for the direct and innocent intention of forgiveness. If the forgiving person, while forgiving, should look at himself and think of himself instead of thinking of the misdeed of the guilty person, and re-sent in echo what he senses, then *ressentiment* and forgiveness begin to become confused a little bit in a single complaisance and a single secondarity. Although, forgiveness serves to liquidate *ressentiment* for us, all sorts of transitions appear between the one and the other. And just as a man who has sincerely felt pity draws from his own pity great cause for satisfaction and savors the tender sweetness of tears, so the man who sincerely forgives cannot fail to know immediately the delights of a good conscience that is well contented. Besides, the instant of innocent sincerity shines on this side of and beyond the present toward the before and toward the after. Just as the consciousness reconstitutes a perimeter of egoism around the point of charity, so a temporality that is retrospective and prospective reintegrates a continuation on both sides of the instant. Not only does the luminous point of the intention *take up space* but also the spark of the intention is *epoch-making* and *takes time*. The blink of an eye of the good movement is continued thanks to repercussion and to anticipation, and will actually have a certain duration; the innocent instant, then, overflows into the interval. At first, recollection and retrospection enrich forgiveness by looking toward the past, by evoking the great, solemn instances of forgiveness from history. The man who remembers the memorable examples recorded in the chronicles authenticates his own clemency and takes pleasure in spelling out in it the undeniable signs of grandeur of soul and moral sublimity. Plutarch and the *De Viris,* the *Epitome,* and hagiography are thus an inexhaustible source of good conscience for magnanimous people. Enough about an aftertaste. And now for the foretaste: consciousness squints not only toward the past but also toward the future. It anticipates the effects of forgiveness and foresees the conversion of the one whom it pardons. Thus, the summit of the soul tapers in forgiveness, but chronological succession and the reflection of consciousness, which are the two dimensions of complaisance, substitute a "peak state" for the fine point. Now, there is a point, but there is exactly no state! Is it not precisely in this respect that pure forgiveness is a normative ideal? Such is pure disinterestedness for Kant. Even if no one since the world has been the world has ever forgiven without reservations, without afterthoughts, without mental restrictions, or without an infinitesimal amount of *ressentiment,* it suffices that the possibility of pure forgiveness is conceivable; even if it has never been attained in fact, the limit of pure forgiveness would still designate our duty for us, would determine and orient our efforts, would furnish a criterion for permitting us to distinguish the pure and the impure,[5] and would give a standard of measure to evaluation and a direction to charity. The one who never attains the ideal (the ideal being made precisely for never being attained) can get infinitely nearer to it. It is what the *Phaedo,* speaking of intelligible essences, calls *eggutata ienai,* "to go closest."[6] Or, in other terms, to say that the forgiveness-limit is the horizon of an infinite quest or that immediate proximity is the ideal of an asymptotic approximation or of an endless approximation comes back to admitting implicitly the possibility of a quick-as-lightning encounter with pure innocence. Between absolute unreachability, with which pessimism menaces us, and the chronic, physical, and extensive contact that optimism promises us, there undoubtedly is instantaneous tangency. Tangency, but not touch! These imponderable and impalpable "touches" are analogous to the ones of which Saint Francis de Sales speaks. Forgiveness is not a tangible thing, but it is not an unreachable ideal either. Man brushes against the limit of pure love and this lasts for the instant of a fugitive spark, a spark *brévissime* that alights as it goes out and that appears in disappearing. That which lasts an instant does not last at all. And in spite of all of this, that which lasts an instant is not nothing! Let us call it the I-know-not-what.[7] Here, the I-know-not-what, which is *barely something* on its verso and is *almost something* on its recto, is the event reduced to its pure coming to pass; the I-know-not-what is the surging or the flickering of lightning reduced to the fact of coming to pass, which is to say, to a fulguration itself. So the objective negativity of forgiveness turns into lived positivity. The fine point, which in the order of historic and psycho-

5. [Jankélévitch published a book by the name of *The Pure and the Impure.* See Vladimir Jankélévitch, *Le Pur et l'impur* (Paris: Flammarion, 1960/1978). Reprinted in *Vladimir Jankélévitch: Philosophie morale,* ed. Françoise Schwab (Paris: Flammarion, 1998), 585–813.]

6. *Phaedo,* 65e, cf. 67d. [65e: "whoever of us prepares himself best and most accurately to grasp that thing itself which he is investigating will come closest to the knowledge of it." 67d: "Therefore, as I said at the beginning, it would be ridiculous of a man to train himself in life to live in a state as close to death as possible, and then to resent it when it comes." *Phaedo,* trans. G. M. A. Grube, in *Plato's Complete Works,* ed. John M. Cooper (Indianapolis: Hackett, 1997), 59, 58.]

7. [The I-know-not-what or "je-ne-sais-quoi" is an important notion that recurs in Jankélévitch's writings. See the three-volume work *Le Je-ne-sais-quoi et le presque-rien* (Paris: Presses Universitaires de France, 1957 and Paris: Éditions du Seuil, 1980).]

logical abstractions seemed to us to be quasi-nonexistent, corresponds, in the order of the lived, to the most real of events. Certainly charity and sincere disinterestedness are never the habitual residence of man. For we can never remain on vertiginous peaks, or on the tapered summit of forgiveness or of love; a prodigious equilibrium would be necessary to maintain oneself there . . . It is down below, in the expanse of the plain or in the continuation of the valleys, that the inhabitants of the empirical establish their domicile! Also, the idea of a virtuous perpetuity or of a domiciliation in virtue offers the widest target to the sarcasms of a La Rochefoucauld: hypocrisy and other-worldliness, indeed, claim to restore a sort of moral continuation or virtuous chronicity across the intermittences of intention. But, on the other hand, the instant of disinterested forgiveness is not radically inaccessible, on the condition that by the word *accede,* we mean not to make oneself comfortable in one's furniture but to find and to lose again at the same moment. The miracle is that the instantaneous advent is capable of inaugurating a future, of founding a new life, of instituting new relations among men; the miracle is that an era of peace could outlive the joyous instant.

What is true is that a forgiveness that is lightly bogged down in pretenses or thickened by conscience would be, for second philosophy,[8] an object that is more manageable, and, for discourse, a food that is more substantial. As long as it is a question of excusing, then very well! for we have a lot to say: one never comes to the end of explaining the implicit reasons, classifying them, or ordering them hierarchically according to their importance; for that which is motivated offers a rich material for development, for descriptions, and for analyses. The excuse naturally sparkles; the excuse abounds, takes up space, and renders loquacious those who set out to put forth proofs and arguments. Nothing is more garrulous than a letter of excuses enumerating the "becauses" and detailing mitigating circumstances: nothing, unless it is the judgment of a tribunal, when this judgment enumerates the preambles and the "reasons." On the contrary, there is almost nothing more to say about the *acumen veniae;* it is impossible to have a discourse on the ineffable, inexplicable, and indescribable instant that is wholly contained in the pure quoddity of the word *grace.* For grace, which is the spark and fluttering of the eyelids, says nothing, or better yet, says one single word, and

---

8. [See Jankélévitch's *Philosophie première* (Paris: Presses Universitaires de France, 1953/1986), a work that is supposed to be a foundation of philosophy but that goes well beyond traditional texts in metaphysics because of the scope of subjects that it addresses.]

this monosyllable of grace seems itself to be in the image of a fine point that is without thickness, just as it is in the image of a punctual instant that is without an interval. In the suddenness of the instant, the alpha and the omega coincide; no logos has the time to unfold the discursive succession of its concepts between the two. And likewise, the philosopher's discourse on grace is finished just as quickly as it was begun. In addition, the grace of forgiveness, which is similar in this respect to a pure, sincere love, renders mute and silent the reasoning people who would be tempted to speak of it; it makes them be quiet; it forces the words back into the throat of the prolix orator. Such is the mute eloquence of the gnosis according to Plotinus. In pure forgiveness, there is a sort of supernatural terseness. The word of grace is often pronounced in silence and has no other commentary than the paradoxical kiss, the unjust and incomprehensible kiss, the scandalous kiss given to the persecutor. But the kiss is not a word, any more than tears are a "language." The accolade is much more of a gesture, like the laying on of hands in the Cathar Consolation of which the kiss (*aspasmos*) is the conclusion. The Ordained and the novice, having said the *perdonum,* which is the demand for grace, and having recited *Parcite nobis* ... actually separate upon this salutation of peace.[9] *Aspasmos* is neither a gauge of nor a symbol for love. Aspasmos is itself and immediately Agape. At the end of *The Power of Darkness,* Nikita falls to his knees, prostrates himself on the floor, and cries out: "Listen, Pravoslaves! I am guilty ... Forgive me for the love of Christ!" His father, Hakim, transported, embraces him and says to him, "God will forgive you, my dear child."[10] Nikita does not look to excuse the inexcusable, or to plead an undefendable cause, or to justify himself. And the forgiveness that forgives him simply says: "I forgive you," without any other explanations, since, indeed, there are no reasons for absolving ... And if we developed these reasons, without a doubt there would be as many reasons for not absolving as for excusing; and if one were to speak instead of silently giving the kiss of peace, it would be in order to roll out objections against forgiveness, to argue against forgiveness, to prove the entire responsibility of the guilty person, or, completely on the contrary, to demonstrate the necessity of indulgence and to make the case for mitigating circumstances. For

9. Cf. René Nelli, *Écritures cathares* [Paris: Éditions Planète, 1968], 237. Deodat Roché, *Études manichéennes et cathares* [Arques: Éditions des Cahiers d'études cathares, 1952], 181.

10. Leo Tolstoy, *The Power of Darkness* [trans. Anthony Clark (New York: Theater Communication Group, 1991)], 5.2.

we speak in order to accuse—and we also speak in order to excuse when the accused is innocent of the crime of which we accuse him. In short, only forgiveness of the guilty person has nothing to say. But because people are at ease only when they can have a discourse, they willingly transform mute forgiveness into a motivated excuse. A garrulous forgiveness is as suspect as a garrulous lover; the one who speaks too much loves himself and loves love while believing that he loves his beloved. By dint of primping and examining the interesting particularities of one's beautiful loving soul in detail in front of the mirror, one ends up by forgetting the second person and abandoning this accusative of love, which is the immediate raison d'être of the loving intention. It is no different for forgiveness. A loquacious forgiveness is interested in itself more than in the sinner; maybe its complaisance hides, who knows? ulterior motives or some minuscule *ressentiment* which one cannot admit with regard to the sinner. Sententious volubility dissimulates lack of sincerity just as it serves to veil bad conscience. This is why we can have a discourse about forgiveness only by speaking of other things; by speaking around it, and incidentally by saying first what forgiveness is not. And for example, a lot of time and words are necessary to show that forgiveness is not the excuse. But this apophatic philosophy is perhaps only a vast circumlocution around the ipseity of forgiveness. Is it not time finally to abandon these puribund periphrases and to aim for forgiveness in itself?

III. "Venia Pura": The Forgiveness-Limit

There is, thus, a forgiveness-limit that is a hyperbolic forgiveness and that forgives without reasons. This unmotivated movement can only be an efferent, pure *élan,* deprived of any psychological perimeter and lived substantiality.—Forgiveness quells the vindictive reflexes of the talion, but evidently this does not suffice—for it could suspend vengeance in order to delay it, transform vengeance into vendetta, and save itself for long-term reprisals. And the rancorous person comes off as no better than the vindictive person. He could also abstain from long-term reprisals themselves and have the offender legally judged and punished. This would not be forgiveness either. Not only does the one who forgives not avenge himself now, not only does he renounce all future vengeance, but he renounces justice itself! And he renounces much more yet. It is an understatement to say that he does not harbor even an atom of self-esteem. He does not even hope that the guilty person who is pardoned today, and gratuitously pardoned, will later care about meriting his grace. Let us understand, however, that this absence of hope or of perspective as regards a possible amelioration of the sinner is not despair strictly speaking; for this would be to admit that despair is alone in being pure, that purity is necessarily desperate ... With forgiveness, it is not a question of this despair, which is an agonizing absurdity and an unlivable real life experience. The man who forgives renounces neither the continuation of his very being, nor even, like the "gnostic" of the *Maxims of the Saints,* his spiritual future. He sacrifices neither his vital future nor his glorious or eschatological future. We know that this sacrifice, according to Fénelon, would characterize the purity of pure love. Having become capable of renouncing not only this margin of vital hope that ceaselessly reconstitutes a futurition in front of us, but also the very hope of salvation, a love that is free from every ulterior motive is collected in a point and is concentrated in the present instant. Like the tribulations of Abraham or Job, this spiritual suicide was, without a doubt, an impossible supposition that was finally refuted. However, it suffices that the vertiginous and scandalous hypothesis of an evil genius,[11] of an impenetrable justice, and of radical evil, has been tangentially grazed. A love without hope, which is not only the misappropriation of the will itself, but also the total elimination and ecstatic loss of the ego, is for this very reason theoretically possible; the lover, ceasing to exist for himself, loses himself in his Other. Actually, forgiveness does not ask us to sacrifice all of our own being or to become ourselves the sinner himself; forgiveness does not demand that much! Forgiveness simply asks of us, where an offense is concerned, to renounce spite, passionate aggression, and the vindictive temptation, and where sin is concerned, it asks us to renounce sanctions, tit-for-tat considerations, and the most legitimate exigencies of justice. All in all, forgiveness is more disinterested than radically desperate. Of course, forgiveness is very much a type of "despair," in the sense that remorse is a despair. Despair would not be despair, but rather a theatrical *disperato,* if it squinted toward redemption of which it is perhaps the forerunner and if it were counting on this forerunner as if on a promise. Nothing prevents grace from possibly redeeming the despair of remorse on the condition that this despair has not expected this grace, and on the con-

---

11. [René Descartes, *Meditations on First Philosophy,* in *The Philosophical Writings of Descartes,* vol. 2, ed. John Cottingham, Robert Stroothoff, and Dugald Murdoch (Cambridge: Cambridge University Press, 1984), 15 (Meditation One).]

dition that this person, feigning desperation, did not put on the act of remorse wholly on purpose. And nothing prevents, either, the grace of forgiveness from converting the sinner, provided that this grace did not aim
expressly at this conversion like a recompense that was due on account of
its generosity, provided that forgiveness has not forgiven in the hope of redemption, and provided that forgiveness did not have the express intention
of saving the immortal soul of the guilty person! We have already criticized
the subtle hypocrisy of a forgiveness that speculates about the conversion of
sinners ... There is then a relation between forgiveness and the transfiguration of the guilty person, just as there is a relation between moral shame
and redemption: but this relation does not need to be devised; and this
relation is entirely undeliberated and indirect. The condition of the efficaciousness of despair, whether it is called *remorse* or *forgiveness,* is the perfect innocence of the hopeless person. Fénelon already knew it: grace is offered uniquely to those who have not sought it out. In these matters, the
pretension to efficaciousness is, then, the most common cause of failure,
whereas the innocent acceptance of the failure alone renders forgiveness
and remorse efficacious. For whoever wants to find salvation will miss it.
The good will, here, is one with the bad conscience, just as a conscience that
is too good is one with ill will. However, it is best not to push this parallel
between remorse and forgiveness too far. In remorse, the supernatural and
unforeseeable grace of redemption rises up from despair itself, while in forgiveness, grace is granted to the sinner by someone else. Of course, the remorse of the sinner, even in forgiveness, gives its full meaning to grace, but
it is no longer the determinate cause of forgiveness since grace comes from
outside, and because it is freely granted. In remorse, the desperate person is
himself the guilty person, and this desperate person, if he is sufficiently sincere, spontaneously redeems himself all alone; for despair is already an expiation; the man who committed the misdeed and the man who suffers for
it and who repents because of it are one and the same man. In forgiveness,
the guilty person is not the one who forgives but the one whom we forgive;
and this guilty person is not always so desperate. The man who bestows
grace is often much more desperate even though he has nothing for which
to be reproached! And consequently, remorse is a monologue and a solitary
rumination: the prostrated sinner stagnates in his own past and holds a
grudge against himself, and depends only on himself. Remorse is a soliloquy, but forgiveness is a dialogue, a relation between two partners in which
one waits for something from the other. Instead of the remorse-filled man

suffering without waiting for anything and passively sinking into the hell of his sterile regrets and of his autoscopic confinement, forgiveness, relating the first person to the second person, opens a breach through the wall of guilty intimacy, especially when the guilty person has a bad conscience. So forgiveness breaks the enclosure of remorse. For it is in itself a liberating act, and it posits the foundations of a new era. Forgiveness forgives in the night just as remorse suffers in the night, but this night is the *pressentiment* of a dawn; but this night is never the black night of hopelessness. If forgiveness is without mercenary hope, then it is, however, not without joy.

IV. The Secondarity of Forgiveness: Pity, Gratitude, Repenting

Joy is the symptom of creation. How do we explain therefore that forgiveness always has a character that is more or less "reactive" and in some respect "secondary"? Indeed, this is a fact: forgiveness is in the same situation as is pity, gratitude, or remorse, as opposed to spontaneous, initial, and thoughtful charity. It echoes a scandal that we call sin or offense according to the situation, and it is a way of responding to sin or offense: a paradoxical response, if you please, an unexpected, surprising, and unmerited response, but in the end a response all the same! In order for forgiveness to find a use, it is necessary that someone commit a misdeed. The secondary love named forgiveness is born on the occasion of the misdeed or of the offense, the secondary love named pity is born on the occasion of misery, and the secondary love named gratitude on the occasion of kindness. Secondary love has need of sin in order to forget and to forgive it, has need of misery in order to cry for and to assist it, and has need of kindness in order to recognize it. Kindness, misery, and sin are the three forms of food from which this love is fed. Purely spontaneous love, if we can use these analogies, would be a forgiveness without sin, a pity without misery, and a gratitude without kindness. Pure love has pity for man in general, pity for his finitude, and it loves others for the kindness that it has not received. The relation of love to forgiveness in the ethical order is analogous to the relation of love to pity in the pathic order. Secondary pity, like every emotion, depends on an exterior occasion that gives rise to it or triggers it. We say that the merciful person is "touched"—touched by an encounter, by an incident at which he was the spectator, or by a fortuitous situation. Pity comes to life in the face of the spectacle of the misery of the other, at the sight of his rags, of his frozen garret, of his suffering, and of his solitude. A charity that loves all men, rich or poor, fortunate or unfortunate, and loves them in all circumstances, independently of their dramatic situation or of their tragedies, such charity has no need of adventitious disturbances or of a posteriori provocations. But pity has need of its beggar ... Without the spectacle of rags, pity would perhaps never have the opportunity of having pitied. Precisely in this, pity, like forgiveness, is an event rather than a disposition; in this, pity, an instantaneous and reactive charity, is in opposition to charity that is a type of habitual pity or virtuous habit. It is true, indeed, that we say that mercy supposes a merciful heart, and compassion supposes a compassionate nature; but this is because charity keeps alive their fervor; for charity alone is perpetuity and chronicity. Charity constantly keeps watch and never sleeps; charity always keeps its lamp illuminated. But pity is not so loyal, and its straw fires hardly survive the spectacle that kindles them. The attributes of misery, which in some way constitute its combustible nature, have barely disappeared, and already the brief blaze goes out. Barely is the beggar out of the field of our vision, barely does he have his back turned, and already we have forgotten him. Ephemeral and superficial, the emotion does not persist beyond its cause. Mercy disappears with the misery of the miserable person and pity with the pitiable thing, just as fear normally vanishes with peril! Will pity still love its poor person when he has become rich? As for the excuse, we were saying: no sin—no forgiveness ... And likewise, we should now say: no misery—no pity!—This "secondarity" characterizes gratitude just as much: no kindness—no recognition! That is clear. That pity is a fugitive movement and that gratitude is a loyal attachment does not change anything about their common secondarity. Certainly gratitude is founded on the cordial, good memory of kindness, while forgiveness, on the contrary, in fighting against *ressentiment,* supposes the forgetting of offenses ... But as this forgetting is just as costly, just as difficult, and consequently just as positive as that memory, the two cases are analogous; the secondarity of forgiveness is even more coarse—for gratitude goes at least in the natural direction of dilection, whereas forgiveness has an instinct of hatred to surmount. Forgiveness has need of a material for its work of forgiving, which is agonizing forgetting, and gratitude has need of a material for its labor of gratitude, which is faithful recollection. "Thank you" and "I forgive you" are both second movements responding to a first movement, which is a service rendered or a misdeed committed. Gratitude is born on the condition that there is a benefactor and a kindness, and only on this condition ... Conditions! what does that mean? Would it be that love has need of kindness in order to love? would love not love if it did not receive gifts? And, if you please, what is a love that loves "conditionally"? We respond: this is precisely a conditional love, and thus hypothetical and mixed with reservations; and consequently this is not love. Furthermore, gratitude is not this efferent and purely gratuitous love that never sets conditions or that expects any advantage, and far from loving with a love of recognition as we normally do with our benefactors, it loves much more with an unreciprocated love, as we paradoxically do with our persecutors. In the measure in which cordial gratitude says "thank you" to the benefactor and gratuitously adds the infinite, unevaluable, and imponderable weight of its recognition and its dilection to the sum that is due, in the measure in which the juridical obligation of reimbursement is haloed by love, in which an aureole of gratuity and of superfluity, in which an "in-addition," and, as the Gospel says, a *perisson*,[12] render our quietus more evasive, gratitude, indeed, goes hand in hand with grace, and it is a little "charitable" in its way. But in the measure in which it pays its debt, it pertains to commutative justice, and even mercenariness. It is thus the intermediate between the order of the gratuitous gift and the order of the "tit for tat." Forgiveness that loves the insulting person is in this respect closer to the gratuitous gift, and the gratitude that loves the benefactor is further away. Forgiveness *is* not, however, an absolutely gratuitous gift, since it is necessary to have committed misdeeds in order to merit it. Forgiveness does not concern faultless people; forgiveness is reserved for the privileged category of persecutors.—And finally, repentance itself has need of the misdeed in order to have something for which to repent. The goal of the repentant person is certainly not to love but to be reconciled with himself ... However, repentance, like forgiveness, echoes a contingent initiative of freedom: it is the counterblow to it and furnishes it with a response. Is its reactive and reflexive character not obvious?

Let us first fear that forgiveness, tagging behind the misdeed, is without a day after. A forgiveness that is desirous of forgiving has need of a forgivable act, a misdeed or offense, in a word, something to forgive and a rancor to liquidate. In order to have the occasion to practice the forgetting of offenses, it is still necessary to have been offended ... A forgiveness that neither has anything to forgive, nor someone whom to forgive, a forgiveness

---

12. [*Perisson:* "fullness" or "abundance." See John 10:10: "The thief comes only to steal and kill and destroy; I came that they may have life, and have it abundantly."]

that has nothing to put between its teeth, wastes away and dies of hunger, that is, of indifference. If there were no sinners here below, then what would remain of forgiveness? Will it be necessary to start sinning ceaselessly anew in order to find work for forgiveness so as to avoid unemployment for it?— This is not the whole of it. Just as commiseration discovers the miserable person on the occasion of misery and the person in connection with misfortune, so forgiveness goes from the act to the agent. In order to find its being it makes a detour via manners of being and modalities, or, better yet, it discovers being on the occasion of doing. Even more than the distress for which pity has pity, the forgiven misdeed is a thing. For distress can be vague, impalpable, and somewhat atmospheric, whereas the misdeed is an assignable thing and is always clearly circumscribed. Likewise, the pity that the general lot of all creatures inspires in us was able to become, for Schopenhauer, a type of cosmological sympathy. Forgiveness goes from the singular act to the person, and love itself goes directly and immediately to the person, and goes to work on him without waiting, in order to love him, whether he is unfortunate or guilty. For love is the shortest path from one heart to another. For this, it has need neither of misery, nor of a misdeed, nor in general of the misfortune of existing. Furthermore, it neither runs the risk of becoming enamored with the misdeed in itself like a forgiveness that is greedy for sin or like a lover of injustices, nor loves misery while forgetting the miserable person, like a somewhat complacent pity that discovers its own treasures of tenderness on the occasion of this precious misery, and that feels flattered, in its good conscience, to have an immortal soul.

V. The Organ-Obstacle: Gift and Forgiveness[13]

We were asking: would the person who forgives have loved his neighbor if his neighbor had been beyond reproach? Does the person who forgives not love his own generosity? Okay, let us accept this criticism . . . Perhaps sin, after all, is the form under which we discover another person. Without a doubt, we had need of the effect of relief and of dramatic antithesis in order to love. The negativity of misery, of the misdeed, and of the offense put the finishing touches on our initiation into loving positivity. However, it is necessary for us to distinguish here between merciful initiation and the heartrending

13. [L'organe-obstacle: don et pardon.]

effort of forgiveness. In spite of it all, pity implies the path of least resistance. And forgiveness, itself, does not slip down the inclined plane of easy tenderness. It does not know the sweetness of merciful tears so dear to the sentimentalism of the eighteenth century. Surmounting the obstacle of the sin, forgiveness can only make tearful commiseration . . . Secondarity itself renders forgiveness more meritorious in a sense, and more difficult than love. Forgiveness poses problems that a love without fetters, pushed by favorable winds, by propriety or by reciprocity, could not truly know. Forgiveness, if there is love, would rather be a love that goes against the current, a love that is thwarted and prevented. So the love that we bring to our enemies can be brought closer to the forgiveness of offenses; so the love by which we love the detestable can be comparable to the forgiveness of sins. However, even in this form, the love that is thwarted by the obstacle still has something diffuse in comparison with forgiveness. A love for that which is detestable defiantly loves those who are the most deprived and the least worthy of love, it loves those whom no one loves . . . But no matter what it does, it is not as provocative as the forgiveness of sins. For love after all can love the lovable as much as the detestable; that is not forbidden to it; while forgiveness is specialized in sin, this is its raison d'être, its vocation, and its dear intricacy: it chooses this and prefers this to all the rest! It is forgiveness that poses the true moral dilemma. It is forgiveness that provokes the acute scandal! For forgiveness, it does not suffice to love wicked people in general: forgiveness aims at the thing that the wicked person did, an act that the evil person committed, a wrong that the evil person bears, or a misdeed for which the evil person made himself responsible. Forgiveness does not only forgive the being, it forgives the doing, or rather the having-done. It forgives the ravages of this being; it forgives the being for these ravages. Better yet, it forgives the evildoings of this malevolence, and it forgives malevolence for this evildoing. For the forgiveness of sin is an act that expressly absolves another act. Forgiveness has a misdeed to pardon, an injury to surmount. It must fight against specific repugnances and must combat a particularly energetic aversion. Forgiveness is a heartrending and dramatic decision. And although forgiveness and love for the detestable both rest on the effect of relief and are both *a contrario,* forgiveness makes a more startling contrast with sin than does love with the detestable. And the path from sin to forgiveness itself, too, is infinitely longer in spite of the instantaneity of the decision, since it has to face a rupture and traverse the trial of radical conversion. It does not matter how paradoxical the love that is addressed to the wicked person is—it loves the wicked person after all! Forgiveness, in the moment in which it forgives, has to make a violent effort over itself in order to absolve the guilty person instead of condemning him. Absurd forgiveness of sin is a defiance of penal logic.—It is of little importance finally that forgiveness depends on and is born of an occasion, from the moment that forgiveness opens itself up to the infinite and allows us to glimpse the horizon of grace; and for that, a disproportion, an irrational asymmetry between the sin, however serious it may be, and the immensity of forgiveness suffices.—No less equivocal are the relations of forgiveness and of the gift. Forgiveness is both more and less than the gift: it is evidently less than the gift—for, as far as "giving" is concerned, it "gives" nothing. It is happy to forget the injury; it indeed wants not to take the injury into account; it considers the injury as null. It is necessary to admit that the remission of a debt is a gift that is quite negative. This "gift," if there is a gift, is more metaphorical! The gift, giving at least something, is less reactive and more generous than forgiveness. But maybe here is the place to recall a famous paradox of Kant's: there are cases in which negativity is more positive than positivity, in which Less is more than More! Without a doubt the remission of a debt is not materially a gift; but it is better than that since for the debtor it is the end of a servitude, the relief following anguish, and for the creditor, it is the renunciation of a right. First, here is the point of view of the guilty person: joy is in liberation more than in liberty, in the passage from pain to health more than in health itself. According to Schopenhauer, is not the cessation of pain the sole pleasure to which a man can lay claim? And as there is more joy for the convalescent at the end of his trials than for a man who is doing well, more joy for the prodigal son who has come back to the fold than for the son who is quite wise, or more joy for a repentant tax collector than for nine hundred ninety-nine model children, so the beneficiary of forgiveness, disburdened of a deserved punishment, will know joys that the simple gift procures for no one, and first of all the joy of deliverance at the cessation of oppression. For the guilty person, forgiveness has more intensity and fervor than the gift; for the person who forgives, it is particularly more costly, for it entails a drama and must resolve a crisis. It is not that the gift is necessarily a spontaneous expansion or an effusion without obstacles; it is not that the resources of the giver always overflow in such a generous fashion and by the sole effect of their overabundance; it is not that the generous person scatters his liberalities blindly in the way that nature squanders its flowers and fruits: it happens that the gift implies a sacrifice. But even in this case,

the sacrifice concerns only the possessions and the adhesions of the one giving. The possessor is separated in a costly manner from his possessions; that
is that. On the contrary, forgiveness, which is a gift without something being given, a *datio* without *donum,* must in all cases clear an obstacle and pass
over a barrier. And whether it is a barrier or an obstacle is a function of
whether the issue concerns the injury suffered by the offended person or
the misdeed committed by the sinner: in the first case, the one who forgives
confronts the difficulty that is erected by philauty and self-esteem, and by
the vindictive instinct and passion; in the second case, he meets the prejudices of a narrow morality that is founded on justice alone. In neither the
first nor the second case is it a matter of the property of a proprietor. The
one forgiving has need of all his courage in order to sacrifice not a part of
his possessions but his being itself, and even more to brave social taboos,
to challenge the duty to punish, and to support himself in so-called moral
dilemmas. We will see how the decision to forgive opposes the hyperbolic
paradox of *a total gift* to the partitive gesture of giving, otherwise referred
to as offering this or that. Aristotle, himself, knew the gift; but only the Bible
truly knew forgiveness.

VI. Because Innocent, Even Though Guilty, Because Guilty. Gratuitous Forgiveness.

This secondarity subordinates forgiveness in the eyes of those alone who
misjudge the "dialectical" function of it. The sharp contradiction of the inexcusable is, in some manner, the trampoline from which forgiveness takes
its *élan* in order to transfigure the guilty person. Forgiveness is rendered pa-
thetically possible by the very antithesis that prevents it.

1. In the first place, can we say that forgiveness implies the positive,
simple, and direct motivation of the *Because*? Does the normal, slippery etiology according to which the effect is in direct proportion to the cause apply
to forgiveness? Not by a long shot! The relationship of forgiveness to the excuse is the same, in this sense, as the relationship of love to esteem. Esteem
appreciates *because,* and it therefore has its reasons for that; the motive of
esteem is called the estimable. The man gifted with reason proportions his
esteem to the merits of the estimable thing. The fervor of the one thing is
given out according to the value of the other. It is thus that a man who measures his fervor esteems the things of median value a little bit, precious

things passionately, and vile things not at all. Love based on esteem, too, claims to legalize itself with empirical explanations. It would love its beloved because this beloved is "lovable," which is to say, worthy of love; the median *kindness* is the cause of small loves or, if you please, the motive behind our daily passing fancies. And supreme *lovability* is the cause of sovereign Love. In Platonic dogmatism, for example, as in theological dogmatism, it goes without saying that preference prefers that which is prefer*able*, *aireton*,[14] which is to say, it chooses that which is morally choos*able* and that which is the supreme elig*ible*. So justice gets something out of these recompenses! Such is, after all, the case with pity, whose secondarity seemed to us analogous with the secondarity of forgiveness; it now appears that the relation of forgiveness with the misdeed is in no way comparable to that of pity with misery. Sin is the material for forgiveness, but it is not the "cause" of it. Cause—it would rather be the cause of rancor! Misery, on the other hand, is indeed the grounds for pity very much as danger is the grounds for fear, and the receiving of a bachelor's degree is the grounds for the joy of the candidate. And even more, terror, when it is justified, is explained by what is terrible, just as pity is explained by what is pitiable. Actually, pity is an emotion whereas forgiveness is an act, and this emotion is of the same meaning and of the same sign as its cause. There is a type of relation and a relative resemblance between distress and pity. But between the misdeed and the absolution of the misdeed, there is rather antithesis, shocking collision, and scandalous contradiction. There, cause, if there is a cause, operates like a foil, and *a contrario*. What is true is that the effect can be disproportionate to the grounds; the grounds are no more than a pretext or an occasional cause in an unreasonable etiology. The sight of misery releases the indivisible, impulsive, and unreasoned *élan* of commiseration—but, for all that, the causal link does not disappear. To love one's neighbor because he is "lovable" or because he is unfortunate is, in both cases, to love "because." In all cases, the Because removes the raison d'être of forgiveness. When the guilty person is exonerated, which is to say, proven and recognized as innocent, then the task

14. [*Aireton:* "choiceworthy."] Aristotle also says: *diokton* (*Nicomachean Ethics,* 1097a32). ["We say that an end pursued in its own right is more complete than an end pursued because of something else, that an end that is never choiceworthy because of something else is more complete than ends that are choiceworthy both in their own right and because of this end. Hence an end that is always choiceworthy in its own right never because of something else, is complete without qualification." *Nicomachean Ethics,* trans. Terence Irwin, 2nd ed. (Indianapolis: Hackett, 1999), book 1, chapter 7, §4.]

is all done and forgiveness finds itself without a job. The innocent person does not have need of our forgiveness and has no need of our nobility of soul; he requires only that justice be done. In this case, the magnanimous person would be as ridiculous as a charitable benefactor giving away as alms the salary of his employee, to which the salaried employee has full rights. What good, then, is forgiveness? whom does it forgive? and for which misdeeds? If it is suitable to call esteem the so-called love that we feel for the lovable, then it is suitable to label the so-called forgiveness that we "grant" to the innocent person, the excuse.

2. Neither love nor forgiveness being truly "because," we are tempted to say that love loves *even though,* and that forgiveness all the more so forgives *even though;* the being who is loved and the misdeed that is forgiven, indeed, are not strictly speaking the reason for forgiveness and for love; they are much more the anti-reason and even sometimes insanity. In principle, they would be the obstacle to this forgiveness and to this love. Must we here replace "causality" with "concession"? In as much as it is relative to its negation and to a resistance, Merit, by its very definition, supposes this "concessionary" *Despite* ... In this respect, fidelity is without a doubt the prime example of "concessive" sentiment. For fidelity is always, in one form or another, fidelity-despite, fidelity despite becoming and the disaffection that this becoming encourages, fidelity in spite of the deceiving about-faces of the partner, fidelity through the trials that the inconsistency of our neighbor imposes on us, and the fidelity of a faithful man against winds and tides. *To maintain* fidelity, *to stay* intransigent among caprices, *to keep* one's faith among renegades, such are the forms under which the constancy of virtue-despite is affirmed.—Are forgiveness and love, despite, too? And, for example, is forgiveness despite the misdeed, is altruism despite the ego, in the very sense in which courage is courageous despite danger and in relation to danger? Between the misdeed and forgiveness, there is the barrier of rancor, which is the condition of forgiveness (for in order to forgive, we must first remember), just as there is the barrier of fear between danger and courage, and just as there is a barrier of egoism between the ego and sacrifice. For it is fear that makes courage and egoism that makes disinterestedness! Does forgiveness have a vocation other than surmounting a negativity? It is the opposite that is true; forgiveness is not only contra, but also for. The "although" always implies a "because" which is the recto of this verso and the "obverse" of this reverse, a because of which it is, in its way, like an implied

inversion. *"Even-though-detestable"* implicitly implies *"because-lovable."* The "concession" is, then, a shameful etiology and an ideological causality that does not dare to say its name . . . When we profess love for someone, *even if* it is someone detestable, *even if* he is odious, *despite* his stupidity and wickedness, we indirectly suggest this: the detestable person is normally worthy of hatred, and consequently, by right, the lovable person alone deserves to inspire love. With kindness being the respectable and natural grounds for all love, the model child theoretically should love only what is lovable and detest what is detestable. And if however, if nevertheless, if *despite everything* we persist in scandalously loving what we logically should hate, this love of what is detestable, because it is love despite the obstacle, confirms the love of the lovable, far from invalidating it. Unmerited and unmotivated love, far from refuting love that is reasonable, normal, and motivated, is an homage to this love. The paradox is an homage to common sense. Is the even though not nascent paradoxology? The antithesis of the lovable and the detestable by itself implies the most reassuring system of reference and the most ordinary tables of values. And consequently, the even though tacitly supposes, as if self-evidently, the preexistence of the object that does or does not carry these values. It is thus necessary to admit a type of inexplicable dissonance between the value worthy of love and absurd love, an irrational dissonance that finds an echo in the "concession" itself. We love that which we *should* hate!—And not only does the Despite lead to a virtual Because that gives it all of its meaning, but, even more, the Despite immediately announces unwillingness and bad grace, lack of warmth, and the absence of enthusiasm and spontaneity. In sum, is this not the concessive and consequently resigned style of Leibnizian optimism? Leibniz's sage, indeed, adapts to a necessary evil against which God himself could do nothing, and of which God made merely the least evil, for the best world is only the one that is the least bad. The sage employs a good heart against bad luck. The sage will be in a good mood *even so,* despite the misery of finitude; but this "even so" quells an *Alas* with difficulty! Love-despite, too, consents to loving *even so.* I love you even though you are detestable . . . What does this mean? Would it be that effectively there are beings who are worthy of being hated? Would it be that in my nobility of soul, and despite the protests of evidence, I indeed want to condescend to closing my eyes to their faults? The magnanimous person deigns to love wicked people, notwithstanding all the reasons that he believes to have for hating them. The *quamvis*[15] expresses here the immensity of the concession and the clemency of the great lord rather than spontaneous love. One should say thank you to the great master for the honor that he gives to the quite unworthy and very humble object of his love. Who would not feel the price of such a sacrifice? who would not be flattered by it? Certainly the most meritorious and the most disinterested love is the one that loves despite the resistance of an obstacle; still, it is necessary that it be not overly aware of the obstacle, for love is not a duty. And a love that would contemplate too much about defeating resistance would end up by no longer distinguishing itself from the Categorical Imperative. What would you think of the lover who said to his beloved: you are ugly, stupid, and wicked, but nonetheless I love you? Without a doubt, you would respond that this is a quite unsettling lucidity and a very strange halfheartedness. And with justification, you would think that this love is too full of reproaches to be a sincere love, that it is a little forced, that the heart is not in it,[16] and that it loves reluctantly.[17] A love that loves with such bad grace, that does such severe violence to itself, that confesses with such a regrettable assiduity, and that enumerates with such a visible complaisance the obstacles *despite* which it condescends to love is a love that is almost necessarily suspect. Would we give the name "love" to a charity that routinely sets out, by the spirit of simple mortification, to "love" the most repugnant things, and that specializes exclusively in the love of evil and envious people and of creeps and ne'er-do-wells? The ascetic and the specialist in creeps indirectly confess, but we cannot do more, that alone the lovable is worthy of our love. This nuance of *unwillingness* is equally perceptible in the will to stay faithful nonetheless, in spite of all the deceptions and despite all the refutations of experience. Unshakable fidelity, too, is also an implicit defeat and a mute confession. The faithful person recognizes, without saying it, that in the behavior of others there would be something that frees him from his word of honor. The unfailing friend prides himself on never having disowned the one whom he had many reasons to disown, the one for whom he would have been excusable one thousand times over for disowning, the one who would have so merited being betrayed. And the more that the attachment is unmerited and absurd, all the more desperately does the faithful person cling, and the more he scores a point of honor for

15. [Although.]
16. [*Le coeur n'y est pas.*]
17. [*À contrecoeur.*]

himself in holding to the impossibility of his commitment. This fidelity that nothing discourages is also a reproach! Besides, fidelity, by its obstinate refusal of all evolution, allies itself much more with rancor than with forgiveness. But forgiveness especially, in spite of what we might believe, does not forgive "despite." Strictly speaking, it does not forgive *notwithstanding the obstacle.* But it no more forgives just because the innocence of the accused has been proven: we have shown that in this case it would serve no purpose. It is the excuse, we were saying, that establishes the nonculpability of the man who is wrongly considered as guilty. Forgiveness, indeed, goes against the stream of the misdeed. However, forgiveness does not forgive solely the guilty person even though he is guilty. A forgiveness-"despite" would, indeed, occur grudgingly and with ill will, as with a judge who, without conviction, forces himself toward leniency and who acquits the accused with a heavy heart. Forgiveness-despite would be the child of misfortune, since it is linked to the misery of the obstacle . . . Here, again, the even though leads us to the because. To plead for a forgiveness-despite is tacitly to suppose that a forgiveness that is granted to the innocent person is alone normal and natural and alone goes without saying. Thus, a forgiveness that is granted to the guilty person would be a type of particularly meritorious sporting achievement. But is forgiveness of the innocent person not an absurdity?

3. Since forgiveness forgives the accused person neither *because he is innocent* (forgiveness would then be superfluous), nor *even though* he is guilty, the only possibility that remains is that forgiveness forgives the accused precisely *because he is guilty.* And in a wholly analogous fashion, it would be necessary to say that since love loves its beloved neither because he is lovable (love would then be esteem), nor although he is detestable (love, then, would be begrudging and would confirm the love of the lovable), the only possibility that remains is that love loves its beloved . . . *precisely because* he is detestable! But just as a moment ago the even-though implied and confirmed the because, likewise and reciprocally, the because can now have the correlative even-though as a consequence; the one who loves his beloved because he is detestable, and for this reason alone, can arrive at loving him even though he is lovable, and excuses himself, and perhaps feels some confusion, just as if in this backward world kindness were paradoxically a reason for not loving, and vice versa wickedness were an indirect reason for loving, as if merit were an obstacle to love! This complication with an exponent is nothing other than complaisance and coquetry, and it flows from an etiology that is counter to nature, of which the following is the profession of

faith: I love him because it contradicts love, because he is not worthy of being loved. To love an object that contradicts the relation of love—here already is a paradoxical chiasmus; for it is already paradoxical that the recipient of love merits being hated, but to make such a contradiction the very reason for loving, that takes the cake! This is scandalous! Is it not a type of insolence to confer the dignity of grounds and cause upon that which is absurd? This irritating and even somewhat provocative because is a challenge to common sense. After the normal and natural, simple and direct, and foreseen and awaited because, which is, as is expected, the because of love motivated by what is lovable, here is the slightly cynical because of scandalous love. After the model child here is the perverse child, the one who loves what is detestable on purpose and uniquely because it is detestable, and by virtue of a formal preference for everything forbidden or illegal. Illegal, the love of the detestable? All the better! the perverse child would reply. The perverse child makes things worse for himself, doubles the paradox, and abounds in scandal. We see the cynical *quia*[18] that is not limited to fighting the repulsion that the detestable inspires in every normal man. For this combat rather represents the part of the *quamvis* that expresses a surmounted disgust, the cleared obstacle, and overtaken prejudices . . . No! the cynical *quia* does not fight against aversion; it transforms aversion into attraction. And the obstacle? it searches it out. Difficulties? it demands them. The love of the detestable is no longer a "concession" for it, but rather a vocation. If the *quamvis* is a confession of a difficulty, then the *quia* proclaims, against all good sense, that this difficulty is an additional ability. Between *amo quamvis odiosum* and *amo quia odiosum,* there is all the distance that exists between asceticism and masochism—the former surmounts pain and the latter makes pain into pleasure. Whereas the ascetic belief in pain endures suffering valiantly, the masochistic belief in pain acquires the taste of pain and treats it as an end in itself. The object of general repulsion has to remain repulsive for the ascetic who trains himself to tolerate it, whereas it has become attractive for the masochistic perversion. Consequently, if the ascetic who endures pain beats records of endurance and of analgesia, then the masochist who takes pleasure in this pain beats all the records of the former. In forgiveness, there is an aspect of moral athleticism. This is the reason for holding a grudge against the sinner, who is absurdly the reason for forgiving! Forgiveness forgives only the guilty person, and only because the guilty

18. [Because.]

person is guilty, and insofar as he is guilty—for forgiveness evidently would not have anything to forgive if the accused were innocent; more still than love, it is specialized in evil. Indeed, forgiveness is expressly and occasionally necessitated by the contingencies of sin, whereas love is linked to the existence of the wicked person.—But, in reaction to the motivated because, is this not going a little too far in the direction of the "cynical" because? To say that forgiveness forgives the sinner on account of the sin of the sinner and in honor of the sin itself is, indeed, to express oneself as if the one who forgives had a taste for guilt in itself and as if forgiveness had need of its guilty person. And this is to allow it to be understood that the person forgiving is perhaps a lover of guilty people, a sort of collector, and that he searches out guilty people like a maniac, in order to give himself the pleasure of forgiving them and, all in all, in order to be of use: in order to have someone to forgive for something. Do sinners not gratuitously offer us the occasion to feel ourselves virtuous, magnanimous, and beyond reproach? The maniac has such a calling for this providential sin that if necessary he would invent it there where it does not exist. For him, forgiveness is more of a sport than a cruel ascesis. It is thus that champions of sacrifice search out lepers on purpose in order to embrace them and thus to beat all the records of charity. It is thus that women in high society search out poor people because they are inspired by good works, a misery here to be coddled, a distress over there to be cuddled. They search out precious beggars of which their benevolence and their professional compassion have need, just as Frederick II[19] looked for tall men so as to make grenadiers out of them. Is this complaisance not a derision?

4. In reality, forgiveness is beyond the *quia* just as it is beyond the *quamvis*. In this respect, forgiveness is in the same situation as faith and love. Faith is neither exclusively because, nor unilaterally even though. In no way does faith believe because: neither because the article of faith is proven and demonstrated to be reasonable or only plausible (*credo quia credibile*)—for if there were such an apodictic certainty in these matters, then faith would be superfluous and even a little ridiculous; nor because the article of belief is unbelievable or undemonstrable (*credo quia absurdum*).[20] It is thus that

19. [Frederick the Great, who ruled Prussia from 1740 to 1786.]

20. [This is a reference to a famous thought generally attributed to Tertullian (160–220 CE), but it really represents a misquotation (Jankélévitch was by no means the originator) of verse 4 of chapter 5 of Tertullian's *De Carne Christi* (On the Flesh of Christ). The passage actually reads: "*credibile est, quia ineptum est.*"]

love loves the beloved neither because it is lovable (*amo quia amabilis*)—for it would thus be only esteem, nor because it is detestable (*amo quia odiosus*). It is thus that forgiveness forgives neither because the accused is innocent (*ignosco quia innocens*)—for forgiveness would thus be only an excuse, nor expressly because he is guilty (*ignosco quia peccans*). In no way, either, does faith believe even though: neither even though the thing believed is absurd (*credo quamvis absurdum*), nor even though it is believable (*credo quamvis credibile*). The first "although," as we showed, refers to a latent because. Under the *quamvis absurdum,* there is a very normal *quia credibile.* For the one who believes "although" absurd or "in spite of" the absurdity of this absurd thing indirectly admits by this that absurdity would rather be a motive for incredulity or an obstacle to credence. In allowing the paradoxical and somewhat desperate character of his fidelity to show through, he recognizes, without saying it, that absurdity is normally a reason for mistrusting and not a reason for believing. Absurdity is more of a reason not to believe, and even to believe the contrary! Such is what the principle of the Excluded Middle requires. This fidelity is, then, faithful despite mistrust; this concession is, then, an indirect homage to the logic of common sense. If the *quia absurdum* is a profession of faith, and a profession that is a little cynical, then the *quamvis absurdum* is rather a confession . . . The latter is an admission, whereas the former is a challenge! And as for the other *quamvis*—I believe, "even though" it is reasonable—it is nothing more than an affectation and a simple overbidding; it feigns admitting that credibility is an obstacle to belief! Is this not a shocking and scandalous exaggeration? And in the end, love, like faith, impugns the two "despites" as much as it impugns the two opposite "becauses." In not loving the beloved because of his "kindness," love does not love the beloved despite his odious character (*amo quamvis odiosus*), either. In not loving the beloved because of his detestable character, it does not love him despite his goodness (*amo quamvis amabilis*), either; spontaneous love is beyond these restrictions and these effects of relief.— Let us show how faith, love, and forgiveness in particular are equally foreign to the two opposite "becauses." Are the normal because and the cynical because not two equivalent varieties of one same etiology? A *quamvis* transformed into *quia* does not at all differ from the direct *quia.* "I believe because that is absurd . . ." The thesis is absurd? All the more reason! All the less reason, all the more reason! It is, then, "insanity," or at least counterreason, or at least the absence of reason that is reason. Irrationalism, thus, in the measure in which it is the philosophy of *reason without reasons,* is more of a reverse rationalism than a true suprarationalism. Right side out or backward, is not rationalism always rationalism? To make a reason out of the objection or to make an objection out of reason is simply to invert the true and the false and to walk on one's hands; this is not to institute a revolutionary metalogic beyond the logic of identity. So, in an upside-down world, but one that is not profoundly disrupted, superficial paradoxes and false scandals in general turn into bourgeois conformism and into orthodoxy: if the ugly is beautiful, then the beautiful is ugly, and a nocturnal dogmatism succeeds diurnal dogmatism; if pleasure is pain, then pain is pleasure, and masochism, which is an inverted or perverted hedonism, succeeds what is contradictory to it. And likewise, antireason, far from opening onto the folly of faith, reverts to this reason that it simply inverted. In all this, it is not a matter of a conversion to the wholly-other-order of the true novelty; it is a matter, at the very most, of an inversion, or maybe of a perversion. Is absurdity directly and in itself a reason for believing? That would still be too simple, and Pascal himself does not even go that far. For it is not necessary to exaggerate anything! First, for Pascal, the object of faith is not unilaterally absurd or a univocal absurdity; it is essentially equivocal. God is not absolutely hidden, but almost hidden, *fere absconditus,* half hidden, and consequently veiled.[21] He shows himself in a dubious manner and conceals himself under revelatory equivocations; he is proven and unproven. We know what Pascal says about the deceptive imagination: "It would be an infallible rule of truth, if it were the infallible one of the lie."[22] For it would suffice to take the opposite view of it in order to reestablish this truth. According to Pascal, the Scriptures do not want to trick us; they want to test us, and they are addressed to those for whom improbability and contradiction are not always objections but in certain cases

21. Isaiah 45:15 ["Truly, thou art a God who hidest thyself"]. Cf. Pascal, *Lettres à Mlle. de Roannez* (1656), Brunschvicg, pp. 214–15. *Pensées,* IV, 228; VIII, 557, 559, 575, 576, 578, 585, 588. [The only passages from Pascal's *Pensées* that are similar to the aforementioned passage are paragraphs 584—which Jankélévitch does not cite—and 585. §584: *"That God has willed to hide Himself* . . . God being thus hidden, every religion which does not affirm that God is hidden, is not true; and every religion which does not give the reason of it, is not instructive. Our religion does all this: *Vere tu es Deus absconditus."* §585: "Thus, it is not only fair, but advantageous to us, that God be partly hidden and partly revealed; since it is equally dangerous to man to know God without knowing his own wretchedness, and to know his own wretchedness without knowing God." *Pascal's Pensées,* intro. by T. S. Eliot, trans. W. F. Trotter (New York: Dutton, 1958), 161–62.]

22. Pascal, *Pensées,* §82. ["For it would be an infallible rule of truth, if it were an infallible rule of falsehood." *Pascal's Pensées,* 24.]

supplementary proofs: "all the more reasons"! Now, the object of faith is something indemonstrable that can sometimes appear probable. This very ambiguity prevents fideism from turning into "absurdism," or put in a different way, into a systematized absurd. And just as ambiguity, in its turn, is infinitely ambiguous, just as ambiguity is ambiguous and unambiguous at the same time, it itself thwarts the systematization of an "ambiguism." The amphibole itself is amphibolically amphibolical . . . But rightly, Pascalian faith is dialectically torn between the provocative *quia* and everyone's *quamvis*, between scandalous profession and agonizing confession; in one respect, it professes contradiction, endorses all the reproaches of obscurity, and defies and braves common sense; but in one way it stays hopelessly faithful *in spite of* the absurd, as if a vague rationalist nostalgia were holding it back; and it remains, by this very confession, in a position of weakness, which is to say, on the defensive. For the one who *believes despite* resists the temptation not to believe, and similarly the one who *loves despite* reacts and fights against the temptation not to love. Happily, the one who believes despite is aided somewhat by the vaguely convincing marks of faith: the one who believed *quia absurdum,* and afterward began to believe *quamvis absurdum,* will then begin to believe secondarily *quia credibile*! What is beyond is obscure, but, thank God, only halfway . . . It would be better still if this clear-obscure were completely clear!—Pure love, like faith, lies beyond the two becauses. Also, we have to dismiss love motivated by merit and love motivated by demerit, motivated love and countermotivated love, without pronouncing in favor of either. Love your enemies, say, it is true, the Sermon on the Mount, and Isaiah before it: *agapate tous echthrous.*[23] What does this mean? Must I love only my enemies? Certainly not, Jesus did not want to say with that: Love only your enemies, and for the sole reason that they are your enemies, for no other reason than because they detest you and persecute you. For such a love would be nothing other than masochism, morose delight,[24] and passion of the martyr. Is a man who thirsts for persecution, a man in love with his torturers, an "underground" man, as Dostoevsky calls him, more disinterested than another? Is the taste for humiliation as gratuitous as a movement of charity? Certainly nothing is less pure than this love whose grounds are too shameful to mention; and nothing is more impure than this love whose grounds are called groundless. Love your enemies,

---

23. [See Matthew 5:44; Luke 6:27; Isaiah 62:44.]

24. [In French, in the original; it refers to the Latin *delectatio morose.*]

then, because that is decidedly sublime, but, out of grace, love your friends
a little. You have to love those who detest you, but this is not a reason for de-
testing those who love you! Allow us sometimes the right to prefer the preferable, to love very naively and very humbly that which is lovable . . . We
should not have prejudices, even against what is worthy of being loved! The
fact that our partner is worthy of love is not, all the same, a reason for having a grudge against him! It is not necessary to fall from one extreme into
another or to renounce the simple and direct complaisance toward the merits of the beloved for backward complaisance. No, simply to have changed
complaisance, that would not be worth the trouble. Maybe the Gospels only
wanted to say this: in view of the decay and the impurity of the psychosomatic being, his finitude, his lamentable weakness, and his egoism, we are
never certain that a lover who gets something in return does not obey motives of vanity and self-esteem. The creature is so dominated by concupiscence and personal interest and is so susceptible to flattery that every reciprocal and shared love is a priori suspect. Better yet, let us say that when we
love the lover, the friend, or what is lovable, it is impossible to affirm that
the love goes effectively to the partner, and that flattering vanity, the merits
of the beloved, or very simply tribal solidarity have nothing to do with it.
Would the love that the beloved feels, or said otherwise, the love for the
lover, not by chance be satisfied self-esteem? Is love for the heir, supposing
that it is sincere and innocent, not indiscernible from love for the inheri-
tance? Kant often said that we are never assured that a duty accomplished
out of duty but *with pleasure* is not a duty accomplished *for pleasure.*[25] In
this case, it is "pathology" that is at issue. Just as we cannot know if an intention is pure, so a lover who loves his own lover perhaps would seem to
obey a type of justice of mutuality . . . What criteria, then, would permit us
to distinguish the equilibrium of commutation from pure and simple mercenariness? There where we were expecting disinterestedness, we suspect
an ulterior motive of exchange. To love those who love us, *agapan tous
agapōntas,* to detest those who detest us, *misein ton echthron,* to repay each
person in kind, as much as he merits it, to give to each person an eye for an
eye and a tooth for tooth, or to give each person the same thing back again,
this is within reach of those with souls of iron and lead. This is not to go

25. [See the first two paragraphs in the second section—entitled "Transition from the Pop-
ular Moral Philosophy to the Metaphysics of Morals"—of Kant's *Foundations of the Metaphysics of Morals.*]

beyond talion justice; it is to give in order to receive, *ina apolabōsin ta isa perisson,* and consequently, to lend so that the gift is given back to us. According to the Gospel of Luke, if you do good to those who do good to you, where will the "willing" be? *Ean agathopoiēte tous agathopoiountos poia humin charis estin;*[26] grace begins with the *surplus,* the *perisson.*[27] If you do good to those who do you bad, and if you bless those who curse you without hoping for anything in return, *mēden a pelpizontes,* then very well! In these chiasmuses, the paradoxical, supernatural, and miraculous asymmetries of charity become clear. It is natural to greet honorable citizens, but it is supernatural to greet, as did Fevronia of Kitezh,[28] the drunk and miserable person who betrayed you.—However, love does not systematically take the opposite view of motivated love, for in this case it would be as alienated as this love. Love for the friend yields the first position to love for the enemy. But the Sermon on the Mount does not say that hatred for the enemy has to give way to hatred for the friend; for, in general, it is necessary to love everyone, friends and enemies, and not to hate anyone, neither enemies nor friends. The Sermon on the Mount does not say that it is necessary to detest one's brother; it says that it is not necessary to love *only* one's brother, *tous del-*

26. Luke 6:27–35 ["But I say to you that hear, Love your enemies, do good to those who hate you, bless those who curse you, pray for those who abuse you. To him who strikes you on the cheek, offer the other also; and from him who takes away your coat do not withhold even your shirt. Give to everyone who begs from you; and of him who takes away your goods do not ask them again. And as you wish that men would do to you, do so to them." "If you love those who love you, what credit is that to you? For even sinners love those who love them. And if you do good to those who do good to you, what credit is that to you? For even sinners do the same. And if you lend to those from whom you hope to receive, what credit is that to you? Even sinners lend to sinners, to receive as much again. But love your enemies, and do good, and lend expecting nothing in return; and your reward will be great, and you will be sons of the Most High; for he is kind to the ungrateful and the selfish."]; Matthew 5:43–47 ["You have heard that it was said 'You shall love your neighbor and hate your enemy.' But I say to you, Love your enemies and pray for those who prosecute you so that you may be sons of your Father who is in heaven; for he makes his sun rise on the evil and on the good and sends rain on the just and the unjust. For if you love those who love you, what reward have you? Do not even tax collectors do the same? And if you salute only your brethren, what more are you doing than others? Do not even the Gentiles do the same?"].

27. Matthew 5:47. ["And if you salute only your brethren, what more are you doing than others? Do not even the Gentiles do the same?"]

28. [Rimsky-Korsakov, *The Legend of the Invisible City of Kitezh,* an opera in four acts, from 1907, to which Jankélévitch makes frequent reference.]

phous monon,[29] and that we should surround the neighbor (*ton plēsion sou*) and those not so close to us in the same love. Indeed, a sincere love is always praiseworthy, whoever the beloved may be, and even if the loved one merits it (which is a saddening irony, one that stems from our misery)! A love, even a repaid love, is better than the "law of the fist" and everyone-for-himself. All that we can say is that unreciprocal or unilateral love, being the most meritorious, is also the most characteristic: when love is asymmetrical there is an additional chance that we are dealing with a disinterested lover. If, then, man is reduced to loving what is detestable in order to prove a sincere disinterestedness, then it is by reason of his congenital frivolity and his incurable superficiality. Also, we can conceive, at the limit, of a state of rights that would render the chiasmus useless: in a city of grace, in a republic of pure spirits in which all men would be brothers and would love one another, in which universal proximity would bring together the most distant people to make neighbors out of them, in such an ideal city, the love that we bring to our enemies would no longer have a raison d'être. With no one, indeed, being the enemy of anybody anymore, no one would have to do himself the violence of loving what is detestable. Even better, in the purity of a transparent world in which souls are not only close to each other but present to everyone, no one knows what is an ulterior motive any longer, and hypocrisy is unknown. All love is thus of genuine worth. Why would the sincerity of a shared love be placed in doubt? This is not all: even in our world of enmity that is dug full of hiding places and subterranean galleries, it happens that a humble and naïve mutual love authentically wins the upper hand over the false heroism and the false saintliness of an unreciprocated charity. When hyperbolical charity itself becomes embroiled in the complications of the exponent of conscience, and muddled in the subtleties of virtuistic complaisance and of affection, then it is mutual love that is the true, pure love!

The same goes for forgiveness as for love. This is why Christ's Sixth Commandment, which prescribes love for enemies, is linked to the Fifth Commandment, which proscribes the commutative *anti* of the talion. Forgiveness transcends every causality, and initially the most stereotypical causality, the one that is at work in the most conservative reactions of the vengeance reflex or of remuneration that is just. The surprising and supernatural gesture, the counter-to-nature gesture of forgiveness inhibits the

29. Matthew 5:47.

natural and long-anticipated reaction that makes us respond to the same with the same and that is the servile echo and stupid counterpunch to sin. The generous man unilaterally decides that the scandal will remain uncompensated, the injustice unredeemed, the offense unexpiated, and that the excess that is imputable to wicked pleonexy will not be leveled. It is absurd to profess contradiction, but it is scandalous to defy the moral axiom of corrective justice; and reciprocally, it is reasonable to honor the principle of identity, but it is also just to annihilate that which should not be. In opposition to the eye-for-an-eye of the Decalogue, the Sermon on the Mount commands us to turn the other cheek; that is to say, far from leveling the injustice that sticks out, it doubles the scandal scandalously. In opposition to justice, forgiveness claims neither to neutralize the disequilibrium of pleonexy, nor to compensate the asymmetry of the sin. But, on the contrary, it aggravates this asymmetry and this disequilibrium, and in aggravating them, it cures them. In its way, forgiveness annuls sin, not literally and by inverting the direction of evil through punishment, and by returning violence to the violent person, like a player who sends the ball back to his partner, but rather by inverting and converting at the same time the intentional quality of the act and the direction. An unforeseen development, one that is paradoxical above all! The generous person gives back the good that he did not receive in place of the evil that he received. He exchanges an offering of love for the bad behavior of malevolence; he thus makes himself capable not only of neutralizing the evil act but of reforming, of transfiguring, of converting the malevolent intention. This chance of amelioration carries a risk, indeed! Let us here distinguish between four attitudes: the first two are intensifications, the last two are chiasmuses. Expiation returns *Evil for Evil,* as justice would have it; Gratitude returns *Good for Good,* and, consequently, it is gracious justice or just grace, just charity. Ingratitude returns *Evil for Good,* and it is thus grace in reverse, which is wickedness. Finally, forgiveness, returning *Good for Evil,* represents that right-side-out grace of which Ingratitude is the symmetrical opposite.—But Good-for-Evil itself can be a serious hypocrisy, a subtle transaction, and an interested speculation if it proceeds purposely from a desire to maintain I do not know what impossibility or to succeed at I do not know what tour de force. Forgiveness that forgives expressly for the pleasure of appearing sublime or for the amendment of the guilty person is a simple calculation. Forgiveness never forgives because: neither because there is innocence, nor because there is a misdeed. If the accused is innocent, then it is the innocence that achieves everything and that vindicates itself without the help of anyone; in this case, forgiveness no longer has anything to do. And if the accused is guilty? If he is guilty, the misdeed of this guilty person is evidently, by definition itself, the primary material of forgiveness and the raison d'être of forgiveness. The more egregious the misdeed is, the more offensive the offense is, then all the more is forgiveness irreplaceable. In the city of grace, there would evidently be nothing to forgive, or at the very most a few small misunderstandings that are dissipated just as quickly as they are formed, like little clouds in an unchanging serene azure. So, if you wish, the misdeed is then the condition without which there would be no forgiveness. In this sense, forgiveness has "need" of the misdeed; without the misdeed, the very word *forgiveness* would not exist! But that does not at all mean that forgiveness has a predilection expressly for the misdeed. In reality, forgiveness does not forgive the misdeed as much as it forgives the guilty person. It is thus that gracious gratitude is addressed to the benefactor beyond the beneficence; if it simply said thank you for the gift, then it would be nothing more than a symbolic and conventional manner of being debt-free and a way of repaying the debt, not by giving back the sum itself, but by pronouncing a ritual, magic word. Gratitude would then be a simple appendix to justice, a justice that is a little evasive around the core of strict justice. But, indeed, gratitude aims at the being of the person beyond the having, at the ipseity of the donor beyond the given thing. Open to an infinite horizon, gratitude is the equal not only of a benefit, nor only of a beneficence, but of a benevolence for which there exists no quietus; for the beneficiary of a kindness that nothing exhausts or compensates, such a beneficiary is an eternal debtor. Ingratitude, under this relation, is not strictly speaking "unjust"; it gave what it owed, and what it does not give, i.e., gratuitous recognition, is exactly that which it is not required to give! And in the same way, love for the wicked person is not love of the wickedness of this wicked person; for in that case, it would be more of a diabolical perversity than a love. Love for the wicked person is quite simply love of the man himself, love of the man who is the most difficult person to love. When the beloved is completely disinherited, deprived of every lovable quality and of every virtue that can justify the attachment, when there is no hope of love in sight and when the love that we persist in bringing to him nevertheless is an unmotivated love, when, in the end, we love the beloved without reason and without attraction, then perhaps it is the moment to say: my love is addressed to the pure hominity of the man and to the naked ipseity of his person in general. And likewise, in the end, the forgiveness of sin is not, strictly speaking, a quietus granted to the sin of this sinner, but truly a grace accorded to the sinner of this sin. In no way is it a matter of approving or admiring the evil of guilt.[30] The one who forgives, far from rallying around evil, decides instead not to imitate it, not to resemble it in any way, and without having expressly willed it, to negate it with the sole purity of a silent love. Far from loving the guilty person *because of* his misdeed in forgiving him *despite* the misdeed, the person who forgives forgives the guilty person *because* of the misdeed, and he loves the guilty person *despite* this misdeed. Sadism cuts out the wickedness of the wicked person in order to love it separately, by virtue of a chosen love and of a scandalous preference; but forgiveness, by contrast, undividedly loves this wicked person, who after all is a person; it manages to recognize immediately the poor man in this guilty person and the misery of the human condition in this sin.

VII. Neither Despite, Nor Because. At the Same Time Because and Despite.

The ironic contradiction of the *quia* and the *quamvis* is, then, infinitely more acute in the case of forgiveness than in the case of faith. For faith, for the believer, is absurd only in a manner of speaking and in the perspective of common sense. According to Saint Paul, the folly of faith is profoundly reasonable even though it seems unreasonable. The misdeed, on the contrary, is essentially bad; the irrationality of this scandal resists exegesis and anthropodicy. The misdeed is nourishment for forgiveness, but it is also an obstacle to it; the misdeed is the material for forgiveness, but at the same time it is also the antithesis of it. It serves, so to speak, as a foil for it. Forgiveness forgives, thus, *a contrario* and absolves the sin by taking its *élan* from the trampoline of this contradictory thing. The antithesis does not thus engender antipathy, even though it does not at all imply sympathy . . . In one sense, the person who forgives very much has "need" of sin—for it is only in the wake of sin that forgiveness appears here below; but at the same time, he suffers on account of sin. The misdeed is the occasion of his birth, but at the same time he has to make an immense and agonizing effort over himself in

30. [*Le mal de la coulpe:* see Thomas Aquinas, *Summa Theologica,* Ia IIae, Q. 39, Art. 4 and Q. 75.]

order to absolve the misdeed. And in such a way, the melange of joy and pain that is characteristic of forgiveness can undoubtedly be explained. Forgiveness forgives from gaiety of heart and begrudgingly at the same time. Better yet, forgiveness forgives *at the same time* because and although, and *at the same time* it forgives neither because, nor although; *utrumque* and *neutrum* at the same time! Its ambiguity is, then, itself ambiguous . . . This ambiguity of an ambiguity, this ambiguity with an exponent is more than an ambiguity to the second power; for it is, all in all, ambiguous to infinity. Neither of the two inverse unilateralities, neither of the two adialectical regimes, neither the obstacle without an organ, nor the organ without an obstacle, is suitable for forgiveness. The fact remains that its natural regime is the dialectic of the organ-obstacle; for it is entirely commanded by amphibole.—Above all, forgiveness obeys neither the causality of the lovable, nor the causality of the detestable; it is unleashed neither by a preexistent value, nor by a countervalue; it trails behind nothing. We do not even forgive "because" love is the supreme value . . . Every *because* announces, indeed, a pressure, a motivation, a determinism. Heterodox or orthodox, paradoxological or rational, causality is, indeed, causal in the two cases; and just as the spirit of contradiction is as servile as the spirit of imitation, of which it is the reversal, so the influence of the absurd because is as alienating as the influence of the because that is right side out. It does not then suffice to say that forgiveness renders good for evil, and that in that consists the unmerited in-addition, the miraculous *perisson* of which the Sermon on the Mount speaks, according to Saint Matthew; this in-addition itself would be neither creator, nor truly gracious, nor by consequence charitable, this in-addition would have nothing of the character of "grace" (*charis*) if it had been determined by the existence of evil, if forgiveness, in search of forgivable material, showed itself to be partial to wrongdoings and to infamies. This is all the more reason why forgiveness is in no way anticipated by the causality of value, of merit, or of innocence—and we say "all the more reason" because such a causality is evidently the most normal. Not only is it not because the accused is innocent that forgiveness forgives him (innocence, on the contrary, rendering forgiveness superfluous), rather it is much more because forgiveness forgives that the guilty person becomes innocent. On the condition of being innocent itself, of claiming nothing, forgiveness converts the sinners whom it pardons to innocence. This paradoxical reversal of the bourgeois "because" is just as perceptible in love and in faith. It is not that which is lovable that is the cause of love, as the rules of etiquette would require and as the Bibliothèque Rose claims: it is love that renders what it loves lovable. Proper love, love that is official and respectable, would gladly say to the one it loves: I love you *despite your faults* (which is to say, although you do not merit it), or—which, in the end, amounts to the same!—I love you *because of your qualities.* Now, truth is wholly other. If the lover loves the beloved, then this is not because of the merits of the beloved, but of course it is not any more *on account of his faults.* It is not in honor of his demerit! After all, demerit is not a reason for loving, even though it is not a reason for hating and for scorning; and, in turn, merit is likewise not a reason for hating or scorning, if it is not a reason for loving ... Instead, we must say: first, the lover loves someone blindly and without any reason for loving, and at the same time he transforms the faults of this person into qualities. And from that moment on, if he became static, he could begin to love the beloved a posteriori for these imaginary qualities that he himself created. This would be an illusory causality, but it would still be a causality. Also, he prefers to create and recreate incessantly the qualities that will legitimate him after the fact. This work of alchemical transmutation does not have an end. We know that Stendhal gave the name *crystallization* to loving transfiguration[31] ... This inversion of etiology is no less discernible in faith. In the *Euthyphro,* Plato wonders if holy things are holy because we revere them or if we revere them because they are holy.[32] And we guess that Greek dogmatism had to judge the first eventuality as being particularly injurious to the objectivity of the Idea. Pascal, in discovering an "order of the heart,"[33] will give the true modern solution to this alternative. He pushes the paradox of M. de Roannez to the extreme: "the reasons come to me after"[34] ... Bergson, in turn, and with such lucidity, will show how the thoughtful decision arouses after the fact retrospective deliberations in order to justify itself. However, if forgiveness resembles, in this aspect, the passionate decision, faith, and love, then it is not identical to them. Passionate faith, faith that nothing discourages, turns objections themselves into arguments and into *additional reasons:* all

31. [Stendhal, *Love,* trans. Susan Sale and Gilbert Sale (New York: Viking Press, 1975).]

32. [*Euthyphro,* trans. G. M. A. Grube, in *Plato's Complete Works,* 10 ff. (10d ff.).]

33. [*Pascal's Pensées,* 80 (§283).]

34. [Ibid., 78 (§276): "M. de Roannez said: 'Reasons come to me afterwards, but at first a thing pleases or shocks me without my knowing the reason, and yet it shocks me for that reason which I only discover afterwards.'"]

that is commanded by this attentive faith, indeed, becomes a reason for believing, the For and the Against, and the proofs and the difficulties; for that
which refutes still proves, yet involuntarily and indirectly. Faith is then crys-
tallizing, like love. But in forgiveness we do not encounter this power of illusion of the lover and of the believer: in culpability, forgiveness does not
seek, even retrospectively, for reasons that would justify absolution; it forgives with complete lucidity; it courageously faces the misdeed of the guilty
person and looks the misdeed in the eyes, straight in the face, without
deceiving itself with myths and chimeras. There is even a wholly efferent
forgiveness, a heroic forgiveness for which this agonizing sacrifice no longer
costs anything. Jesus, remarks Max Scheler, does not say to Mary Magdalene: "If you promise to sin no more, I will forgive you" . . . But *first* he
forgives—*apheōntai sou ai hamartiai,* "your sins are forgiven,"[35] and then
unconditional forgiveness renders Mary Magdalene capable of getting back
up. In order to forgive, forgiveness itself did not set conditions, did not have
reservations, required neither promises nor guarantees! As for the guarantee, it is rather the act of forgiveness that creates it! And before forgiving,
forgiveness would still like assurances? As in the remarks mentioned by
Pascal, First and Then are reversed. It is in forgiving, in supposing that the
problem is resolved, that we render the guilty person innocent. Forgiveness
forgives the guilty person even though he is guilty, precisely because he is
guilty, because at bottom and in the last analysis, he maybe is innocent, and
all of this contradictorily and at the same time! In sum, forgiveness forgives
because it forgives, and again it is similar to love in this respect: for love too
loves because it loves . . . And we say again, the lover loves his beloved because it is he and because it is she:—as if that were a reason for loving! But
yes, it is a reason for loving; for a reason without reasons is the most profound of all. Love is literally *causa sui,* or conversely: the effect is explained
by itself, founds itself, and itself is its own cause. This is what theologians
call *aseity.* The because refers, thus, to a why. But this circular causality is
neither a tautology, nor a statement of the obvious; and this circle is not a vicious circle. On the contrary, it is a *circulus sanus.* This *petitio principii* is the
holy *petitio principii* of spontaneous love. To the diallel of love responds the
diallel of transfiguring forgiveness, which always begins with itself.

35. Luke 7:48. ["And he said to her, 'Your sins are forgiven.'"]

VIII. An End That Is an Event, a Relation with the Guilty Person, a Total and Definitive Remission

In this centrifugal and spontaneous *élan,* we finally recognize the heart of forgiveness for which we were searching in vain in heartless temporality and in the excuse. This cordial forgiveness would actually be an event, a relation with the person, and a total remission. And first, it is an event—for forgiveness is something that comes to pass, and insofar as it comes to pass it is on the same scale as sin, which is to say, as the contingent clinamen and as the "could have been otherwise." The intellective excuse, we were saying, does not come to pass: it is neither an act nor a decision, but rather the simple recognition of the nothingness of the misdeed. It only notices and records the continuation of a preexistent innocence; it understands, all in all, that the sin has never been committed: freedom, which is at work in gracious remission, does not even find the chance to intervene here: a lucid analysis permits the accuser to excuse the accused—or rather, it is the so-called guilty person who exonerates himself all alone. The excuse is thus a small conversion: it does not create a truly new order; it effaces the phantom of sin, it passes the eraser not over a nonexistent misdeed, but rather over an unjustified grievance. The recognition of misjudged innocence (perhaps Aristotle has said: *anagnōrisis*) is the only notable event here, and it is a wholly subjective event. The conversion itself would be indeed the advent of a new order: but the conversion is too often rational and motivated to be truly creative, for in general it implies the adhesion to a preexistent dogma or to an article of faith whose truth we recognize; and it can give its reasons, like a neophyte who decides to adhere to this or that party, because the arguments of the new doctrine have won his conviction; the new doctrine is judged as being preferable to and more well-founded than the old one. Forgiveness excludes this well-reflected-upon consent. Forgiveness, like repentance, rather implies an arbitrary event that is always synthetic in comparison with the old life: as opposed to so many apparently sudden conversions, ones that a long and invisible process has in reality been preparing for a long time, the decision to forgive is contingent. It does not mature little by little, does not emanate in any way from the past by an immanent and continual evolution, or does not result from a progressive incubation . . . This decision is an end that is a beginning. And first of all an end: forgiveness turns the page and suspends the drivel of rancorous continuation, the vindictive person will no longer keep trotting out his obsessive refrains. But if it were only about liquidation and termination, then the excuse would be as good as forgiveness. In fact, forgiveness is at the same time the omega and the alpha; the conclusion is, in the same blow, an initiative; it is in this way that death, according to eschatological hope, is in the same instant the end of life and the threshold of the afterlife, the conclusion of the anterior order and, ipso facto, the debut of a wholly other order. Terminal and initial all at once, the event that is called *forgiveness* closes a continuation in order to begin another one. The instant of forgiveness terminates the anterior interval and founds the new interval. So it supposes courage: courage, taking the offensive, faces the danger, and forgiveness, daring to offer peace, forgets the insult. Forgiveness is literally *epoch-making* in both senses of the word: it suspends the old order, it inaugurates the new order. We were saying that the excuse, in recognizing the poor grounds of the accusation, takes back its complaint and abandons every pursuit: it reestablishes the status quo in its ancientness. The excuse, by pronouncing a dismissal, refers us to the state that preceded the accusation. But forgiveness, excluding every dismissal, refers us to the state that preceded the misdeed, which is to say, to prelapsed innocence. The dismissal does not imply the salvation of a lost soul: this salvation is called Forgiveness. It is forgiveness that fishes out from the dark lake the person shipwrecked in the great moral shipwreck. The excuse, by operating in the continued plenitude, is not a resurrection; it is forgiveness that resuscitates dead people; the dead person, or, said otherwise, the guilty person, is revived from his nothingness and from his lonely depths. "My son was dead, and has come back to life, he was lost and he has been found again," *Outos ho huios mou mekros ēn kai anezēsen, ēn apolōlōs kai ehurethē.*[36] After the excuse, the continuation assumes its normal path, as if nothing had happened. And, indeed, there was never anything that happened, nothing ever came to pass. The projections of faulty freedom have never troubled the serene and irreproachable existence of the stay-at-home son. For of what can we indeed forgive this irreproachable son? But the model son, having known neither perdition, nor temptations, nor the Wily Women,[37] will not

---

36. Luke 15:24 ["for this my son was dead, and is alive again; he was lost, and is found! And they began to make merry"]; cf. Luke 15:32 ["It was fitting to make merry and be glad, for this your brother was dead, and is alive; he was lost and is found."].

37. Prokofiev, *The Prodigal Son*. [*The Prodigal Son*, op. 46, a ballet in three scenes, written in 1929.]

know joy either,[38] joy reserved for those who have rebounded from nonbeing into being. That which succeeds the excuse, renewing contact with the previous life, is the commencement of this life again. But forgiveness announces a rebirth or, better yet, a new birth. The runaway child who reenters his foyer as absolved, forgiven, and repentant will never be the one he was before his departure: the circuit of adventures is now finished, but an invisible, differential element, but an inalienable richness, forever distinguishes the prodigal son from the stay-at-home son. This differential I-know-not-what is the gratuitous surplus that we were calling, with a term borrowed from the Gospel, the *perisson*. Indeed, the gift, when it is not simple restitution, is epoch-making just like forgiveness. The gift will have consequences, and especially if it inaugurates the era of reconciliation and of peace. However, the in-addition here is an asset that is too palpable to be miraculous: it is the remission of a sin, despite its negative character, that is the veritable More and the true pneumatic miracle. And thus forgiveness institutes a new era, institutes new relations, and inaugurates a *vita nuova*. The night of the misdeed, for the person who is pardoned, portends a wholly new dawn; the winter of rancor announces, for the one who pardons, a wholly new spring. It is the time of renewal and of a second youth. *Hic incipit vita nuova*. Here, the great thaw and the happy simplification, which forgiveness announces, receive all their meaning. In this forgiveness belies resignation. For if resignation is an adaptation to what is insoluble, then forgiveness is a solution, even though the misdeed is not a problem to be "resolved" . . . We resign ourselves to destiny, we forgive the misdeed. Whoever resigns himself to the misdeed, as if it had been destined, is an accomplice to the sin and is of Machiavellian ill will. Whoever forgives destiny as if he had been the guilty person is a boor. Resignation is made for the destiny to which it resigns itself, forgiveness for the misdeed that it forgives. Also, resignation is destined just as destiny is of a resigning nature. And forgiveness, like sin, is an initiative. The person who resigns himself adapts to the coldness of inflexible and rigid destiny; like a hibernating animal he makes his hole in the ice and becomes embedded in it so as to make his eternal winter livable. This resigning accommodation to the frozen situation is what we call wisdom. On the other hand, the folly of forgiveness, unresigned forgiveness, resolves the frozen relations of man and of evil. The forgiven offense resembles, after the fact, a misunderstanding. Forgiveness liberates, liquidates, and

38. Joy: Luke 15:32 (*charēnai*).

liquefies the running water that rancor held prisoner; it helps out the conscience that is blocked in ice. This general debacle, this mobilization of the
past, are the very initiative of the generous man; the generous man goes out
to meet his offender, takes the initiative, and takes the first step. Who will
take the first step? This considerate step, these unilateral and arbitrary advances entice the new season: so the rancorous person is ashamed of allowing himself to be left behind and of not himself having taken the initiative of this armistice. It is indeed necessary that someone begin, is it not?
Forgiveness, preaching by example, seems to whisper for the benefit of rancorous people: Do as I do, who am outside of legality, who do not go right up
to the limit of my rights, who do not exploit my titles, who reclaim neither
reparations, nor damages, but rather clear all my debtors of their obliga-
tions; in a word, do as I do who forgive without being obliged to do so. And
the communicative warmth of this generosity and the radiance of this
warmth thaw frozen men, sullen ones and wicked ones. And a great emulation of peace takes possession of all beings.

Moreover, forgiveness sets us in relation with someone other, something
that repentance does not do! Repentance, a purely personal drama, calls into
question only my own redemption and my own destiny. Above all, then, it
concerns moral intimacy and solitary perfection; it is, indeed, the same person who sinned and who repents: the misdeed to be redeemed is one's own
misdeed. Also, it is much more a matter of contrition than of expiation. Forgiveness, on the other hand, is not a monologue but a dialogue; forgiveness,
being a relation of two, entails a supplementary hazard: this adventurous
element stems from the presence of the other. The springtime of the guilty
person, as we were calling it, no longer depends on the guilty person alone
. . . Without a doubt, sincere repentance, too, repents in poignant inquietude
and in the innocence of despair, which is to say, without any guarantee of
amendment; and even repentance is efficacious only if it gives up hope of
its own efficacy. However, in it there is a type of reassuring finality that forgiveness lacks. The offender receives forgiveness as the repentant person
repents: in the night. But, indeed, when even the offender would not be desperate, black shadows would still envelope him, for his dereliction is in a certain way more poignant than that of the repentant person; restlessness is
here coupled with an incertitude, and the incertitude itself is suspended by
this free gesture of pardoning, which is the whole essence of forgiveness.
Forgiveness is an adventure not only for the guilty person; the one who forgives exposes himself too to hazards of which every relation with the Other

is composed. In advance, he accepts the risk of ingratitude. Forgiveness, qua relation between two ipseities, poses problems of social or pedagogical efficacy. Is it dangerous? is it beneficent? A casuistry of the law of grace can be constituted around this alternative . . . For everyone knows that the new man does not arise infallibly and automatically from the old one.—Forgiveness supposes two partners. In forgiving the misdeed, it forgives the person guilty of this misdeed. Nonresistance to evil is a relation with the wicked act, and by chance with the author of this act; vice versa, forgiveness is a relation with the agent with regard to an act of this agent. Also, nonviolence, in renouncing fighting, is a pure, abstaining negativity, a simple exterior facade, a privative comportment, and an intransitive gentleness, whereas forgiveness, in looking the foreign ipseity in the eyes, possesses an intentional soul. We forgive someone, not Vesuvius or an anonymous necessity before whom a man can only bend his knee. We were saying that gratitude, in extending beyond kindness, invokes the very ipseity of the benefactor. Gratitude is turned toward the being who is on the horizon of all having, toward the person who is at the limit of all belonging, and toward the donor who is at the limit of the gift. In doing this, recognition becomes blurred, diffuse, and atmospheric, and evaporates into the infinity of love. In the same way that the Thank You of cordial gratitude is a word of love that infinitely exceeds the tangible materiality of the gift, so the grace of forgiveness is a movement of love that surpasses the punctual and atmospheric reality of the misdeed. To forgive a lie is essentially to forgive the liar for this lie. "Te absolvo a peccatis tuis."[39] With an infinitive totalization, absolution spreads from the isolated misdeeds to the guilty subject who committed them.

Forgiveness, which sets us in relation with the person of the sinner, forgiveness, which is an instantaneous event, is then by that very fact an unlimited remission: this sudden forgiveness is simultaneously total and definitive. To forgive is neither to change one's mind on the score of the guilty person, nor to rally around the thesis of innocence . . . Quite the contrary! The supernaturality of forgiveness consists in this, that my opinion on the subject of the guilty person precisely has not changed; but against this immutable background it is the whole lighting of my relations with the guilty person that is modified, it is the whole orientation of our relations that finds itself inverted, overturned, and overwhelmed! The judgment of condemna-

39. ["I absolve you of your sins." In the Roman Catholic tradition, this phrase forms part of the formula of absolution that a priest proclaims when one confesses one's sins.]

tion has stayed the same, but an arbitrary and gratuitous change has intervened, a diametrical and radical inversion, *peristophē*, which transfigures hatred into love. To pardon is to turn one's back on the direction that justice indicates to us . . . For forgiveness is not simply a relative conversion of contrary to contrary, but a meta-empirical conversion of contradictory to contradictory, which is to say, an acute inversion. The dramatic and so strongly contrasted antithesis of dark regions and light, which is such a strong contrast, is always recognizable by this effect of relief, by the coup de théâtre that we call forgiveness. Forgiveness, the revolutionary inversion of our vindictive tendencies, initiates a change *of all into all.* And thus, forgiveness is total or not at all! Forgiveness comes under the jurisdiction of the alternative of all-or-nothing, of yes-or-no . . . In contrast, the excuse, as we have seen, allows itself to be expended according to the law of More-or-Less: a lot, a little, nothing-at-all, there is its ordinary scale; all the degrees, all the nuances of the comparative are admissible when it is a question of the excuse or of esteem. For just as esteem divides up and details itself, so too is the excuse, considering the misdeed analytically, distributed in morsels. It distinguishes the this and the that, hierarchically organizes motives, absolves the excusable, condemns the inexcusable, and multiplies, between the one and the other, all the degrees of rigor and all the gradations of indulgence. Love no longer differs from the excuse when it is mixed with restrictions and conditions, with reservations and a *"distinguo,"* and with expectations and ulterior motives. Love thus begins to quibble; but such a love is a cracked love, a suspect love, and the very conditions that it poses are the proof of its bad faith. Repentance, too, can be a pseudo-repentance: for example, it happens that the repentant person makes a type of progressive atonement of his own redemption; this redemption no longer differs in any way from simple reimbursement in installments of a sum that was lent. Excluding every scalar progression, forgiveness is at the antipodes of such a repentance just as it is at the antipodes of the excuse. Forgiveness, in the end, differs from the gift; for the gift is after all a partitive and fragmented misappropriation. For the donor of this gift never relinquishes anything but his assets or a portion of his assets. Forgiveness, in contrast, forgives in one fell swoop and in a single, indivisible *élan,* and it pardons undividedly; in a single, radical, and incomprehensible movement, forgiveness effaces all, sweeps away all, and forgets all. In one blink of an eye, forgiveness makes a tabula rasa of the past, and this miracle is as simple for it as saying hello and good evening. The obstacle called the *misdeed* vanishes as if by magic! Forgiveness forgives the misdeed and the wrongdoer globally, and in turn it forgives infinitely more misdeeds than the guilty person has committed.—The absence of every reservation, which is the fundamental condition of forgiveness, also has a temporal meaning. No more in duration than in degree does forgiveness *purissime* suffer the least restriction or the least reticence. The restriction, in the order of time, is called *time limit,* or better yet, conversely, *chronological limitation.* Is not the ulterior motive of this limitation quite often the form that an insidious bad will takes? Forgiveness that forgives up to a certain point, *thus far,* and not beyond, is an apocryphal forgiveness; but forgiveness that forgives only up to a certain date is just as suspect. To forgive until there is a new order is not to forgive. Forgiveness does not favor a determinate lapse of time, does not foresee debarment, does not sign provisional armistices, and does not limit itself to suspending hostilities; this genre of truce is made for suspicious, belligerent people, whose hearts are not intimately converted for the benefit of peace. Where a sincere will for reconciliation is lacking, peace is necessarily precarious. Forgiveness, on the contrary, is an intention of perpetual peace. For what kind of grace is a grace whose validity would be temporary? Between validity, which is effectively temporary, and value, which is atemporal, there is an abyss, just as there is an infinite distance between granting a stay of execution and pardoning the condemned person. Forgiveness, forgiving the misdeed once and for all and forever, is opposed in this to curing by forgetting or by temporality alone: a rancor whose progressive extinction is an effect of decay and accumulated years, this rancor is a poorly healed rancor, a rancor exposed to relapses: something like a poorly consoled grief; and, conversely, remission, when it is the work of time, can be put into question again by time: the abscess forms again. The instant of a decision that arbitrarily cuts the temporal continuation is alone definitive. Forgiveness forgives one time, and this time is literally *one time for all!* Precisely because the decision is the arbitrary instant, nothing limits the supernatural gratuitousness of it: to the unmotivated or unmerited decision, there are unlimited consequences. Not only does forgiveness forgive infinitely more misdeeds than the guilty person committed, but it forgives all of the misdeeds that this guilty person would be able to commit or still will commit. It immensely exceeds all culpability, either actual or to come. Its resources are infinite; infinite is its patience. Nothing discourages its inexhaustible generosity; it would wait without becoming disgusted until the end of time. It would forgive seven-and-seventy times were it necessary ... Forgiveness extends unlimited credit to the guilty person. And the perverted man will grow tired of hating and tormenting the generous man sooner than the generous man will grow tired of forgiving the perverted man. It is of little importance if a burst of rancor must someday challenge the absolution. That which will have lasted for only a time wanted, at the time, to last forever, and for centuries and centuries. It suffices that the sincere intention of forgiving has, at the moment of forgiveness, sincerely and passionately excluded every chronological limitation, just as it suffices that love, even if, in fact, it has to be unfaithful and versatile, wanted to be eternal on the day of the oath. One understands, consequently, why forgiveness can be the founder of a future. As much as pity, an emotion without a tomorrow, appears inconsistent and transitory, so much does forgiveness reveal itself capable of instituting a new order. Forgiveness, like inspired intuition, does the work of several generations in one instant. In one single word, in a look and in the flutter of eyelids, in a smile, in a kiss, forgiveness accomplishes instantaneously what it took centuries of forgetting, and of decay, and even of justice to bring to fruition. Violaine forgives Mara[40] at once, for everything and forever. Thus is explained the exaltation of which forgiveness is the cause. That the father of the prodigal son welcomes the repentant son into the house is just and understandable. But to embrace him, to clothe him in the father's best outfit, to kill the fatted calf, and to throw a feast in honor of the repentant son, this constitutes the inexplicable, the unjust, the mysteriously great feast of Forgiveness.[41]

40. [A play by Paul Claudel, *L'Annonce faite à Marie* (1912). See Paul Claudel, *L'Annonce faite à Marie* (Paris: Gallimard, 1993).]

41. [*La mystérieuse grande fête du Pardon:* a reference to the French *fête du Grand Pardon,* or Day of Atonement.]

Conclusion   **The Unforgivable: More Unfortunate Than**
Wicked, More Wicked Than Unfortunate

> Yet another stain. Ah, go away, damned stain . . . Oh, these
> hands will never be clean . . . All the fragrances of Arabia
> could never perfume this little hand. Oh wash your hands . . .
> What is done is done.[1] —*Macbeth (translated by Edmond*
> *Fleg for the opera by Ernst Bloch)*

In one sense, forgiveness extends to infinity. Forgiveness
does not ask if the crime is worthy of being forgiven, if the atonement has
been sufficient, or if the rancor has continued long enough . . . Which
amounts to saying: there is an inexcusable, but there is not an unforgivable.
Forgiveness is there to forgive precisely what no excuse would know how to
excuse: for there is no misdeed that is so grave that we cannot in the last recourse forgive it. Nothing is impossible for all-powerful remission! Forgiveness can in this sense do everything. Where sin flows, Saint Paul says, forgiveness overflows.[2] In spirit, if not in letter, all offenses are "venial," even
the inexpiable ones. The more mortal they are, the more venial they are! For
if there are crimes that are so awful that the criminal who commits them
cannot atone for them, then the possibility of forgiving them still remains,
forgiveness being made precisely for such hopeless or incurable cases. And
as for misdeeds that we readily call "venial" in the current sense of the word,

---

1. ["Out damned spot, out I say . . . What, will these hands ne'er be clean? . . . All the per-
fumes of Arabia will not sweeten this little hand . . . Wash you hands . . . what's done cannot be
undone." *Macbeth*, in *William Shakespeare: The Complete Works* (New York: Viking Press,
1969), 1131 (5.1.32–63).]

2. [See Romans 5:20.]

they do not have need of our forgiveness, forgiveness not being made for these insignificant matters; indulgence suffices. Forgiveness forgives everyone for everything for all times; it protests madly against the evidence of the crime, not by denying this evidence, not even with the hope of redeeming the criminal after the fact, nor out of defiance or out of a taste for scandal, but rather by opposing the paradox of its own infinite freedom and gratuitous love to the abominable crime. And since the crime is inexcusable and unforgettable, at least let the victims forgive it; this is all that they can do for it.—Forgiveness does not know impossibility; and yet we still have not mentioned the first condition without which forgiveness would be devoid of sense. This elementary condition is the distress, the insomnia, and the dereliction of the wrongdoer; and although it is not up to the person who forgives to require this condition, this condition is nevertheless that without which the entire problematic of forgiveness becomes a simple buffoonery. To each person belongs a task: to the criminal belongs desperate remorse, and to the victim belongs forgiveness: but the victim will not repent in the place of the guilty person. It is necessary that the guilty person work toward this himself; it is necessary that the criminal redeem himself all alone. As for our forgiveness, this is not his concern; it is the concern of the offended. The criminal's repentance and in particular his remorse, by themselves alone, give meaning to forgiveness, just as despair alone gives meaning to grace. What good is grace if the "desperate person" has a good conscience and a good mien? Forgiveness is not aimed at contented people with clear consciences, or at unrepentant guilty people, who sleep easy and eat well. When the guilty person is fat, well nourished, prosperous, and takes advantage of the economic miracle, then forgiveness is a sinister joke. No, forgiveness is not made for that; forgiveness is not made for swine and their sows. Before there can even be a question of forgiveness, it is first necessary that the guilty person, instead of protesting, recognize himself as guilty without pleas or mitigating circumstances, and especially without accusing his own victims; not at all! In order for us to forgive, it is first necessary, is it not? that one comes to us to ask for forgiveness. Has one ever asked us for forgiveness? No, the criminals do not ask us for anything, nor do they owe us anything, and what's more, they have nothing for which to reproach themselves. The criminals have nothing to say; this matter does not concern them. Why would we forgive those who regret their monstrous crimes so little and so seldom? This is not all. When on the day after the massacre general frivolity and convenient indulgence were discreetly covering over the crime in silence and forgetfulness, forgiveness became derisory; henceforth, forgiveness is a farce. This eagerness to fraternize with the hangmen, this hasty reconciliation is a grave indecency and an insult with regard to the victims. Certainly not, the epoch is not rancorous! Even if everything has long been finished, even if no one ever held criminals' crimes against them, must we still forgive? By excusing crimes almost immediately, repugnant and cowardly indulgence has rendered forgiveness not only useless and premature but also impossible. Expiation, it is true, also removes the raison d'être of forgiveness: expiation, but not repentance! For if unexpiated crimes are precisely the ones that need to be forgiven, then unrepentant criminals themselves are precisely the ones who have no need of forgiveness. By what right, or by what entitlement, would one now advise us to forgive when the hangmen themselves have never asked us for forgiveness? Let us fear that the occasion of having a pathetic attitude, the temptation of having to play a sublime role, or the complaisance toward our beautiful soul and our noble conscience may one day make us forget the martyrs. It is not necessary to be sublime; it suffices to be loyal and serious.

Without a doubt the unexpiated misdeed, and even more so, evil itself, make up the material for forgiveness. If the existence of evil is not, strictly speaking, the "reason" for forgiveness (for forgiveness does not have *reasons*), then at least it is its raison d'être; if it is not the grounds for forgiveness, then at least it is the foundation of its appearance; the existence of evil is certainly not a reason for forgiving, but neither is it any more of an obstacle to forgiveness: it is rather the mysterious and scandalous condition, or as we were saying, the organ-obstacle of forgiveness. The infinite "forgivability" of the misdeed does not in the least imply the nonexistence of evil, quite the contrary: it is rather this nonexistence that would deprive forgiveness of its daily bread! And we ourselves showed how the intellectualism of the excuse precipitates the decline of forgiveness by making evil and perniciousness disappear. However, there is an Unforgivable, which is perhaps the irreducible residue of an infinite and always unfinished reduction. This organ-obstacle can become, at the limit, an absolute impediment, a metaempirical impediment. Malevolent freedom, ill-intentioned freedom, which is not strictly speaking the "source of" evil, but rather the only conceivable evil or evil itself (for there is no other evil than the willing of evil), is infinitely the organ-obstacle. Or, better yet, the organ-obstacle is, infinitely and in its own right, sometimes organ and sometimes obstacle. Were we not saying that the equivocal, far from being univocal, is itself infinitely equivocal? First, it is quite evident that "to understand" freedom is to explain the mechanism of this freedom, which in turn is to deny all will of evil, as does the excuse; explanation by causes transforms freedom into necessity. Schelling, for his part, thought that freedom can never be an element in a system.[3] And more precisely, the decision ceases to be free for the person who analyzes its motives and impulses, or who demonstrates the cogs and springs of mental machinery, or who demonstrates them by explaining the misdeed in terms of ignorance or stupidity, in terms of blindness or delirium of the senses. Up to this point, intellectual indulgence suffices for excusing sin. To explain is to excuse. But if the excuse boasts of understanding the determinism behind freedom, then forgiveness would rather attempt to uncover the freedom behind determinism. The excuse exonerates the guilty person due to the fact that it understands. And forgiveness does not forgive *because* it understands; but first it forgives without reasons, and then, in a certain way, it understands or guesses. We were saying that to understand is not at all to forgive: and now we must admit that to forgive is in a certain respect to understand. Forgiveness understands and it does not understand. At first, it does not understand. But not to understand is, indeed, to forgive! In this first point of view, to forgive without understanding is the only way of forgiving: for if we *can* understand without forgiving, we *should* in certain respects forgive the unforgivable without having understood it. You made a mistake of an hour: I understand and I excuse you. You did not *want* to arrive on time. You did it *on purpose*—and I forgive you (or do not forgive you . . .). Here, all of your excuses will be for naught: for an evil will neither can be interpreted, nor admits of nuances, and there is no way of "understanding" it. Perhaps it is necessary to hurry up and forgive prior to understanding for fear of not doing it when one has understood: for sometimes we understand only too well! But on the other hand, it may also be necessary to understand many things before finally forgiving without understanding. And in this second sense, forgiveness forgives comprehensively and thus renders itself capable of regenerating the sinner. It fears having understood; it vaguely understands something, something that is nothing or that is more of an I know not what. What exactly did it understand or learn by forgiving? To tell the truth, it did not understand wicked freedom (for no

3. [See Vladimir Jankélévitch, *L'Odyssée de la conscience dans la dernière philosophie de Schelling* (Paris: Alcan, 1933). This work is the doctoral dissertation that he defended in 1933.]

one understands the incomprehensible), but it understands *that there is* wicked freedom. Without being able to respond to the question *Quid?* it emphasizes the *quoddity* of the bad intention; it understands *that* there is an incomprehensible; it understands *that* there is in the end nothing to understand! It *understands that,* but it does not know how to say *what* it understands; it understands without knowing *what.* And just as Mélisande does not know what she knows, so forgiveness does not understand what it understands and understands what it does not understand. This empty intellection of the incomprehensible is forgiveness itself ... "Understand me" is what, in one look, the inexcusable sometimes says to us ... Now, this supplication is in reality not a call to impossible comprehension; it is rather a desire to be loved ... Who knows? maybe the wicked person is wicked because he has not been loved enough ... When the wicked person is irreducibly wicked he can, indeed, do nothing more than implore our love. But from this point on, understanding ceases to be analytic; it comes to pass, on the contrary, like an intuitive and sudden glimpse that reveals to us, in the instant, the irreducible, qualitative simplicity of the bad intention and the indivisible mystery of freedom. In this indemonstrable freedom, which is the ultimate presupposition of all moral evaluation, we recognize, as Kierkegaard might have called it, the "mystery of the first thing." Transparent opacity and opaque transparency, the mystery of the first thing is not without analogy to the *akataēpton*[4] or the Incomprehensible of John Chrysostom;[5] for it is, like this *Akatalepton,* evident in its "*quoddity*" and obscure in its *quid.* In the presence of this straightforward mystery, two pieces of evidence, contradictory and yet each as evident as the other, confront each other in a collision from which there is no escape: considered respectively, each one leads back to itself and only itself, but on the other hand, the sporadic nature of the two pieces of evidence is precisely that which sends our mind incessantly from one to the other. In a manner of speaking, the collision changes for us into oscillation. After the first two moments of oscillation: the indulgence, which excuses, would claim that "they are *more*

---

4. [See Saint Gregory of Nyssa, *Commentary on the Song of Songs,* Archbishop of Iakovos Library of Ecclesiastical and Historical Sources, no. 12 (Brookline, Mass.: Hellenic College Press, 1987). The French text leaves out the *l* in *akatalēpton.*]

5. [Saint John Chrysostom, *On the Incomprehensible Nature of God,* trans. Paul W. Harkins, The Fathers of the Church, no. 72 (Washington, D.C.: Catholic University Press of America, 2002).]

stupid than wicked," and the rigorous attitude of condemnation would affirm that "they are *more wicked than stupid"*; here is the first evidence of forgiveness: they are wicked, but it is necessary to forgive them for precisely this reason—for they are *more unfortunate than wicked.* Or better yet, it is their wickedness itself that is a misfortune, the infinite misfortune of being evil! We understand and excuse the fated evil for its absurdity: but barring the creation of despair, the evil associated with scandal can only be forgiven. This first piece of evidence, which spontaneously inclines the accuser and the outraged person to forgiveness, conveys our irresistible and fraternal sympathy for human misery: however much that the abuse that the wicked person makes of his free and infinite power is voluntary, it is no less one of the forms of this miserable condition, of this distress. Before the power itself, which is attentive, there was the possibility of this power, which is preexistent and always pregiven; before freedom, there was the fact-of-freedom. It is in this that the wicked person is a poor person just like each one of us, a poor person sworn to death like all of us, a solitary person like all of us, and infinitely more alone still, a poor, guilty person who has much need of our help. This is what the marvelous gentleness of forgiveness implies. Forgiveness whispers in a quiet voice: *Et ego!* Me, too . . . *De vestris fuimus.* You are sinners, well, I am another one of them, too. I, as well, I sinned or will sin. I could have done as you did; maybe I will do as you did. I am like you, weak, fallible, and miserable. There is a principle of pride in the ruthless rigor of the person who does not forgive: to refuse to forgive is to reject all resemblance to, and all brotherhood with, the sinner. The irreproachable person considers himself as being of another essence than the guilty person and of an origin that is infinitely more elevated; he places himself on a wholly other plane and decides a priori that he is above sin. He was impeccable in the past and will stay that way for the duration of the future; he neither says *"peccavi"* nor *"peccabo"*; these sinful affairs do not concern him at all. It is not that the offended in pleading for himself forgives himself virtually for the sins that he would have committed or those that he still intends to commit; for if he was simply striving after acquittal for his previous misdeed or credit for misdeeds to come, then he would resemble the hypocrite who feels pity for himself in seeming to feel pity for others. Let us admit straightforwardly, the person who forgives abstains from denying his essential similarity with the guilty person; he does not exploit the advantageous position that his innocence confers upon him; he does not keep for himself the privilege of alone being infallible, impeccable, and irreproachable, and he rejects any monopoly that he may have upon this position; he thus sacrifices this very fleeting and precarious superiority that may have arisen by sheer luck . . . Likewise, he will not abandon the wicked person, his brother, this wicked person in distress and in peril of death. Pitied for the profound misfortune of being wicked!—But the power that is attentive, when it has its chance, forestalls the preexisting possibility: they are still *more wicked than unfortunate.* There is nothing indeed to understand in the mystery of gratuitous wickedness except that the wicked person is wicked. This tautology makes the irreducibility of pure hate come to light: for the aseity of freedom responds to the aseity of love: here, the circular "because" would, then, express the scandal of a freedom that is absolutely unjust and absolutely malevolent and incredibly wicked, of a freedom that is free to the point of sacrilege, of a freedom that is the only radical evil here below. This totally wicked freedom would be bad will itself . . . "I take you as a witness that this man is wicked!" Besides, there is no reason for the oscillation to stop: the misfortune of this radical wickedness can, in turn, be the object of an exponential forgiveness; and the wickedness of this misfortune becomes a hyperbolic Unforgivable. If in becoming petrified this unforgivable were to remain ultimate and definite, then it would be nothing other than Hell: the Hell of despair. Is not the idea of an irremediable evil and one that would have the last word literally an "impossible supposition"? Fortunately, nothing ever has the last word! Fortunately, the last word is always the penultimate word . . . so that the debate between forgiveness and the unforgivable will never have an end. The moral dilemma that ensues is insoluble, for if the imperative of love is unconditional and does not have any restrictions, then the obligation to annihilate evil, and if not to hate it (for it is never necessary to hate anyone), at least to reject its negating force, to put it out of action or to damage its destructive rage, such an obligation is no less imperious than the duty to love; of all the values, love for humans is the most sacred, but indifference to crimes against humanity, but indifference to crimes against the essence and hominity of the person is the most sacrilegious of all misdeeds. And we have no means either for choosing one of these superlatives over the other, or for honoring them together: the choice of one Absolute necessarily leaves the "other Absolute" outside, the combination and conciliation of the *two Absolutes* is impossible; the sacrifice of one Absolute gives birth to misgivings and remorse in us; the synthesis of the two Absolutes would be a miracle: for the Absolute is plural and irremediably torn apart. Likewise, the finitude and irrationality of our situation give us three solutions of which the first condemns us to impotence, while the other two are unilateral and shaky: either moral judgment will hesitate indefinitely before the amphibole of an intention that is both malevolent and unfortunate, before this equivocation of the wicked-miserable; or we will choose to forgive the miserable person although it may mean the establishment of the reign of the hangmen for one thousand years; or, in order that the future be saved and that essential values survive, we will agree to prefer violence and force without love over a love without force. Such was, as we know, the heroic choice of the Resistance. Is not the fight against fanatics the least of all evils by far? It is better to disavow oneself in punishing than to contradict oneself in forgiving! This insoluble conflict of duties and this always approximate solution are the consequences of the debate that opposes forgiveness to unforgivable wickedness. Incessantly, the tireless, inexhaustible goodness of forgiveness surmounts the insurmountable wall of wickedness, and incessantly the wall reappears ahead of this goodness. Just as the incurable nature of death reconstitutes itself beyond the curable sicknesses, so the incorrigible nature of mortal sin and fundamentally wicked freedom continues to reconstitute itself beyond forgiveness . . . However, all misdeeds are forgivable to infinity, just as all sicknesses are curable to infinity. The same reciprocity sends us endlessly from the thought of death to the death of the thinking being, from the enveloping and enveloped thought to enveloped and enveloping death, and vice versa, from triumphant death to the thought that thinks this death, denies it, and surpasses it. The human spirit oscillates between these two triumphs that are simultaneously true, yet alternately conceived: for they contradict one another. And the reciprocity of these two contradictories is reciprocal to the point of vertigo . . . No! there is no last word. As is the case with thought in the face of death, love is, in some manner, the spirit of life in the face of evil. The spirit of life is invincible in a wholly other sense than is death: for death is more inexorable than invincible. Above all, death is the *ametapeiston*,[6]

6. ["Inexorable" or "unable to be persuaded": the reference is to a passage in Aristotle's *Metaphysics*. See *Metaphysics* in *Basic Works of Aristotle,* ed. and trans. Richard McKeon (New York: Random House, 1941), book 5, chapter 5, 1015a31–33: "And necessity is held to be something that cannot be persuaded—and rightly, for it is contrary to the movement which accords with the purpose and with reasoning." Leon Shestov refers to this term in *Athens and Jerusalem,* a book that Jankélévitch cited in chapter 1. See Leon Shestov, *Athens and Jerusalem,* trans. Bernard Martin (Athens: Ohio University Press, 1966), Second Foreword and also book 4, §66.]

and this is why we say precisely that death does not "forgive." And the human, on the contrary, forgives so as not to resemble death, that is, so as to be invincible in a wholly other sense than is death. Like the thought of death, or like the willing that morally can do all that it wills (for to will is to be able to) but cannot do all it wills literally, forgiveness is simultaneously omnipotent and impotent. All of its redeeming and absolving power cannot make it so that the action that occurred did not occur . . . "Out damned spot!" But the damned spot does not go away. For if the bloodstains of the action done are capable of being washed away, the accursed stain of the having-done is indelible, and no amount of polishing will wash it away. And nevertheless, in another truly pneumatic and incomprehensible sense, it is the very miracle of forgiveness that in a burst of joy annihilates the having-been and the having-done. By the grace of forgiveness, the thing that had been done has not been done. Is this *coincidentia oppositorium*[7] any more miraculous than the "miracle of the roses" of which Franz Liszt's *Saint Elizabeth*[8] speaks? And since the two forces are equally all-powerful, we can say: the infinite force of forgiveness is stronger than the infinite force of the fact of something's having-done, and reciprocally. To infinite evil, infinite grace, and reciprocally. Always reciprocally! Love is stronger than evil and evil is stronger than love; each is stronger than the other! The human spirit does not know how to go beyond . . . That is why the *Song of Songs* says that love is strong *as death: krataia hōs thanatos agapē.*[9] It does not say that love is stronger, and indeed it cannot say this, since the lover has to die one day. Love is strong like death, but death is strong like love. In truth, love is simultaneously stronger than and weaker than death, and it is thus just as strong. This extreme and almost heartrending tension is that of the mad forgiveness that is accorded to the wicked person. Where misdeed flows, grace overflows.[10] Besides—what Saint Paul did not add—where

7. [See *Nicholas of Cusa on Learned Ignorance: A Translation and an Appraisal of De Docta Ignorantia,* trans. Jasper Hopkins (Minneapolis: A. J. Banning Press, 1985); and see Nicholas of Cusa, *Vision of God,* trans. Emma Gurney Salter (New York: Dutton, 1928).]

8. [Franz Liszt's oratorio *The Legend of Saint Elizabeth* (1857–62). Saint Elizabeth is the patron saint of the poor and downtrodden in Hungary.]

9. [Song of Songs 8:6: "Set me as a seal upon your heart, as a seal upon your arm; for love is strong as death; jealousy is cruel as the grave. Its flashes are flashes of fire, a most vehement fire."]

10. Romans 5:20: "*ou de epleonasen hē hamartia, upereperisseusen hē charis.*" ["Law came in, to increase the trespass; but where sin increased, grace abounded all the more."]

grace overflows, evil overflows in response and submerges this overflowing itself, with an infinite and mysterious outbidding. The mystery of irreducible and inconceivable wickedness is, at the same time, stronger and weaker, weaker and stronger than love. Likewise, forgiveness is strong like wickedness; but it is not stronger than it.

Appendix   Jankélévitch's Philosophical Works

Henri Bergson. Paris: Alcan, 1931.

L'Odysée de la conscience dans la dernière philosophie de Schelling. Paris: Alcan, 1933.

Valeur et signification de la mauvaise conscience. Paris: Alcan, 1933.

L'Ironie ou la bonne conscience. Paris: Alcan, 1936. Reprinted as *L'Ironie* (Paris: Flammarion, 1964).

L'Alternative. Paris: Alcan, 1938. Reprinted as chapter 2 of *L'Aventure, l'ennui et le sérieux* (Paris: Aubier-Montaigne, 1963), and in *Vladimir Jankélévitch: Philosophie morale*, ed. Françoise Schwab (Paris: Flammarion, 1998), 816–990.

Du Mensonge. Lyon: Confluences, 1942. Reprinted as chapter 9 of the complete reedition of *Traité des vertus* (Paris: Bordas, 1972), and in *Vladimir Jankélévitch: Philosophie morale*, ed. Françoise Schwab. (Paris: Flammarion, 1998), 203–88.

Le Mal. Paris: Arthaud, 1947. Reprinted as chapters 13 and 14 of the complete re-edition of *Traité des vertus* (Paris: Bordas, 1972), and in *Vladimir Jankélévitch: Philosophie morale*, ed. Françoise Schwab Paris: (Flammarion, 1998), 289–371.

Traité des vertus. Paris: Bordas, 1949.

Philosophie première: Introduction à une philosophie du presque. Paris: Presses Universitaires de France, 1953.

L'Austerité et la vie morale. Paris: Flammarion, 1956. Reprinted in *Vladimir Jankélévitch: Philosophie morale*, ed. Françoise Schwab (Paris: Flammarion, 1998), 373–582.

Le Je-ne-sais-quoi et le presque-rien. Paris: Presses Universitaires de France, 1957.

Henri Bergson [complete reedition]. Paris: Presses Universitaires de France, 1959.

Le Pur et l'impur. Paris: Flammarion, 1960. Reprinted in *Vladimir Jankélévitch: Philosophie morale,* ed. Françoise Schwab (Paris: Flammarion, 1998), 583–813.

L'Aventure, l'ennui et le sérieux. Paris: Aubier-Montaigne, 1963. Reprinted in *Vladimir Jankélévitch: Philosophie morale,* ed. Françoise Schwab (Paris: Flammarion, 1998), 815–990.

La Mort. Paris: Flammarion, 1966.

La Mauvaise Conscience [reedition of *Valeur et signification de la mauvaise conscience*]. Paris: Aubier-Montaigne, 1966. Reprinted in *Vladimir Jankélévitch: Philosophie morale,* ed. Françoise Schwab (Paris: Flammarion, 1998), 31–202.

Le Pardon. Paris: Aubier-Montaigne, 1967. Reprinted in *Vladimir Jankélévitch: Philosophie morale,* ed. Françoise Schwab (Paris: Flammarion, 1998), 991–1149.

Traité des vertus [full reedition]. Vol. 1: *Le Sérieux de l'intention.* Paris: Bordas, 1968.

Traité des vertus [full reedition]. Vol. 2: *Les Vertus et l'amour.* Paris: Bordas, 1970.

Pardonner? Paris: Éditions Le Pavillon, Roger Maria, 1971. Reprinted as *L'Imprescriptible* (Paris: Éditions du Seuil, 1986).

Traité des vertus [full reedition]. Vol. 3: *L'Innocence et la méchanceté.* Paris: Bordas, 1972.

L'Irréversible et la nostalgie. Paris: Flammarion, 1974.

Quelque Part dans l'Inachevé (with Béatrice Berlowitz). Paris: Gallimard, 1978.

Le Je-ne-sais-quoi et le presque-rien [complete reedition in three volumes]. Paris: Éditions du Seuil, 1980.

Le Paradoxe de la morale. Paris: Éditions du Seuil, 1981.

Sources. Ed. Françoise Schwab. Paris: Éditions du Seuil, 1984.

Penser la mort? [interviews]. Ed. Françoise Schwab. Paris: Liana Levi, 1994.

Premières et dernières pages. Ed. Françoise Schwab. Paris: Éditions du Seuil, 1994.

Une Vie en toutes lettres [correspondence]. Ed. Françoise Schwab. Paris: Liana Levi, 1995.

Vladimir Jankélévitch: Philosophie morale. Paris: Flammarion, 1998.

Plotin, "Ennéades" I, 3: Sur la dialectique [Jankélévitch's master's thesis]. Ed. Jacqueline Lagrée and Françoise Schwab. Paris: Éditions du Cerf, 1998.

Glossary

aseity: *aséité*, something that exists completely of and by itself; absolute independence. The term was often used in relation to God.

to come to pass: *advenir*. Jankélévitch employs this verb because of its relation to the French term *avenir*, "future," and the French verb *venir*, "to come." In turn, these terms are related to Jankélévitch's view that time is unidirectionally oriented toward the future.

decay: *usure*. Jankélévitch employs this term to indicate a false substitute for forgiveness: allowing anger to subside over the course of time. *Usure* can also mean "usury," and thus there is the sense that if one allows the passing of the years to do what forgiveness could do in an instant, one lives on "borrowed time." Likewise, whereas forgiveness has a proximity to the gift and true giving, allowing the passing of time to quell anger is much more akin to usury.

disinterested: *désintéressé*, selfless; the opposite of self-interest.

forgiveness: *pardon*. Jankélévitch emphasizes the proximity, not only etymologically but also ethically, between forgiveness (*pardon*) and giving or the gift (*don*).

futurition: *futurition*, looking toward or relating to the future.

hapax: from the Greek *hapax legomenon*, a word that is used only once in a work or corpus. Jankélévitch employs the term in relation to an event that comes to pass only once.

the having-been: *l'avoir-été*, the fact that something was or existed in the past.

the having-done: *l'avoir-fait*, the fact that an action was undertaken or finished in the past.

ipseity: *ipséité*, selfhood; one's being a self.

miscomprehension: *mécompréhension*, to fail to understand something.

misunderstanding: *malentendu,* to mistake one thing for another.

naturality: *naturalité,* the rawness or state of being basic or foundational that something possesses. For example, something may be natural because of a naturality that underlies it.

organ-obstacle: *organe-obstacle,* something that gives rise to an occasion at the same time as it hinders. Evil can hinder forgiveness, but without evil, there can be no forgiveness.

the other: *l'autre.* This word is used to mean any other person than oneself. However, the self and what is other, or the same and the other, are on the same plane ontologically and ethically. The term refers simply to the fact that another person is not the same as oneself.

the Other: *autrui.* Following how the term has been translated in Lévinas's works, the Other indicates radical alterity or that about something which cannot be reduced to categories, descriptions, or language.

to pardon: *gracier,* literally, "to give grace." Jankélévitch uses this term as a synonym for forgiveness and not as a synonym for clemency.

philadelphy: *philadelphie,* literally the love that one has for a friend or family member.

philauty: *philautie,* love of self (see "self-love"). Jankélévitch will often use this formulation of the term when he uses other words beginning with the prefix *phil-*.

pleonexy: *pléonexie,* insatiability, the desire to have more than others.

pneumatic: *pneumatique,* from the Stoic term for "spirit" or "soul."

quiddity: *quiddité,* a thing's essence or "whatness." When one defines something, one lists "what" the thing is.

quoddity: *quoddité,* something's "thatness," the fact that it exists. This fact cannot be described in terms of reason, language, and categories. "That" something is here remains indescribable.

right side out: *à l'endroit.* Most often this term relates to the fact that time can unfold only in one direction, that is, it must unfold as it does, even though we think that we can return and undo what has been done.

self-interest: *intérêt-propre,* seeing something in terms of what one, oneself, will procure from that thing. This does not mean selfishness. One can do something for another because one will obtain something in return for the kind action. Charity, benevolence, and so on can all be kind acts, but someone may do these with an eye to what he or she will receive.

self-love: *amour-propre,* pride; being overly concerned with oneself; literally, self-ishness.

self-will: *volonté-propre,* in the Stoic sense, the realm over which one has control as opposed to the external world.

semelfactive: *semelfactif,* a term taken from linguistics meaning a form of a verb that indicates that an action took place only once.

to ununderstand: *décomprendre,* no longer to comprehend something; to analyze to the point where one does not see the object for what it is.

Index